Exploring Techniques of Analysis and Evaluation in Strategic Management

Exploring Techniques of Analysis and Evaluation in Strategic Management

Véronique Ambrosini

with Gerry Johnson and Kevan Scholes

THE
STRATEGIC
PLANNING
SOCIETY.

Prentice Hall Europe

London New York Toronto Sydney Tokyo
Singapore Madrid Mexico City Munich Paris

First published 1998 by
Prentice Hall Europe
Campus 400, Maylands Avenue
Hemel Hempstead
Hertfordshire, HP2 7EZ
A division of
Simon & Schuster International Group

Typeset in 10 pt New Century Schoolbook
by Fakenham Photosetting Ltd, Fakenham, Norfolk

Printed and bound in Great Britain
by Biddles Ltd, Guildford

Library of Congress Cataloging-in-Publication Data

Available from the publisher

British Library Cataloguing in Publication Data

A catalogue record for this book is available from
the British Library

ISBN 0–13–570680–7

1 2 3 4 5   02 01 00 99 98

Contents

Figures and tables

Tables

Strategy in action – illustrations and case studies

Illustrations

Case studies

Foreword

When Gerry Johnson approached me with the idea of inviting leaders from the Society's workshop programme to contribute chapters for this book, I had no hesitation in agreeing. What was especially gratifying was the positive response from many of those leaders to accept the invitation.

The Strategic Analysis, Strategic Choice and Strategy Implementation model set out in *Exploring Corporate Strategy* has proved a powerful framework within which to promote the Society's workshops. It has also proved to be a source of new topics to enrich the series.

Over the six years I have been associated with the Society's programme, most of the themes have struck chords with our members and others. They have clearly been of positive, practical help to them as they have wrestled with the challenge of strategy formulation and implementation.

So having access to the essence of the workshop programme in a single volume, with the benefit of other perspectives and topics, was a very attractive prospect for the Society. Used as a background reader to the tools and techniques of strategic analysis and evaluation, I fully expect it to become a well-thumbed work of reference on our members' bookshelves.

Neither I nor the Society would be so presumptuous as to suggest that a study of the techniques will produce a winning strategy. However there is no doubt in our minds that exposure to selected techniques will lead to an improved capability in the processes of strategic thinking, planning and management.

It is from such capability that strategic insights spring.

So if you aspire to have a voice at, and make a contribution to, the strategy debate, this book will prove invaluable.

Tom Haddon
Programme Director
The Strategic Planning Society

**THE
STRATEGIC
PLANNING
SOCIETY.**

Preface

Exploring Corporate Strategy by Gerry Johnson and Kevan Scholes is now established as the leading text in its field in Europe and beyond with world-wide sales exceeding 300,000. It is a text for students and practising managers which aims to develop their conceptual under-standing of why and how organisations of many different types de-velop and change their strategies. It does so within a practical context while drawing on best strategic management practice, as researchers, writers and practitioners understand it. *Exploring Corporate Strategy* is not a book of analytical techniques, although it explains in depth where and how techniques can contribute to both the understanding and practical application of strategic management.

With so many managers and students now familiar with *Exploring Corporate Strategy* we have responded to the requests for material which takes the themes and concepts of strategic manage-ment further, in a way that is not possible within the confines of a broad textbook on the subject. Prentice Hall Europe have agreed to publish a series of short practical books which build on the basic framework of *Exploring Corporate Strategy*. This book, on *Exploring Techniques of Analysis and Evaluation in Strategic Management*, is one of the first two books to be published in this series. The other is *Strategic Financial Management* by Tony Grundy. Further books are in preparation or planning. All the books are developed under the edi-torial guidance of Gerry Johnson and Kevan Scholes and have the fol-lowing aims:

- to provide further depth on aspects of strategic management which should already be familiar to readers of *Exploring Corporate Strategy*;
- to do this in a practical and applied way while drawing on best prac-tice from researchers, writers and practitioners.

For this particular book in the series, Véronique Ambrosini, Gerry Johnson and Kevan Scholes have brought together or commissioned a series of 17 chapters which provide further depth for readers on a range of important aspects of analysis and evaluation of strategy. In all cases there is an emphasis on moving beyond 'knowing what' (i.e. 'what is the technique about?') to 'knowing how' (i.e. 'how do I use the technique?') to produce useful insights or to guide decision-making in the organisation. In summary, *Exploring Techniques of Analysis and Evaluation in Strategic Management* is about developing one's practical capabilities in strategic management and hence is to be used in conjunction with *Exploring Corporate Strategy*, which provides the conceptual understandings of the various tools and techniques.

The 17 chapters of this book are all of direct relevance for practising and future managers. Each chapter deals with one technique useful for effective strategic management. This means that the present book can be valuable to students, tutors and managers:

- Students can find here a practical supplement to their textbook, *Exploring Corporate Strategy*.
- Tutors, who may require support with the practical aspects of strategic management, may use *Exploring Techniques of Analysis and Evaluation in Strategic Management* in parallel with the textbook, and this should allow them to show students the tools that are available in strategy.
- *Exploring Techniques of Analysis and Evaluation in Strategic Management*, being practically oriented, is a useful tool for managers dealing with strategic management issues.

The book is divided into four main themes, following the broad structure of *Exploring Corporate Strategy*:

- Analysing organisational resources and capabilities
- Analysing the business environment
- Analysing organisational culture and stakeholders
- Evaluating and choosing strategic options.

The chapters provided for the first theme – organisational resources and capabilities – have received considerable attention by writers and practitioners over the last five years or so and this was reflected by significant changes in the coverage of this area in the fourth edition of *Exploring Corporate Strategy*. Véronique Ambrosini has collected five chapters which, between them, explore this theme extensively. They are all concerned with techniques that have received significant coverage and should be familiar to many managers: core competences, value chain analysis, financial appraisal, benchmarking and business process re-engineering. Again the purpose of each chapter is to move readers from a general understanding of the technique to a capability to undertake a useful analysis.

The second theme, analysing the business environment, covers the important topics of scenario planning, competitor analysis and SWOT analysis. These are all approaches which managers have told us look deceptively simple, while in fact they can be difficult to undertake in practice without a framework to rely on. We hope these chapters help.

The third area of organisational culture and stakeholders is a core theme of *Exploring Corporate Strategy*. It appears throughout the book, but particularly in Chapters 2, 5 and 11. Four important aspects have been chosen for further development: mapping and re-mapping culture (using the cultural web), stakeholder mapping, corporate responsibility audit and strategy development process. Important connections have also been provided between themes which are discussed in separate places in *Exploring Corporate Strategy*; for example, how stakeholder mapping might quote political tactics during strategy implementation.

The final theme of evaluation and choice covers a series of topics from Chapters 6, 7, 8 and 9 of *Exploring Corporate Strategy* – again providing practical guidance on how to evaluate and choose strategic options. These are portfolio analysis, gap analysis, shareholder value analysis, corporate parenting, and creative thinking.

The book has been compiled to provide a collection of analytical techniques which are essentially free-standing, so readers should be able to select chapters in any sequence. However, it is recommended that if readers are to gain most benefit from a particular technique, and to avoid the pitfall of choosing and applying techniques inappropriately, they should bear the following in mind:

- They should have a good conceptual understanding of the broad area of strategic management within which the particular technique 'sits'. This is provided by the appropriate sections in *Exploring Corporate Strategy*. The brief introduction to each chapter provides some guidance on these connections.
- It is desirable to be familiar with other techniques on related topics within the broad theme. For example, value chain and core competence analyses are clearly connected to each other and to benchmarking and business process re-engineering. A knowledge of each will benefit an understanding of the others.

Finally, we would like to thank all the authors – Mahen Tampoe, Andrew Shepherd, Tony Grundy, Geoff Tomlinson, Stuart D. Francis, Patrick G. Alley, David Mercer, Gerry Johnson, Cliff Bowman, Peter Rudd, Tony Jacobs, Jill Shepherd, Kevan Scholes, David Clutterbuck, David Faulkner, Jon Billsberry, Roger Mills, Andrew Campbell, Michael Goold, Andy Bailey, Clare Avery and Stephen Reid – for their contributions, and MCB and Elsevier Ltd for their permission to reproduce their articles. We would also like to take this opportunity to thank those who have helped us in the preparation and completion of this book. In particular, Tom Haddon at the Strategic Planning Society: *Exploring Techniques of Analysis and Evaluation in Strategic Management* has been prepared with the assistance of the Strategic Planning Society, and several of the chapters have been prepared by their workshop leaders. We are also grateful to Alison Southgate at Cranfield School of Management and many of our colleagues, notably John Darwin from Sheffield Business School, who have commented on drafts of our own chapters.

Véronique Ambrosini
Gerry Johnson
Kevan Scholes
January 1998

The authors

Patrick G. Alley. Patrick is currently clinical associate professor of surgery at the Auckland University School of Medicine and is clinical director of surgery at North Shore Hospital in Auckland. Besides his clinical duties he has, since 1994, chaired a patient-focused review group, examining the delivery of surgical services to a population of 400,000. In addition to the publications on clinical matters, his recent literature includes an examination of the reaction of senior medical staff to stress generally, and particularly the process of reform that has taken place in the United Kingdom, Australia and New Zealand.

Véronique Ambrosini ISEG sup, DBA, MBA. Véronique is a research fellow in strategic management at Cranfield School of Management. She holds an MBA from the University of Birmingham and studied for her first degree at the ISEG, a French Business School. Her current research interests include the resource-based theory of the firm and tacit knowledge.

Clare Avery BSc, MSc. Clare is a researcher at Cranfield School of Management. Having trained in applied psychology, her research work looked at the middle manager's experience of organisational change. She is currently researching processes of strategy development in organisations.

Andy Bailey BSc, MSc. Andy is a lecturer in strategic management at Lancaster University. He was previously a senior research fellow at Cranfield School of Management. He is a psychologist by training and his current research interests include the processes of strategy development and organisational change within both public and private sector organisations.

Jon Billsberry BA (Hons), MBA. Jon is a lecturer in organisational behaviour at the Open University Business School. He is the course team chair of The Effective Manager, responsible for all academic matters on one of Europe's largest management courses. His research

interests are in the subjects of recruitment and selection, organisational entry, and person–organisation fit. Before turning to academia, he spent six years as a manager in the financial services and
manufacturing industries, including periods as a financial analyst at
Citibank and Morgan Grenfell. Following these appointments, he
worked for four years as a headhunter with Scott Collins Ltd. His first
book, *Finding and Keeping the Right People*, was published in 1996 by
Pitman. In addition, he edited a collection of readings, *The Effective
Manager: Perspectives and Illustrations*, for Sage which was also published in 1996.

Cliff Bowman BA, MBA, PhD. Cliff is professor of business strategy
at Cranfield School of Management. After graduating, Cliff joined
Shell UK in marketing and sales. He then moved to the UK Civil
Aviation Authority as an economist, where he worked in airport planning and airline economics. Since 1979, he has been engaged in management development. Before joining Cranfield, he was head of the
School of Business at Humberside College of Higher Education. He
has undertaken strategy consultancy and management development
work for a wide range of private and public sector organisations in
Europe, USA, Brazil, India, Australia and South East Asia, specialising in strategy process consulting with top teams. Client organisations include APV, Bass, Boral, DHL, Burmah Castrol, Northern
Foods, Christies, HSBC, KPMG, Mercers, Natwest, UPN, Trygg
Hansa, Harrisons and Crosfield. He is the author of numerous books
and articles. Recent publications include *The Essence of Competitive
Strategy* (Prentice Hall, 1994), *Managing Strategy* (Macmillan, 1996)
and *Competitive and Corporate Strategy* (Irwin, 1996). His current research interests include competitive strategy, strategy processes and
organisation structures for delivering sustainable advantage.

Andrew Campbell. Andrew is a founding director of Ashridge
Strategic Management Centre and active as a consultant on strategic
issues for major corporate clients. He is also a visiting professor at City
University. Previously he was a fellow in the Centre for Business
Strategy at the London Business School. Before that he was a consultant for six years with McKinsey & Co., working on strategy and organisation problems in London and Los Angeles. He also spent three years
as a loan officer with Investors in Industry. Andrew holds an MBA from
the Harvard Business School where he was a Harkness fellow and a
Baker scholar. His books include *Core Competency-Based Strategy*
(1997), *Breakup!* (1997), *Corporate-Level Strategy* (1994), *Strategic
Synergy* (1992), *A Sense of Mission* (1990), *Strategies and Styles* (1987).

David Clutterbuck. David is chairman of The ITEM Group plc, an
internal communication company, director of Clutterbuck, Palmer,

Schneider Ltd and The Winning Streak Ltd. He is a trustee of the European Mentoring Centre and the charity Children's Aid Direct. He has authored or co-authored more than 30 books on management topics including the best-selling *The Winning Streak* (Weidenfeld, 1983) and its recent sequel *The Winning Streak Mark II* (Orion, 1997). His books in the field of social responsibility include *Working with the Community* (Weidenfeld & Nicolson, 1990), *Actions Speak Louder* (Kogan Page, 1992), *The Charity as a Business* (Directory of Social Change, 1996).

A graduate of London University, his career includes a lengthy period with *International Management*, eventually as editor. He has founded several management journals, including *Strategic Direction* and *Technology Strategies*. He is a visiting fellow at several business schools and associate professor at the International Management Centres. He divides his time between research, writing, lecturing around the world and running his various entrepreneurial businesses. His current projects include a study of how different types of team learn, a study into the success patterns of 'whacky' companies, and the development of boardroom competence.

David Faulkner BSc (Econ), MA (Oxon), DPhil, FIMC. David is an Oxford educated economist by background, who has spent much of his career as a strategic management consultant and business builder. He is an official student (tutorial fellow) at Christ Church, Oxford, and an Oxford University lecturer in management studies (strategic management). Having moved into academic life seven years ago, he became a lecturer in the Cranfield Strategy Group in the School of Management, and gained a doctorate from Oxford University (DPhil), researching into conditions for success in International Strategic Alliances.

He is currently a visiting fellow at the Judge Institute at Cambridge working with Professor John Child on research into partnerships between British and foreign firms with emphasis on changes in management methods resulting from them. He has published and is publishing widely with a number of academic refereed articles and conference papers. He has published three books, *The Challenge of Strategic Management* with G. Johnson (Kogan Page, 1992), *The Essence of Competitive Strategy* with C. Bowman (Prentice Hall, 1994) and *International Strategic Alliances: Cooperating to Compete* (McGraw-Hill, 1994) and has further books in preparation.

He carries out management consulting and lecturing activities with a wide range of companies including both public and private sectors on all topics concerned with strategy. He is a director of Oxford Management Research Limited and Strategic Partnerships International Limited. He has worked for both a number of PLCs and government bodies, including the Home Office. In his earlier career he spent seven years with McKinsey as a strategic and organisational consultant, and was head of strategy consulting for Arthur D. Little Ltd. He was also managing director of the UK office of SIAR (The Scandinavian Institute for Administrative Research), the Stockholm-based international strategic consulting group.

Stuart D. Francis. Stuart is a senior consultant within the Health Care Consulting Group of Ernst & Young New Zealand. His experience includes business process redesign and implementation, information system design, development and implementation, and management team and strategy development in a variety of industries and companies. Prior to joining Ernst & Young, Stuart project managed a re-engineering project of surgical services in a Crown Health Enterprise. The project involved extensive clinician involvement and redesigned several core processes. The redesign incorporates some internationally innovative solutions in the delivery of secondary surgical services. Stuart lectures for the Diploma in Business (Quality Management) for the Executive Programmes, Auckland School of Business, University of Auckland and has also lectured for the Auckland Institute of Studies. Stuart has eight years' experience as a qualified volunteer ambulance officer for the Auckland Ambulance Service and holds a Master of Commerce from Auckland University.

Michael Goold MA, MBA, PhD. Michael is a director of the Ashridge Strategic Management Centre. His research interests are concerned with corporate strategy and the management of multi-business companies, and he runs the Centre's programme on Group Level Strategy. His publications include *Corporate-Level Strategy: Creating Value in the Multibusiness Company* (John Wiley & Sons) and *Strategic Control: Milestones for Long-Term Performance* (Financial Times/Pitman).

Prior to establishing the Centre in 1987, he was a senior fellow at the London Business School. During this time, he undertook research into the role of the corporate centre in diversified companies that led to the publication of *Strategies and Styles* (Blackwell, 1987). He also taught business policy on the Master's programme and on executive courses.

Michael has extensive consulting experience with senior management. From 1971 to 1983 he was a member of the Boston Consulting Group, and in 1978 was elected a vice-president of the firm. He continues to consult with a variety of clients in addition to his research and teaching responsibilities. Michael holds an MA with First Class Honours in PPE and a PhD in Philosophy from Merton College, Oxford, and an MBA with distinction from the Stanford Business School, California.

Tony Grundy MA, MBA, MSc, MPhil, FCA, PhD (*Strategic Planning Society workshop leader*). Tony is senior lecturer in strategic management at Cranfield School of Management. After graduating from Cambridge he worked in line management at BT and ICI and in a European retailer. He consulted with KPMG and ICI before forming his independent strategy consultancy, where he works with major blue chip clients. He has a PhD from Cranfield School of Management and higher degrees in management and organisation from Warwick Business School, City University Business School and the University of London. He is author of *Corporate Strategy and Financial Decisions* (Kogan Page, 1992), *Implementing Strategic Change* (Kogan Page, 1993), *Strategic Learning in Action* (McGraw-Hill, 1994), *Breakthrough Strategies for Growth* (Pitman, 1995) and *Exploring Strategic Financial Management* (Prentice Hall, 1998). He is also co-editor (with K. Ward) of *Business Finance* (Kogan Page, 1996).

Tony Jacobs. Tony has industry experience of retail and international banks. He joined the research staff of Cranfield School of Management in 1996 and contributed to *Exploring Corporate Strategy* (4th edition) and associated projects. He is currently at the School of Strategic Management at Bristol Business School and is involved in both teaching and research in strategic management.

Gerry Johnson BA, PhD. Gerry is professor of strategic management at Cranfield School of Management. After graduating from University College, London, he worked for several years in management positions in Unilever and Reed International before becoming a management consultant. He has also taught at Aston University Management Centre, where he obtained his PhD, and Manchester Business School. He took up his appointment at Cranfield in 1988. Professor Johnson is co-author of Europe's best-selling strategic management textbook *Exploring Corporate Strategy* (Prentice Hall, 4th edition, 1997), is author of *Strategic Change and the Management Process* (Blackwell, 1987), editor of *Business Strategy and Retailing* (Wiley, 1987), *The Challenge of Strategic Management* (Kogan Page, 1992) and *Strategic Thinking* (Wiley, 1993). He is also author of numerous papers on strategic management and is a member of the editorial board of the *Strategic Management Journal*. His research work is primarily concerned with processes of strategy development and change in organisations. He has also worked extensively as a consultant at a senior level on issues of strategy formulation and strategic change with many UK and international firms.

David Mercer. David is senior lecturer at the Open University Business School, Europe's largest business school, where he chairs the team of academics responsible for the long-range planning element of the MBA programme. He was the first head of its Center for Strategy and Policy, and now directs its Futures Observatory (which has superseded the previous 'Millennium Project') – in partnership with the Strategic Planning Society.

His previous career included brand and marketing management for a range of multinationals, in the consumer goods sector, and general management in the manufacturing and retail sectors; as well as 15 years with IBM. Most recently he has also advised organisations and international bodies overseas, as well as governments. He was director of the School's prestigious programme, teaching the MBA at presidential level.

He is the author of one of the United Kingdom's best-selling MBA marketing textbooks, *Marketing*, published by Blackwell, as well as co-author of its equivalent selling in the United States, along with two popular books on marketing (*New Marketing Practice*, Penguin, and *Marketing for Managers*, Orion). His new book in the field of long-range (marketing) planning is *Marketing Strategy: the Challenge of the External Environment*, published by Sage, and his more popular introduction to the results of the Millennium Project is *Future Revolutions*, published by Orion.

Roger W. Mills BTech (Hons), MSc, PhD, FCMA, FCIS, FCT (*Strategic Planning Society workshop leader*). Roger is professor of accounting and finance at Henley Management College where he is head of the accounting and finance faculty. He has a Bachelors degree in psychology, sociology and economics, a Masters degree in management studies and a PhD in finance. He trained as an accountant in industry and is a chartered management accountant. He is a fellow of the Chartered Institute of Management Accountants (FCMA), a fellow of the Chartered Institute of Secretaries and Administrators (FCIS), and a fellow of the Association of Corporate Treasurers (FCT). He is the author of a book on strategic value analysis, co-author of a text for managers on accounting and finance, and is the author of numerous articles in journals, such as *Management Accounting*, the *Treasurer*, the *Journal of General Management*.

Roger has undertaken numerous consultancy assignments within the financial services, banking and computer industries. He has been an independent consultant for 15 years, the last 10 of which have been in the area of strategic value analysis, an approach to valuation developed and published extensively. Substantial involvement in the area of valuation and cost of capital determination as a consultant both within the UK and elsewhere. Countries in which consultancy services have been provided, including the delivery of value development programmes to senior executives other than the UK, are USA, Norway, Switzerland, France, Denmark, Nigeria, South Africa, Spain,

Holland, Germany, Turkey, Hong Kong, Singapore, Thailand, Malaysia, Indonesia, Brazil and Russia.

Stephen Reid (*Strategic Planning Society workshop leader*). Stephen graduated in genetics and cell biology at Manchester University in 1975. He also has become a skilled painter with a distinctive style. On the commercial level Stephen has a solid track record of running successful operations in the UK, northern Europe and the Middle East with Eli Lilly, Johnson & Johnson and Fisons. Most of his assignments were characterised as complex and difficult and because of his creative, strategic and marketing skills Stephen was highly competent in producing and directing change. In 1995 Stephen set up Spring Business Innovation to deliver thinking workshops that would help managers to be more creative or to facilitate innovation.

Stephen's institutional clients have included Ashridge Management College, Nottingham Business School and the Strategic Planning Society. In addition, he has found that delivering thinking workshops works best with functional teams and, as a consequence, has led Creative Decision Making workshops in USA, Italy, France, Germany, Portugal and England with senior management teams. Stephen has also conducted basic research into employee suggestion schemes and intends to publish in 1998.

Peter Rudd Peter holds an HNC in electrical power engineering and a CIM advanced certificate in marketing and is currently studying for the CIM diploma in marketing at the University of Central England. He has several years of experience within the electrical engineering industry and is currently employed as a marketing engineer responsible for product development, direct marketing and market research.

Kevan Scholes MA, PhD, DMS, CIMgt, FRSA. Kevan is a visiting professor of strategic management and formerly director of the Sheffield Business School, UK. He has considerable experience of lecturing, consultancy and writing in strategic management for both the public and private sectors both in the UK and overseas. He is author of Europe's best-selling text *Exploring Corporate Strategy* (with Gerry Johnson) with over 300,000 sales world wide.

His consultancy and training work includes organisations in manufacturing, professional services, computing, telecommunications, retailing and a wide range of public service organisations. He has regular commitments outside the UK – including Melbourne and Brisbane (Australia), New Zealand and Singapore.

He has also been an adviser on management development to a number of national bodies. He is a Companion of The Institute of Management and a past chairman and currently president of the Sheffield and Chesterfield branch of the Institute.

Andrew Shepherd (*Strategic Planning Society workshop leader*). Andrew gained double honours in mechanical engineering and economics at the University of Birmingham, and an MBA and MA at Stanford University. He is a chartered engineer whose career as a consultant began in the Courtaulds Group in the early 1970s and continued after business school, leading to his current position as a founder of the Alexander Partnership in London.

Andrew has worked in a wide variety of industries, including telecommunications, energy, insurance, electronics, porcelain, glass, alloy wheels, animal feed, office supplies, fast food, books, periodicals and soft drinks. Projects typically focus on business strategy, but often include pricing, value chain modification and efficiency studies as parts of a cascading action programme. Besides lecturing at the Strategic Planning Society on value chain analysis, he has also made a significant contribution to the development of neural net software application to solve business problems.

Jill Shepherd BSc, DIC, MBA. Having worked within the pharmaceutical industry Jill became a management consultant for the healthcare industry. Working primarily within multinationals, she focuses on using a mixture of training and process consulting to improve strategy development processes within New Product Development. Her academic research interests include knowledge as the basis for a dynamic theory of the firm, strategy innovation and institutional theory.

Mahen Tampoe (*Strategic Planning Society workshop leader*). Mahen is a consultant and trainer specialising in the strategy formulation and strategic design of Knowledge Based Organisations. After a varied career in ICL, which culminated as Director of ICL's Information Technology Centre in Dublin, he took up consulting, research and teaching. He is a member of the Chartered Institute of Management Accountants, and got his MBA and PhD at Henley. He is also a member of the Strategic Planning Society, the Operational Research Society and a committee member of the Reading branch of the Institute of Management. His academic and research interests are carried out through his links with the Henley Management College where he lectures on their Master programmes and carries out research in interested subjects with other faculty members. He has also lectured at the Civil Service College on the management of specialists. His consultancy work has focused on helping organisations in the newly privatised utilities sector and commercial and financial organisations in the UK and overseas achieve strategic change. He has published a book on using computers in business and many articles on project management, managing knowledge workers and recently on the practical application of the theory of core competences of the organisation. He has also contributed to books on change management and project management. He is a director of Management Metrics Limited, a partnership of academics and consultants supplemented by associates and research assistants.

Geoff Tomlinson. Geoff is a consultant with A.T. Kearney Ltd, based in their London office. Geoff's experience in benchmarking has been predominantly practical – working for a variety of leading FMCG clients internationally to improve their competitive position through benchmarking and process mapping. Prior to joining A.T. Kearney, Geoff held technical and sales management positions with Rank Hovis McDougall, and subsequently completed an MBA at Manchester Business School.

Part I
Organisational resources and capabilities

1

Getting to know your organisation's core competences

By Mahen Tampoe

Editor's introduction

Chapter 4 of *Exploring Corporate Strategy* is concerned with the relationship between strategic capabilities and strategy. The strategic capability of an organisation results from the resources which it owns or can access, the way that these resources are deployed to create competences in specific activities and, crucially, the way in which these separate activities are linked together, both inside and outside the organisation. Together these resources and competences enable the organisation to create products or services which are regarded as good value-for-money by users. However, this is largely a matter of the relative performance of the organisation *vis-à-vis* other providers (competitors) and hence creating and sustaining competitive advantage requires managers to understand the unique resources and core competences which give them advantage.

In practice, it is one thing for managers to understand these general concepts but it is quite another to be able to undertake a practical identification of their own organisation's core competences. Mahen Tampoe's chapter provides a useful extension of Section 4.3 of *Exploring Corporate Strategy*. Managers in service organisations should find his example of the ambulance service particularly helpful.

1.1 Introduction

Organisations that understand their true strengths are better able to compete successfully in a rapidly expanding and competitive world economy. Core competence analysis will help them do this by enabling them to see beyond their end products and served markets to their core technologies and sources of competitive advantage. This chapter sets out to explain how the author identifies core competences and offers an approach which readers may wish to use.

1.2   What is a core competence?

The core competences of the organisation lie in the collective learning in the organisation, especially 'how to coordinate diverse production skills and integrate multiple streams of technologies' (1). Parsons (2), an early proponent of the idea, provides a clue to its whereabouts in the organisation by suggesting that the skills and capabilities of an organisation are embodied in three subsystems: administrative, technical and institutional. John Kay (3) attributes corporate success to four distinctive capabilities: innovation, architecture, reputation and strategic assets, and suggests that the effective blending of these four can contribute to the unique capability of an organisation.

A summary of all these views leads to a definition which says that *the core competence of an organisation is its enabling culture*, as opposed to its relationship culture, where the relationship culture could be likened to its personality and interpersonal skills and its enabling culture to its motivation and applied skills.

1.2.1   Where can core competences be found?

Core competences can be found in single businesses, conglomerates or diversified businesses. They are often a single capability made up of many components, as defined above. They can be hierarchical. A holding company such as Hanson Trust or BTR will have core competences which make it good at managing a diversified business. Each subsidiary may have its own core competence which sets it apart from its parent and other subsidiaries in the group. The core competence of a holding company could be financial control or the ability to rationalise the businesses it acquires or owns. Sometimes, the core competence of the organisation comes from its leader rather than the organisation itself. Examples of leaders who form the core competence of their organisation are Jack Welsh of GE, Richard Branson of Virgin, Percy Barnevik of ABB. Leader-centred core competences make organisations vulnerable. Leaders can leave or, more dangerously, stay on after they have lost their energy, charisma or vision. Institutionalised core competences are more enduring but they too can stifle initiative, innovation and necessary change.

1.2.2   The benefits conferred by core competences to an organisation

The core competences of an organisation are considered essential to corporate survival in the short and long term. They will invariably be unique to the organisation, invisible to competitors and difficult to imitate even when their existence is understood by competitors. As a mix of skills, resources and processes they confer a capability which is greater than the competence of an individual or operational unit. As the essence of the organisation they endure over time and contribute directly and indirectly to the development of core products, end products and services. This becomes more critical as corporations turn from cost management or denominator management (as Gary Hamel would express it) to seeking new sources of revenue and profit to enlarge their earning potential.

Traditional approaches to organisational growth tend to favour acquisitions and mergers. This approach often fails because the acquiring organisation does not have the know-how to manage the acquired business. Attempts at imposing its own enabling culture on the acquired organisation often lead to an erosion of the true value of the acquired business. Companies with core competences which do not match those of a Hanson will find it much harder to grow through acquisitions. STC had to eventually sell off ICL to Fujitsu. The marriage between ICL and Fujitsu has endured because it had a very long courtship and the companies knew each other very well before the current arrangement. Besides, ICL has a history of merging with similar companies and acquiring and exploiting their technology. More recent examples abound. In some extreme cases, because the acquiring organisation was unable to manage its new acquisition successfully, the newer enlarged group has failed, taking both the acquirer and the acquired into the hands of the Receiver. In recent years many large organisations have demerged to reduce their vulnerability to takeovers and found that, by doing this, they have released new energies in both the original (but now smaller and more focused) parent and its offspring.

The core competence approach enables organisations to achieve organic growth by building on their core strengths and unique capabilities.

1.2.3   *The cost of misunderstanding core competences*

The cost of misunderstanding their core competences can have severe adverse effects on a business. It is therefore not a game for amateurs. For example, Mercedes-Benz's foray into expansion through acquisition has cost it dearly. At heart it was a company whose core competence lay in building luxury cars. Using its surplus cash from its car business to enter other businesses in the manner of GE was a mistake as it did not have a Jack Welsh at its head. As *The Economist* (4) says 'Just three years ago . . . Daimler-Benz's then chairman, Edzard Reuter, boasted that he had transformed the firm from a car maker into an "integrated technology group" involved in aerospace, microelectronics and many kinds of transport. That vision is now in tatters.' *The Economist* goes on to suggest that eventually the company, through the divestment of its newly acquired empire and other ratio-nalisations, would 'reach the destination some shareholders wish for it: a return to its origins as a maker of high-quality vehicles'. With a declining share of the German passenger car market, even its core business could be at risk. Attempts at widening its product range may yet return to haunt the company which has, over the years, survived on the cachet and prestige of its larger cars. Mercedes-Benz is not the only company to find that the acquisition trail does not always result in profit and growth. In Britain, many of the newly privatised utilities have also come to realise that surplus cash, in itself, is inadequate for acquisition-led growth. Mercedes-Benz's mistake can also be seen mir-rored by British Aerospace which, for a short period, strayed into the car, construction and executive jet businesses before divesting itself of these and reverting to its core business as a defence contractor. In the words of *The Economist*, BAe has since 'transformed itself from one of Europe's shakiest industrial companies into a solid defence firm with a profitable civil aircraft business'. In other words, it had returned to its 'defence or Forces mentality'. To an outsider working with BAe's senior managers, the difference in culture and attitude between execu-tives of the revitalised Rover Group and those of its defence business was stark. The BAe executives often displayed an 'officer' and 'other ranks' mentality which their Rover colleagues had shed on their way to revitalising the car company. The BAe executives also demonstrated a tendency of wanting to be led rather than to lead – a mentality which is best suited to the industry they serve.

Even companies such as Hanson, who have a track record for acquiring and exploiting the underutilised assets of the businesses they acquire, can fail when they buy businesses they do not under-stand. *The Independent on Sunday* (5) highlights the immense harm that the Hanson approach to profitability can do to a company, such as Ever Ready, which needs to innovate in order to lead its industry. Under Hanson its market share reduced from 80 per cent, when it was acquired, to 30 per cent when it was sold. Its investment in R&D had been pruned soon after its acquisition by Hanson, and this perhaps contributed to the fact that its new owners, Ralston Purina, found that Ever Ready's technology was 10 years out of date. *The Independent on Sunday* also claims that research in the USA has shown that 'only 22 to 34 per cent of restructuring companies increase productivity to their satisfaction'. The research also found that 'net income relative to sales, return on assets and return on equity tend to increase in the first year following job cuts, but not in the next year'. This accounts for the vora-cious appetite of conglomerates for new acquisitions and their willing-ness to shed those weakened by years of under-investment. In no case out of the 210 surveyed did 'post-redundancy performance match the maximum levels achieved before'. These very illuminating statistics are understood more by the managers and staff left behind after the pruning, as it is they who have to meet the still exacting demands of the marketplace and the shareholder with fewer applied skills and resources. When the dismal performance of most computer systems is added to this paucity of skilled staff, we have a situation which needs to be tackled from the ground up and where quick fixes must give way to reasoned and sustained investment in and exploitation of core competences rather than cash cows. What we see when we analyse 'denominator' management is the demonstrated effects of a tragic lack of imagination and a paucity of investment in vision in many board rooms in the USA and the UK.

Core competence analysis, by unshackling the mind of long-held prejudices, can release managers and strategists to think the unthinkable and shed their cash cow mentality.

1.2.4　When is a core competence not a core competence?

It is quite easy to mix core competences with sources of competitive advantage, i.e. differentiators that enable organisations to achieve unique market positions. It is also easy to mix up core competences with key or main products. Core competences are also often confused with strategic assets such as patent rights or exclusive licences to trade, as those offered to the newly privatised companies such as the regional electricity or water companies. The core business of an organisation is not necessarily its core competence, but people do often mix these up.

Sony Corporation created a world-wide reputation for innovation in consumer electronics. In their article, Prahalad and Hamel (1) suggest that 'among Sony's competences is miniaturisation' and that to 'bring miniaturisation to its products, Sony must ensure that technologists, engineers and marketers have a shared understanding of customer needs and of technological possibilities.' They suggest that the organisation's core competence lies beyond its ability to miniaturise and rests within an innovative culture. At a presentation in January 1995 to members of The Conference Board Europe, the strategy manager for Sony Europe explained that Sony's success was derived from a combination of many things. A summary of what he said is given in Illustration 1.1. It helps put core competences in context. It shows how, as a company, it was successful at using its core competence – research, venture/entrepreneurial spirit and global reach – to create breakthrough products. These it then exploited by carefully considered strategic initiatives and the exploitation of its competitive strengths. It has learnt to leverage proven products into new markets and is not afraid to step into the unknown, to take a leap of faith, in order to maximise its position and release new market potential.

Strategy in action

Illustration 1.1

Sony Corporation. Notes of talk by Sony European strategy manager to members of the Conference Board Europe, January 1995

- *Key drivers*
  He saw that there were three key drivers which combined to form its core competence. Research alone would not have given it its pre-eminence in the marketplace. He suggested that the Sony name was probably as well known as Coca-Cola. The three drivers he identified were: research, venture/entrepreneurial spirit, global reach.

- *Key innovations*
  He suggested that in each decade of its existence Sony has capitalised on a single major innovation, and offered the following summary:

  1950   Transistors
  1960   Trinitron
  1970   Betamax, Walkman
  1980   CD
  1990   Games, multimedia, personal computers

  This illustrates the steady exploitation of its core competence, which built a new breakthrough product each decade to enable the organisation to change the basis and source of its revenue and profit. It also shows how rapidly the organisation can mobilise a breakthrough innovation, as it did in 1970 when Betamax failed to become the world standard for video recorders.

- *Key strategic initiatives*
  He saw four strategic initiatives which, together with the key innovations, contributed to the company's success. These were: changing its name to SONY, improvements in manufacturing, overseas manufacturing, and globalisation with three non-Japanese directors on the Board.

- *Competitive strengths*
  He explained that it retained its competitive strength through brand image, miniaturisation, global reach, hardware and software, free spirit (dynamic and risk-taking culture), and its genius founder.

- *Sony culture*
  He explained that while Sony was well managed, staff in its research and innovation laboratories were allowed more latitude and freedom than their colleagues in other parts of the organisation. They sought to be deliberately ambivalent in terms of innovation goals and to give flexibility and reduce bureaucracy in the way the research was managed.

- *Future challenges*
  He suggested that the company had used its three key drivers to migrate from one market to another by moving from consumer electronics to non-consumerism (telecommunications and communications) and from electronics to entertainment, from global to local presence without losing its global identity.

1.3   *Finding the core competence of an organisation*

In most cases the core competences of an organisation are hidden from competitors and from the organisation itself. Few within established organisations have bothered to find out the real source of their true strengths. Today's successful end products and markets dominate corporate thinking, as do the personal biases of leaders and strong influencers who seek to protect their empires. The searcher of core competences must be able to cut through many veils in order to discover the core competences of an organisation. It helps to trace the

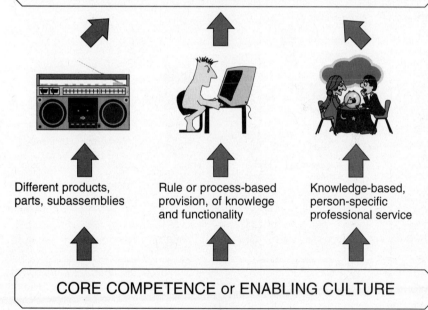

Figure 1.1   *Composition of products/services.*

steps from the known to the unknown. This offers us two methods which lend themselves to systematic approaches. The first is to take a bottom-up approach, which aggregates various materials, processes, etc., into complete products and services, as illustrated in Figure 1.1. This approach more closely resembles the way products and services come into being and is therefore a seductive and, in many senses, an easier route to take.

The second is to use a top-down approach, which decomposes products and services into their constituent parts, much like the work

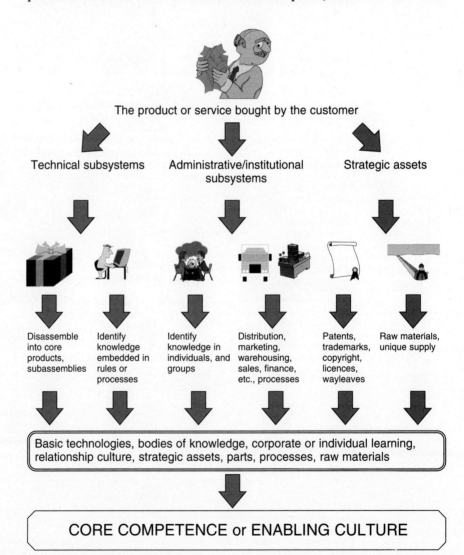

Figure 1.2   Unravelling core competences.

breakdown structure techniques used by project managers to analyse a project and break it down into manageable chunks. This is illustrated in Figure 1.2. The personality and preference of the researcher often determines the approach taken.

The bottom-up approach argues that, as a rockery is made up of stones and plants, anyone who can heap stone upon stone and plant shrubs in the gaps can build a beautiful rockery. The top-down approach begins by appreciating the beauty of the rockery and the designer's flair before delving deeper to determine the stones and plants that were used to create the rockery. On the face of it, it appears that there is really no difference between the two approaches; however, the bottom-up approach starts from the organisation and may not move outwards to the customer because the researcher could get smothered in detail too early and lose his or her frame of reference. The top-down approach begins the analysis from the customer and moves inwards to the organisation. The bottom-up approach may work for product-based businesses, but there is a high risk of missing the core competence when the bottom-up approach is applied to service-based organisations, particularly those selling know-how, such as consultancies. If, for example, you considered an engineering consultancy such as W.S. Aitken or Sir Alexander Gibb and Partners it would be wrong to claim that the core competence of these organisations is the aggregated engineering skills of its many consultants. As the case study discussed later will show, the core competence of a consultancy can reflect a corporate persona which transcends the individual competences of the staff and may be something mundane and unrelated to the core skills of the organisation.

It is the top-down approach that is discussed here. It starts by looking at the rich picture, admiring its beauty, and then moving on to analyse its different components. In doing so it is necessary to pause to consider whether it is the product, the way it reached the market and the way it was conceived and built or resourced (among other factors) which makes up the core competence of the organisation. The steps shown in Figure 1.2 are explained below.

1   Analyse the revenue stream and identify the products and services offered by the organisation to its served markets. To make the process of analysis easier it may make sense to start with those products which make a significant contribution to the organisation's revenue, profit and strategic purpose. However, the tendency to focus on cash cows must be avoided.

2   Using the selected products and services as guides:
    (a) Disassemble them to identify the **core** products and services and then disassemble the core products into their constituent parts to unearth the basic technologies, people skills, processes and strategic assets which combine to produce these core products.

(b) Dissect the services to identify the **core** processes or unique talents that confer unique value to the delivered service. For example, if it is a fast food business, is it the process or the people or the location? If it is a legal service, is it the specialised skill of the lawyer rather than a process?

(c) Relate the products or services to their subsystems: the technical subsystem, the administrative subsystem or the institutional subsystem as defined earlier.

(d) Analyse the subsystem which contributes to the company's market strength to find the basic technologies, people skills, processes and strategic assets which combine to produce these core products. That is your core competence.

3 Test these findings using the three tests proposed by Prahalad and Hamel (1), which are:

(a) Do they 'provide potential access to a wide variety of markets'?

(b) Do they 'make a significant contribution to the perceived customer benefits of the end product'?

(c) Is it 'difficult for competitors to imitate'?

If the core competences you identify meet this criteria you have been successful. If not you will need to start again. This process of reverse engineering is used to understand the business and its prime source of competitive advantage; it must not be seen as confirmation of past strategies and used to consolidate the status quo unless unbiased assessments of market opportunity confirm that course of action.

1.4   *The characteristics of the core competence analyst*

This approach to the extraction of core competences is much more than the application of a 'checklist'. It involves making intuitive judgements as the analysis progresses and the application of imagination and strong lateral thinking to unearth the competences. An ability in systems thinking and soft systems methodology can be a great help. Rigid, android-like cause and effect logic often fails to unearth the magic behind the trick. It often requires leaps of faith and of thinking the unthinkable. If the researcher has an understanding of the industry and the organisation whose core competence is being studied, he or she is more likely to arrive at an answer which intuitively feels right – i.e. engines for Honda. However, it is important that the researcher works closely with the management team and senior executives, preferably in group sessions, as the strong debate that ensues makes it more likely that the core competences will be identified. Group consensus-building techniques such as decision analysis or decision-conferencing techniques can prove very useful.

1.5   Core competence analysis of product-based organisations

Prahalad and Hamel (1) show how products can be dissected to arrive at the core competence of product-based companies. They do this by discussing many companies and illustrating their conclusions in some instances, i.e. Vickers, Canon, with more detailed breakdowns. It seems unnecessary to replicate their work in this chapter.

1.6   Core competence of a service provider

Determining the core competences of service providers can be slightly more difficult to do as the end products – hamburgers at McDonalds or merchandise at a retailer – do not necessarily explain how the 'complex harmonisation of individual technologies and production skills' makes one retailer better in the perception of its customers.

An advertising campaign of the Automobile Association suggests that it is the fourth emergency service next to the police, ambulance and fire services. The Royal Automobile Club does the same. It would be tempting to think that there is little difference between these companies and the emergency services. But is this true? The roadside rescue company needs to arrive soon and repair the vehicle or tow it away for repair. It also needs to transport the passengers who were in the vehicle, which is now non-operational. Is that the same as getting to the scene of an accident and extracting people from the wreckage, stabilising their life and removing them to a hospital after checking that the hospital can receive them and has the equipment to sustain life and cure the injured?

Applying the methodology outlined in Section 1.3, and illustrated in Figure 1.2, it is possible to determine the core competence of an ambulance service. It does make sense to start with the hypothesis that the road rescue service and the ambulance service provide a similar service and may have similar core competences.

The end product of either service is that of rescuing someone from a distressing circumstance. The intensity of the distress may vary, but a person stranded and alone on a highway may feel as vulnerable as someone who has slipped and broken an ankle. Neither would be as bad as someone suffering a heart attack or being seriously injured in a road accident. One situation is far more life threatening than the other and may prove to be an important differentiator. The speed of arrival at the scene of the incident is as important in all cases as getting the motorist mobile again or stabilising the patient. From then on the circumstances can vary. The dilemma for an emergency service is whether its value is in getting to the scene as fast as possible, or its effectiveness when it gets there in saving lives or helping the stranded. An incompetent paramedic is significantly more life threatening than an incompetent motor engineer. If you organised an ambulance service, would it be more important to get to the scene of an emergency, pick up the injured and ferry them as quickly as possible to a hospital or would it be better that, having reached the scene of the emergency, you ensure that the patient's life is saved, and that his or her condition is stabilised before being taken to a hospital? To the ambulance service both are important.

The distinction is very critical to the way an ambulance service is resourced, structured and viewed by the public and its political masters. If it sees itself as a fast and efficient transport service it will structure and resource itself differently to what it would if it saw its job first as a lifesaver and then as a transport agency. As a lifesaver it has a near regional monopoly. As a transport agency it has competitors. As a lifesaver, the paramedics and paramedical skills and equipment are probably more important than the vehicle. Similarly, the command and control system widens its scope from being just a means of routeing vehicles to the scene of an emergency to also providing a life-line and channel of advice to the paramedics. This was the dilemma facing the provider of ambulance services. The solution is, of course, to do both. However, the traditional views held that the job of the ambulance crew was to get the patient to hospital as quickly as possible where the doctors would take over.

A study of an ambulance service revealed that the emphasis on fast arrival at the scene and fast transfer of the patient to a hospital had skewed the resource and skills mix and placed the emphasis of the command and control system on speed as the means of saving life. This emphasis also tended to favour the fleet management and command and control managers in the corporate power battles. Critical evaluation prompted another approach which took, as the basis, saving life. This suggested that medical assistance (rather than speed) at the scene may prove a more meaningful way to save life. Adopting this strategy the power balance, resourcing and service emphasis changed. It also meant that comparisons between the ambulance service and local taxi services were seen as invidious. The unique strength of the ambulance service was now mobile medicine rather than transport and the command and control system was merely a tool to be used in achieving its main purpose of saving lives.

Perhaps, the roadside rescue services are right to call themselves the fourth emergency service.

1.7   The core competence of a consultancy company

Many consultancy companies face the dilemma discussed here. I first met it in ICL Dataskil and in many other consultancies of a similar kind in later years. Many consultancies primarily offer two types of service: hire of specialists to supplement a client skills shortfall (popularly known as body-shopping) and project teams which offer solutions to problems. The staff are totally interchangeable and often could be involved in both types of work in the course of a year. The charging rates reflect the levels of experience of each consultant or team member. The case discussed here is a composite of many similar assignments.

1.7.1   The problem

The problem facing the organisation was how to expand its business while retaining its professional standards and service quality. The consultancy services it offered were not susceptible to process-based management in the way that audits can be procedurised. One of their options was to design a cloning machine to clone their more market attractive consultants, but this was dismissed as non-viable! A shift to project work would enable them to raise revenues and also to gain more leverage from their more senior consultants as the teams could be mixtures of senior and junior staff. In the past it had approached growth as purely doing more of the same. Growth had not been a conscious decision but the result of increasing volumes of placements of consultants. While this worked for a while, in that it resulted in increased revenues, it found that with time this increasing revenue base produced reducing profits and problems with retaining the 'better' staff. The staff were not being offered the variety of work that they desired and nor were the profits sufficient to offer them high bonuses to compensate for the repetitiveness of the work. The other problem it faced was that the market value of the knowledge of its staff could diminish, and therefore the market value of the consultants would reduce even though the company could not reduce the consultants' salaries to the same extent to compensate for the reducing margins from the consultants' work. The problem in summary was:

1   Growth was limited by the inability to find enough of the 'right' people.
2   The market value of the consultants would diminish with time.
3   To maintain salary levels the company had to maintain charging rates.
4   Poor salaries would mean inadequate people and the eventual demise of the business.

The results of the study showed the vulnerability of the organisation to eroding profit margins and client and staff retention. Future growth would need the organisation to build 'monopoly' services by capturing the high ground in specific specialisms and by embodying less valuable knowledge into processes for application by less qualified and experienced staff. It sought to create a new core competence which enabled it to 'productise' knowledge.

It was this realisation which made it take a fresh look at itself. Could core competence analysis offer new insights and help chart a different course for the future?

1.7.2   The analysis

The study to determine a new strategy for the future began by carrying out an analysis of the customers, determining what they bought and analysing the profitability of each revenue stream. The study revealed that 'body-shopping' was mainly the acquisition of high-calibre skills and knowledge. Projects were much more staff substitution in that the client, faced with a one-off task, preferred to out-source work rather than increase staff. Body-shopping was quite lucrative as it meant little management, little risk and, if the consultant knew his or her job and was on amiable terms with the client, potential renewal business which protected revenues, reduced the cost of acquiring new business and minimised risks. Projects, on the other hand, took much more management and had much higher levels of risk with the potential to sour relationships. Significant projects, however, strengthened its position in the market and guaranteed a steady revenue stream. Body-shopping tended to absorb more of the ablest people, thus making the projects more vulnerable. The idea that the consultancy was the aggregation of the skills of its employees and associates was seen as false. The answer needed to be found elsewhere.

1.7.3   Unique value of the consultancy organisation

The next phase of the study set out to determine whether the unique value provided by the organisation was greater than the value of each individual and whether the client paid a premium over the price of the consultant purely for this added value. For example:

1   Did the organisation's name lend credibility to the solutions offered and to the status of the consultant?
2   Did the client feel more confident of the professionalism of the individual, particularly in the areas of ethics and knowledge currency?
3   Did the client feel more confident that the consultant would honour the confidentiality of the information gathered?
4   Did the client feel that there was a pool of resources which could be tapped if any single consultant was ill or unavailable or needed further support?
5   Did the client feel that the management of the consultant was shared between the client and the consultancy company?

It was evident that clients wanted all or many of these added value benefits and were willing to pay a premium to engage the consultants through the consultancy company. Having determined what the clients wanted, it was necessary to determine what unique value the firm offered the consultants, as without them there would be no business. Here the benefits were:

1   Market access and quality of assignments.
2   Pay cheque security.
3   Reputation among clients, colleagues and friends.
4   Training, holidays, short-term sickness, etc., without loss of income.
5   Personal marketability and mobility.

In this respect, the firm fell short. As the organisation grew and the managers and consultants became more distant, and as the pressures of revenue and profit encouraged managers to focus more on high rates of staff utilisation (which meant getting staff to continue doing similar work over and over again), both client and staff member found that the consultancy had ceased to add value to them or to the staff they were assigned.

1.7.4   The core competence

All this led us to the view that while its reputation gave it a competitive advantage in the marketplace and among potential new staff, its value to both its clients and its consultant staff came from its ability to act as a conduit by which knowledgeable people and those who needed their knowledge were brought together. The primary value of the firm seemed to be in its ability to *marry the needs and expectations of its clients to those of its consultants*. This was its core competence.

1.7.5   So what was different in the core competence-based approach?

This way of studying the strengths and weaknesses of the firm differed from previous approaches in many ways. The core competences approach enabled the organisation, for the first time, to take a strategic look at itself to understand its true position in the supply chain between knowledgeable individuals and their potential clients and how it added value by interposing itself between the two. Discovering that being purely a placement service did not deliver it longer term objectives was felt by some directors, but not by all. Convincing the doubters was easier when the core competence analysis was done and the organisation understood that its true enabling culture contributed no more than that offered by an agency providing temporary secretarial staff. They did not realise that that was what they were seen to be doing by their customers. What was worse, their consultants recognised this and felt that it did not contribute to their own marketability – being used and viewed as 'bodies' rather than specialised professional skills.

1.8 Using core competences for strategic planning

Once the core competences are identified they can be used to determine the new markets or product/services in which they can be exploited. Core competences are substituted for products and services in analysing the potential of the organisation to benefit from its core competences. The core competences become inputs into:

- Portfolio analysis (see Chapter 13), but based this time on whether your core competences are being applied to your stars rather than your dogs.
- Studying potential threats to the organisation, which requires that you search for substitute core competences from rival organisations, in substitute products, in new technologies and/or suppliers (Porter (6)).
- Acquisition strategy or strategic alliances where the objective is to complement core competences rather than acquire new core competences which are at variance with the culture and management capability of the organisation.
- Divestment decisions, where those units and subsidiaries which do not exploit or add to the core competences of the organisation are targeted for disposal rather than those which deploy the core competences.

The same logic applies to many other decisions which the organisation needs to make in the areas of process renewal and innovation, personnel policy and skills development, and other related aspects of the business.

1.9 Summary

Many entrepreneurs have an intuitive grasp of the synergy which an understanding of core competence analysis can bring to their business. Managers, on the other hand, particularly those who are not involved in the strategic aspects of the business, will need to employ techniques such as those explained already to unravel the hidden capabilities of the organisations they manage. They ought to start by looking at the markets they serve and the products they sell to these markets. They need to judge the importance of these markets and products to the future of the business. They then need to uncover the subsystems and the combination of skills, processes, technologies and assets which come together within each subsystem to confer sustainable, repeatable and unique competitive advantage. Having done this they should set about applying this knowledge to plan and execute new strategies which continue to build and reinforce these competences, even as they let less attractive products and services wither. The primary objective of the analysis is to optimise the applied capability of the organisation not only to secure profits today but also to position the business for the future and eventually take an industry lead.

References

(1) Prahalad, C.K. and Hamel, G. (1990). 'The core competence of the corporation', *Harvard Business Review*, May–June.
(2) Parsons, T. (1960). *Structure and Process in Modern Societies*, New York: The Free Press.
(3) Kay, J. (1993). *The Foundations of Corporate Success*, Oxford.
(4) *The Economist* (1995). 'Dismantling Daimler-Benz', 18 November.
(5) Bowen, D. (1993). 'Calling up the Future', *The Independent on Sunday*, 8 August.
(6) Porter, M.E. (1987). 'From competitive advantage to corporate strategy', *Harvard Business Review*, May/June and (1979) 'How competitive forces shape strategy', *Harvard Business Review*, March/April.

Further reading

Espejo, R. and Harnden, R. (eds) (1989). *The Viable System Mode*, Chichester: John Wiley & Sons.
Florida, R. and Kenney, M. (1990). *The Breakthrough Illusion*, Basic Books.
Goold, M. and Campbell, A. (1987). *Strategies and Styles, the Role of the Centre in Managing Diversified Corporations*, Oxford: Basil Blackwell.
Hamel, G. and Heene, A. (eds) (1994). *Competence Based Competition*, New York: John Wiley & Sons.
Lorange, P. and Roos, J. (1992). *Strategic Alliances*, Oxford: Blackwell.
Lynn, M. (1992). *The Billion-Dollar Battle*, Mandarin.
Miller, D. (1992). 'The Icarus paradox', *Business Horizons*, January–February.
Morecroft, J.D.W. and Sterman, J.D. (1994). *Modeling for Learning Organisations*, Portland: Productivity Press.
Post, J.E. (1978). *Corporate Behaviour and Social Change*, Reston Publishing Co.
Prahalad, C.K. and Hamel, G. (1989). 'Strategic intent', *Harvard Business Review*, May/June.
Prahalad, C.K. and Hamel, G. (1994). *Competing for the Future*, Cambridge, MA: Harvard Business School Press.
Slatter, S. (1984). *Corporate Recovery*, London: Penguin.
Tampoe, M. (1994). 'Exploiting the core competences of your organisation', *Long Range Planning*, **27** (4), 66–77.
Ulrich, D. and Lake, D. (1990). *Organisational Capability*, New York: John Wiley & Sons.

2 Understanding and using value chain analysis

By Andrew Shepherd

Editor's Introduction

Section 4.3.1 of *Exploring Corporate Strategy* introduces the concept of the value chain as an important way in which managers can start to identify the competences and core competences of their organisation and the links to their competitive performance. Turning these broad concepts into practical management tools requires two things. First, managers must be able to identify the core competences of their organisation, which is not easy as it is likely to be part of the tacit knowledge in the organisation and taken for granted. Second, the need to move from a qualitative description of an organisation's value chain(s) to a detailed and quantified assessment of where both cost and value are being added and lost. As mentioned in *Exploring Corporate Strategy*, this latter approach returns to the origins of value analysis of the early 1960s. Andrew Shepherd's chapter reviews value chain analysis at both the qualitative and the quantitative levels and is a useful addition to the coverage of the value chain analysis in *Exploring Corporate Strategy*.

2.1 Introduction

Value chain analysis (VCA) is a framework for taking knowledge that you have about a business and structuring that knowledge so that it can provide you with new insights into that business. Part of its value as a strategic tool lies in the way it forces you to make explicit what you know. This chapter will cover two levels of VCA.

The first level describes an application of Porter's technique (1), which is strong in preformed structure, and relatively qualitative. We will apply it to the sandwich bar business, to understand the different ways in which customers can be served with lunchtime food, and the implications this has on required business competences.

The second level demonstrates a more detailed and segmented approach (Figure 2.1) which my colleagues and I have been developing over the last ten years. This adapts Porter's concept to construct quantified value chains for each segment of a company's business, reveal-

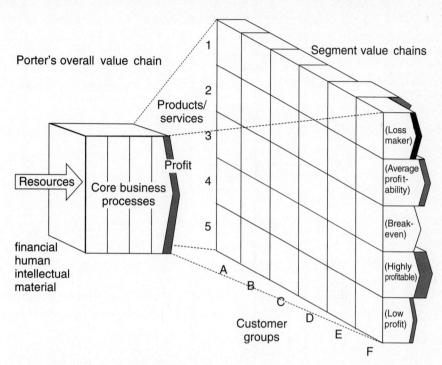

Figure 2.1   *An organisation is a set of processes for delivering products or services to customers.*

ing where value is being created, or destroyed, and so providing the basis for an agenda for change.

2.2   *The Porter approach – to sandwich bars*

In 1982, VCA consisted of little more than staring at a stacked bar chart of a company's management accounts and trying to create ideas to reduce cost or increase customer value. For a traditional 'Italian' family-run sandwich bar this is a very simple picture (Figure 2.2). The Porter framework (Figure 2.3) is richer, requiring us to spell out just what we think the value-creating activities are and to position them accordingly in the format.

It is still somewhat sparse, the lack of significant support activities confirming the simple nature of such a single-site, family-run business. Already, however, Porter's framework is forcing us to think about the business in a different way. Why, for example, have I chosen to place sandwich assembly (in which customer-selected ingredients are placed between slices of bread, and wrapped) in 'Marketing and sales' instead of solely in 'Operations'? If you have ever been a regular

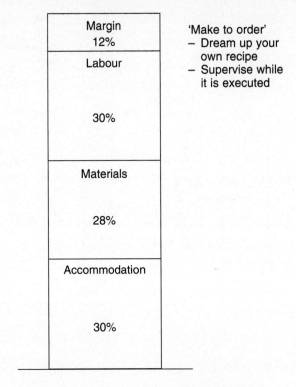

Figure 2.2   Sandwich bar value chain: traditional 'Italian'.

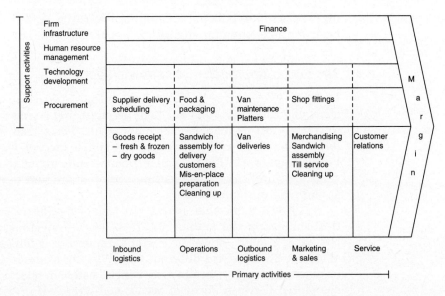

Figure 2.3   Defining the value chain: traditional 'Italian' sandwich bar.

visitor to an Italian sandwich bar you will remember the banter that takes place between customer and staff – and between staff – during this process. Done well, it is a mix of entertainment, relationship building and selling up; done badly, it is just an 'Operations' procedure. The same applies to cleaning up; in an unbranded business, uncertainty about hygiene, and freshness of ingredients for that matter, is difficult to address. Making the cleaning-up process conspicuous, and using a different pair of hands for till service (and the handling of germ-ridden money) from those used for sandwich assembly is a way of sending a *marketing* message.

From a customer perspective, however, this value chain is potentially missing the opportunity to create more value. The best sandwich bars are characterised by long queues at lunchtime, and the recipes selected by customers tend to be safe and, therefore, repetitive. Is there a viable alternative value chain?

The concept shown in Figure 2.4 is for customer self-service of

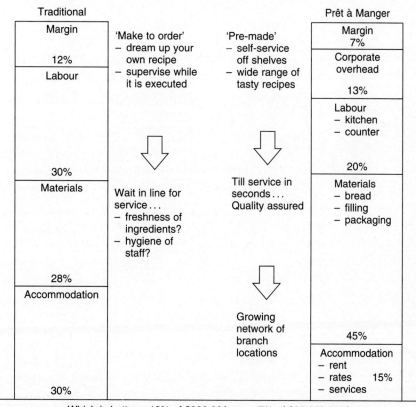

Which is better – 12% of £200,000 pa or 7% of £25,000,000?

Figure 2.4   Sandwich bar value chains.

sandwiches, pre-made to tasty recipes, with a McDonalds style of rapid till service, without queues, building into a branded offer exuding quality and freshness. The simple bar chart value chain seems to offer a much lower profit margin, expressed as a percentage of sales, but this is misleading. If you look at the materials content portion, you will notice that it is 50 per cent higher than for a traditional sandwich sale. If you accept that Prêt à Manger, whose concept this is, are probably not worse at buying sandwich ingredients than Luigi or Victor, then it would seem that better value for money is on offer. All things being equal, this should result in higher local market share and a bigger catchment area per shop – and it does.

Their accommodation piece of the value chain (15 per cent) is not half of the traditional value chain because of lower cost locations or a smaller number of square metres – in fact Prêt à Manger's outlets are typically in prime, higher rent locations, and are slightly bigger than the traditional sandwich bar. The reason is simply that sales per outlet are much higher, driving down the sales unit cost of rent and rates.

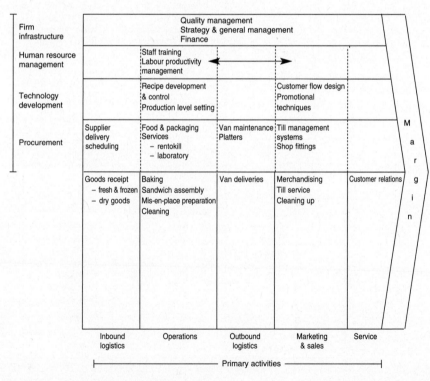

Figure 2.5   Defining the value chain: Prêt à Manger.

Porter's VCA framework now comes into its own, with the support activities in particular revealing more about what makes Prêt à Manger different (Figure 2.5).

If we translate the traditional stacked bar of management accounting costs and margin into Porter's framework, an operating cost value chain map can be drawn (Figures 2.6 and 2.7).

In the simple example shown in Figure 2.7, the importance of managing the purchased inputs is clear. It also emphasises the criticality of production level setting as a technology value activity. If the forecast for today's lunchtime sales is, say, 10 per cent too high, then this morning's sandwich making will consume 10 per cent more purchased inputs than it should, resulting in wastage of 4.5 per cent of sales – wiping out over 60 per cent of today's profits.

Translating assets into Porter's framework can be just as enlightening (Figures 2.8 and 2.9).

What's interesting in Figure 2.9 is the contrasting position of 'Marketing and sales' versus 'Operations'. The source of this can be traced to an imbalance in property leasehold assets, even though half the floor area of a typical Prêt à Manger outlet is kitchen and half is shop. Simple accounting would have allocated the leasehold cost equally, but Porter's framework prompted deeper questions: Why is the property leasehold cost this high? Is it mostly the need for operating space or is it the need for marketing and sales space? The answer is that sandwich making could take place in a low-cost factory unit, but selling needs high-value retail locations.

	Support activities				Primary activities					Margin
	Firm infrastructure	HRM	Technol	Proc'mt	Inbound logistics	Operations	Outbound logistics	Marketing & sales	Service	
Margin										7
Corporate overhead	4	3	3	3					<1	
Labour – kitchen – counter					<1	11	<1	8		
Materials – bread – filling – packaging						45				
Accommodation – rent – rates – electricity – water	No					9		6		

Figure 2.6   Operating costs: Prêt à Manger.

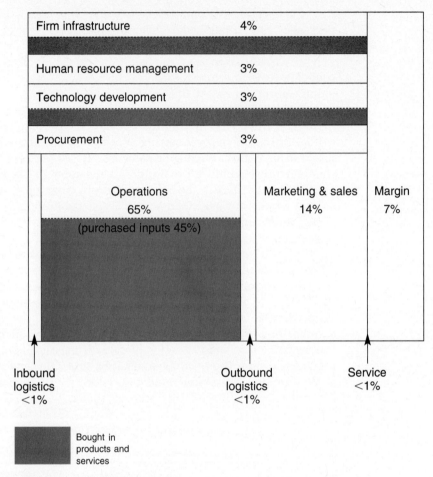

Figure 2.7   *Operating costs: Prêt à Manger.*

The marketing and sales portion of the asset value chain is high because the retail locations are expensive; perhaps the single most important aspect of Prêt à Manger's strategic management support layer is ensuring that these high-cost sites are also high value to the company and its clientele. Prêt à Manger wants to sell sandwiches, not newspapers or jewellery, and so local market research that enables a site's sandwich revenue potential to be closely predicted is extremely valuable. Look at the asset map again; if an outlet's sales turned out to be half the level expected when the site was acquired, would the asset cost change? Hardly at all – the liquid element is tiny, and the bulk of the spend for fixtures and fittings is not transferable to another site.

Cash	Firm infrastructure	HRM	Technol	Proc'mt	Inbound logistics	Operations	Outbound logistics	Marketing & sales	Service
	Support activities				Primary activities				
Debtors								2	1
Stock				3					
Motor vehicles	2						1		
Shop fixtures & fittings		<1	3		5	9		13	
Leaseholds	1	<1				9	1	50	

Figure 2.8   Assets: Prêt à Manger.

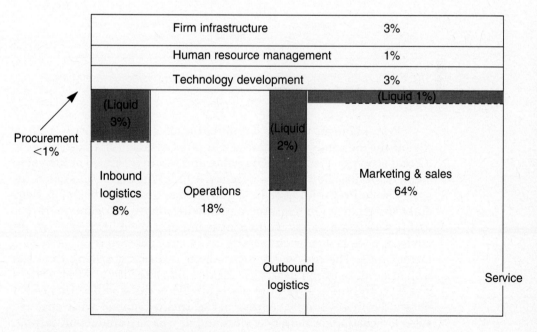

Firm infrastructure	3%
Human resource management	1%
Technology development	3%

Procurement <1%

(Liquid 3%)

Inbound logistics 8%

Operations 18%

(Liquid 2%)

Outbound logistics

(Liquid 1%)

Marketing & sales 64%

Service

Figure 2.9   Assets: Prêt à Manger.

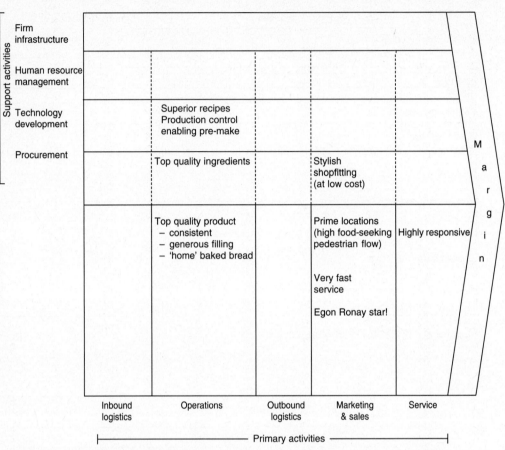

Figure 2.10   Successful differentiation strategy in sandwich provision: Prêt à Manger versus typical 'Italian'.

Prêt à Manger pursues a differentiation strategy (Figure 2.10) in the lunchtime sandwich business, but must also pay close attention to its cost strategy if it is to create value and retain a portion of the value created for its shareholders (Figure 2.11). When I first became involved with Prêt à Manger its turnover was around £600,000 a year, derived from one London shop and a deli-counter in a supermarket – and it was loss-making. Value was being destroyed because of an ill-advised move of sandwich-making away from the two retail sites to a factory unit. The previously high labour utilisation arising from the transition of morning sandwich makers into lunchtime till operators was lost, and retail sites were not available in the smaller size needed for sandwich sales only. A reversal of this, combined with effective sales forecasting for both new sites and day-to-day production setting, saw the business turn over some £25 million from 35 sites in 1995 at

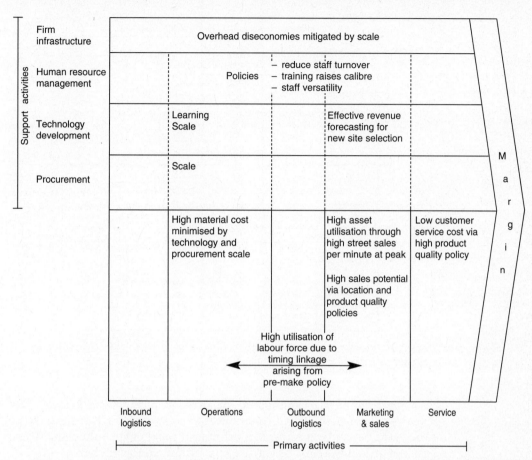

Figure 2.11   *Successful cost leadership strategy in sandwich provision: Prêt à Manger.*

a healthy profit. It is possible to create value while making losses through underpricing, but growing profits are a sure sign that you are on the right path!

2.3   *Categorising activities*

Subdivision of value chains (Figure 2.12) is helpful, but only if it separates activities which:

- have different economics, or
- have a high potential impact on differentiation, or
- represent a significant or growing proportion of cost.

Categorising activities requires judgement – there are no hard and fast rules. If it is thought-provoking, then your understanding is probably being enriched. For example, is order processing for the company

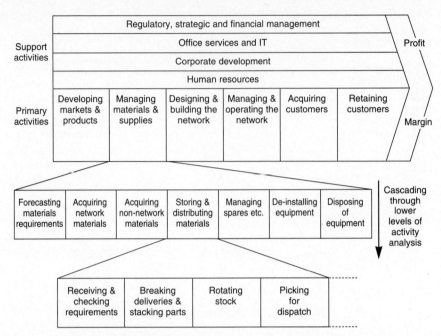

Figure 2.12   *Mercury Telecommunications' value chain structure (Source: Gwynne and Hasworth(2)).*

in question part of outbound logistics or part of marketing? The answer depends on how it contributes to competitive advantage. Order processing may be a routine, mechanised task, or it could be a critical customer-facing role ... as it is in an Italian sandwich bar.

The interaction of value chains between suppliers and customers can also be illuminating. Imagine a heavy truck company seeking to supply an office supplies wholesaler with its new fleet. The truck company has developed a series of differentiators which are intended to secure sales success by adding more value to its customers than its rivals can.

The differentiators can come from almost any part of the supplier's value chain, and their potential impact is similarly dispersed through the customer's value chain (Figure 2.13).

Salesforce skill is the last differentiator on the list shown, but is crucial. Without effective marketing and sales effort, not all of the dimensions of differentiation may be made known to the customer, and some potential value will be lost. Customers may be prepared to pay less for the truck than they might if all the facts were known, and even if they buy the truck, their ignorance of a differentiator may prevent them from exploiting it to create value. Fuel cost savings may become self-evident in a well-run fleet, but reduced goods damage from cargo

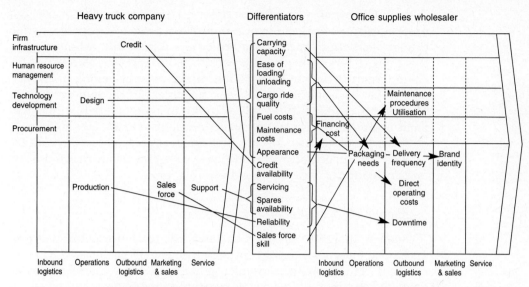

Figure 2.13   *Suppliers create differential value by lowering the buyer's cost and/or raising buyer's performance.*

ride quality improvement may neither be attributed to the truck, nor prompt lower cost packaging choices. Effective communication of value is therefore critical to both buyer and seller.

2.4   *Segmented value chain analysis*

Most businesses, seeking a degree of strategic security, choose to serve many customers with a variety of products (or services). The value chain of the company is adapted to accommodate the new products and customers as the enterprise grows, but the detail of this process is rarely apparent to the people in the business. The real effects of the changing business portfolio may take some time to be reflected in the value chain, and in the company's bottom line.

Segmented VCA is a way of revealing the value chain for each customer and product segment – the elements which have become exaggerated or suppressed, and the profit generated, the value captured. It is an enormously powerful and valuable technique, particularly at the start of a strategic review process. The methodology developed by the Alexander Partnership's team extends Porter's concept by combining it with the basics of activity-based costing.

2.4.1   *Core business processes*

The approach to specifying a company's core business processes is discussed more fully in Chapter 1. In essence we are simply allowing

Porter's five primary and four support activities to be whatever is appropriate for the business in question. We are also taking seriously the primary activities' dotted lines in Porter's framework, extending into the support layers. A potential weakness in applying Porter's value chain format is the tendency to see 'direct' costs belonging in the primary layer and 'indirect overheads' belonging in the support layers. The danger is that little is added to the insights offered by management accounts. Overhead has no divine right to exist – it should only be there for a purpose. Taking a business process perspective disentangles the important overhead layers and provides a rational basis for benchmarking (see Chapter 4).

2.4.2 Segmentation of customers and products

A common analytical pitfall is to delve into too much detail and produce thick piles of numerical output which cannot be digested by management. The purpose of segmentation in VCA is therefore not so much to simplify the analysis as to simplify the understanding which follows.

VCA customer segmentation should be based on different customer groups' needs for, and impact on, core business processes. If we consider the Prêt à Manger sandwich bar business, four customer segments emerge from its five core processes (Figure 2.14).

	Core business processes					
	Find attractive new sites	Open shops quickly and effectively	Make excellent sandwiches efficiently	Sell efficiently, with minimum queues	Develop and refine the formula	Segmentation
Lawyers	Near to office	Effective customer flow design	Satisfying tasting product range	Time critical	Quality and variety	Regular pick-up
Accountants	Near to office	Effective customer flow design	Satisfying tasting product range	Time critical	Quality and variety	
Large merchant banks	One-hour response time from order to delivery	Corporate marketing	Substantial central purchase	100% service fulfilment	Quality and cost	Corporate deliveries
Tourists	Near to shops	Efficient seating plan	Attractive looking product	Somewhere to sit down	Inviting outlets	Eat-in
Selfridges' customers	In third parties' (department?) stores	Thought-through deal structure	Staff utilisation (production only)	(Contracted out to store staff)	Rollout concept	In store

Figure 2.14   *Strategic customer segmentation needs to be founded on different customers' needs for, and impact on, core business processes: sandwich bar example.*

	Goods supply	Storage	Picking & packing	Delivery	Customer service	Segmentation
Staplers	Frequent purchase	Shelved area	Repacked as singles	Straight-forward	No problems	Desk accessories
Post-it notes	Frequent purchase	Shelved area	Repacked in subsets	Straight-forward	No problems	Desk accessories
Calculators	Price drops while in stock	Secure store	Warehouse manager access only	Straight-forward	High returns 'wrong colour'	Office machines
Fax machines	Price drops while in stock	Secure store	Warehouse manager access only	Straight-forward	No problems	Office machines
Computer tables	Obsolescence	Pallet racking	Fork lift picked	Higher risk of in-transit damage	No problems	Furniture
Desks	Range selection & obsolescence	Pallet racking	Fork lift picked	Higher risk of in-transit damage	Range availability for add-ons	Furniture

Figure 2.15   *Product segmentation is similarly based on differentiated impact on the value chain: office products wholesaler example.*

One or more of the core processes of location, site design, sandwich making, selling and developing the formula are differently impacted by each of the customer groups. We have chosen to put lawyers and accountants together, despite the accountants' greater price sensitivity, because they are more like each other than the other segments. If we were to discover later that they each made up 30 per cent of Prêt à Manger's business we might well separate them, but at this stage the analysis is being kept simple.

VCA product segmentation is similarly based on differentiated impact on the value chain. For an office products wholesaler, handling 12,000 different stock-keeping units (SKUs), the simplification of a useful segmentation is invaluable (Figure 2.15). Although I used over 24 product segments in a study of such a company, the three shown here would, with hindsight, have probably been just as useful!

It should be remembered that we are not interested in whether the products bear any functional resemblance to each other, but only in whether they have similar impacts on the value chain.

2.4.3   Costing the business processes, and identifying drivers

Armed with the management accounts of a business, it is a straightforward task to interview department managers to ascertain (a) how much of their effort is spent on each of the core processes, and (b) the principal drivers of that effort.

Strategy in action

Illustration 2.1

Office supplies

Cost centres	£'000
Depots (10, spread nationally)	
Labour	
warehouse	1,000
drivers	700
field sales	600
telesales	700
administration	900
Accommodation	1,400
Vehicles	900
Other	500
Head office	
Finance and administration	900
Computer, etc	1,200
Purchasing	400
Operations management	200
	9,400

Our office supplies wholesaler (Illustration 2.1), for example, has a purchasing department costing £400,000 a year to run. The 'Purchasing' core business process incurs cost from other departments, too. Besides the computing and finance activities that keep track of purchase orders and associated payments, there is also activity in the depots, calling off supplies from centrally negotiated contracts. The total cost of this core business process amounts to some £700,000 per annum (Figure 2.16).

The principal 'drivers' of the purchasing process usually turn out to be the number of suppliers dealt with and the number of stock-keeping units (SKUs) purchased. The number of purchase orders placed with suppliers may also be a factor, but in this simplified example it, and other drivers of purchasing, will be ignored.

The relative weighting of each driver is then needed, and a series of interview questions is usually enough to get close:

Cost centres	Processes								Total
	Purchasing	Goods in	Storage	Goods out	Delivery	Selling	Order proc'g	General fixed	
Depot									
Labour									
– warehouse		200	100	700					1,000
– drivers					700				700
– field sales						540	60		600
– telesales						70	630		700
– administration	100	50	50	100	200	200	200		900
Accommodation		100	1,000	200	100				1,400
Vehicles					900				900
Other		50	50	100	100	100	100		500
Head office									
Finance & administration	100		50			50	600	100	900
Computer, etc.	100	50	100	200	50	50	600	50	1,200
Purchasing	400								400
Operations management				50	50	50	50		200
Total	700	450	1,350	1,350	2,100	1,060	2,240	150	9,400

Figure 2.16   Analysing the value chain: step 1.

- How many more buyers would you need if you doubled the number of SKUs purchased, but all with today's suppliers?
- How many more buyers would you need if you doubled the number of suppliers from whom you purchased, but with today's SKUs?

In the example, the weighting is 50 : 50 between suppliers and SKUs (Figure 2.17).

Note: Fixed costs

Very, very few costs are truly fixed, in a strategic time frame. Most of the added costs are variable in the medium term, with respect to customers, products or both. In our experience the only fixed costs are some statutory accounting and the security guard on the gate. If we

Outputs/ cost drivers	Processes								
	Purchasing	Goods in	Storage	Goods out	Delivery	Selling	Order proc'g	Fixed	Total
SKUs	350		1,000	400		80	140		1,970
Suppliers	350	350							700
Units		100	350	50	600				1,100
Customer orders				400			400		800
Order lines				500		90	1,500		2,090
Deliveries					1,500				1,500
Field sales calls						800			800
Customers						90	200		290
Fixed								150	150
Total	700	450	1,350	1,350	2,100	1,060	2,240	150	9,400

Figure 2.17 Analysing the value chain: step 2.

treat the managing director's costs as fixed, it is only because it saves time and does not materially affect accuracy!

2.4.4 Costing drivers and sorting into customer and product groups

In our office products wholesaler example the number of SKUs does not affect purchasing. It is a major contributor to storage cost, and affects other process costs too. The total amount of cost driven by the number of SKUs is £1,970,000 per annum, or about £164 per SKU per annum, given that 12,000 SKUs are stocked (Figure 2.18).

Once the other cost drivers are similarly analysed, a simple linear equation of the value chain of the business can be written:

Profit = Gross margin − 164 ∗ SKUs − 3,500 ∗ Suppliers − 0.20 ∗ Units − ... − 150,000

Sorting the drivers into customer- and product-related groups is the next step (Illustration 2.2). Ask the question: Will there be more units of this cost driver if I add products, or if I add customers? Judgement is required, since different businesses will generate different mappings. For example, it is usually a safe bet that field sales calls

Strategy in action

Illustration 2.2

Office supplies wholesaler

	Large	Large/ medium	Small/ medium	Small	Total
		Customer groups			
Number	80	155	440	1,400	2,075
Sales (£ million)	16	16	8	3	43
Gross profit (%)	17	23	28	29	22
Sales call frequency					
– field sales	weekly	fortnightly	monthly	monthly –quarterly	22,000 p.a.
–telesales		–––––––––––daily––––––––––– (or more)			
Sample average values (£)					
– order	325	200	80	30	131 (329,000 p.a.)
– delivery	555	430	125	35	199 (216,000 p.a.)
Order lines per order	10	7	4	2	5 (1.65m p.a.)

Product information
Number of units   5.6 million/year
Number of lines   12,000
Number of suppliers   200

are customer related. However, if the company has just diversified into a totally new product area – say, personal computer modems – it may be that a new salesperson has been appointed to service this specialised sector, in which case these costs could be product related.

Some drivers will be judged both product *and* customer related (Figure 2.18). In this example the number of product units despatched and order lines processed per annum are considered to be customer and product related. In other words, if we did more business with the same product range and the same customers, we would expect to process more units and order lines through the system.

The analysis can be summarised on a four-box chart. The results are already useful strategically (Figure 2.19):

- Growing business with existing customers with current products

Outputs/ cost drivers	Total cost £'000	Number of outputs	Cost/unit £	Customer related	Product related	Customer and product
SKUs	1,970	12,000	164		P	
Suppliers	700	200	3,500		P	
Units	1,100	5,600,000	0.20			C&P
Customer orders	800	329,200	2.43	C		
Order lines	2,090	1,652,000	1.27			C&P
Deliveries	1,500	215,700	6.95	C		
Field sales calls	800	21,870	36.58	C		
Customers	290	2,075	140	C		
Fixed	150	N/A				

Figure 2.18   Analysing the value chain: step 3.

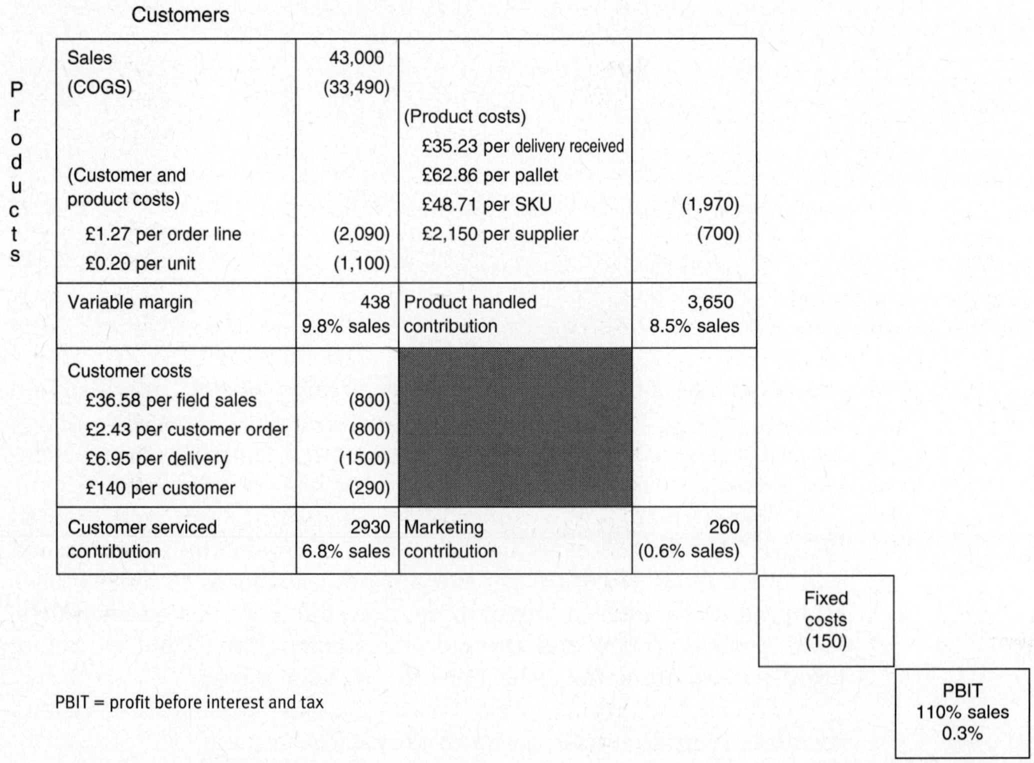

Customers

P r o d u c t s

Sales	43,000		
(COGS)	(33,490)		
		(Product costs)	
		£35.23 per delivery received	
(Customer and product costs)		£62.86 per pallet	
		£48.71 per SKU	(1,970)
£1.27 per order line	(2,090)	£2,150 per supplier	(700)
£0.20 per unit	(1,100)		
Variable margin	438 9.8% sales	Product handled contribution	3,650 8.5% sales
Customer costs			
£36.58 per field sales	(800)		
£2.43 per customer order	(800)		
£6.95 per delivery	(1500)		
£140 per customer	(290)		
Customer serviced contribution	2930 6.8% sales	Marketing contribution	260 (0.6% sales)

Fixed costs (150)

PBIT 110% sales 0.3%

PBIT = profit before interest and tax

Figure 2.19   ABC PBIT structure (£'000).

would earn around 15 per cent of incremental sales (not the 22 per cent average gross margin, because costs *will* rise with volume).

- Adding more 'average' customers will earn around 7 per cent of sales (and average customers are often harder to find than below-average ones!).
- Adding more 'average' products to increase revenues from the same customers will earn around 8 per cent on sales.

Some approximate breakeven analysis is also possible. The smallest order will cost at least £1.27 + £0.20 + £2.43 + £6.95 = £10.85. Given an average gross margin of 22 per cent, orders under £50 are likely to be unprofitable.

2.4.5 Calculating segment value chains

Now that we know the company's value chain equation we can calculate any segment's value chain, given its sales, gross margin and values for each of the driver parameters – units, order lines and SKUs and suppliers for a product segment, or units, order lines and all of the customer servicing drivers for a customer segment.

The basic data given here for four customer size band segments (Illustration 2.3) enables customer group profitability to be calculated

Strategy in action

Illustration 2.3

Analysing the value chain – customer overview

		Large	Large/ medium	Small/ medium	Small	Total
No.		80	155	440	1,400	2,075
Sales (£ million)		16	16	8	3	43
Gross profit	– (%)	17	23	28	29	22
	– £'000	2,270	3,680	2,240	870	9,510
Sales calls	– per year	52	26	12	6	
	– total no.	4,160	4,030	5,280	8,400	21,870
Orders	– value (£)	325	200	80	30	130.6
	– total ('000)	49.2	80.0	100.0	100.0	329.2
Order lines	– line/order	10	7	4	2	5
	– total ('000)	492	560	400	200	1,652
Deliveries	– value (£)	555	430	125	35	199
	– total ('000)	28.8	37.2	64.0	85.7	215.7

		Customer group				Total	Product handling and marketing costs		
		Large	Large/ medium	Small/ medium	Small				
Sales, £'000s		16,000	16,000	8,000	3,000	43,000			
Gross profit %		17	23	28	29	22.1			
Gross profit, £'000s		2,720	3,680	2,240	870	9,510			
Customer and product costs	- units	409	409	205	77	1,100	Product handling costs	– stock-keeping units	1,970
	- order lines	622	709	506	253	2,090		– suppliers	700
Variable margin		1,689	2,562	1,529	540	6,320	Product handled contribution		3,650
Customer servicing costs	- orders	120	194	243	243	800			
	- deliveries	200	259	445	596	1,500			
	- calls	152	148	193	307	800			
	- customers	11	22	61	196	290			
Customer serviced contribution		1,206	1,939	587	(802)	2,930	Marketing contribution		260

(Fixed) (150)

PBIT 110

Figure 2.20   Analysing strategic customer profitability (£'000).

(product group profitability is achieved by a similar process) (Figure 2.20).

As the earlier breakeven analysis indicated, the small customer segment is decidedly unprofitable for this company – its value chain is simply inappropriate for this type of customer, being much more suited to the large/medium-sized group.

2.4.6   Analysing segment profitability

What should the office products wholesaler do? Scrabbling around for extra gross margin by signing up more small customers is not going to restore profitability. Even if another 5 per cent of gross margin had to be given up to win more large and large/medium accounts, the extra business would be profitable, but raising prices for small customers does not look realistic. Just to break even the gross margin would have to nearly double, meaning that, effectively, they would be buying at retail prices.

Some radical rethinking of the value chain serving small accounts is required. Delivery seems to be this segment's Achilles heel; how many small account customers could be persuaded to pick up from the company's depots? Could the business be kept if a £60 minimum order size were introduced? Scrapping field sales calls to these accounts would release a valuable sales resource to attack the really attractive business, too.

2.4.7 Segmented VCA-driven strategy

We looked at core business processes in Section 2.4.1, and we are now in a position to define the core business in terms of products and customers. For the office products wholesaler some further segmentation work revealed that customer location, as well as customer size, was a profit driver, while furniture was a dog of a product for the current value chain (Figure 2.21).

Once the core is identified, it is relatively straightforward to construct an income statement for the core part of a business (Figure 2.22). It is rarely appropriate to downsize a company immediately to this theoretical core: in the short term many costs are fixed, and rather than write these off it is often cheaper to work them off (like vehicle leases, premises leases). Continuing to do business which is unprofitable in the long term can make sense:

- Some may be truly marginal business, as long as investment is not needed to accommodate it.
- Some customers may require that certain unprofitable products remain in the range served, but the cost of such concessions is a marketing expense against that customer's account, not a product-related cost.

Even though the core is the part of the business best served by its current value chain, this value chain may not be the best shape for the

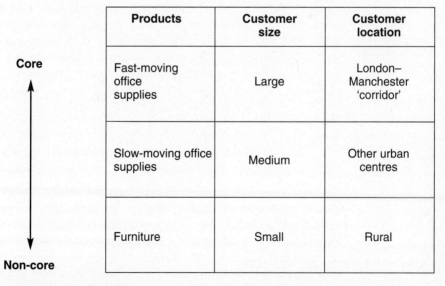

	Products	Customer size	Customer location
Core	Fast-moving office supplies	Large	London–Manchester 'corridor'
	Slow-moving office supplies	Medium	Other urban centres
Non-core	Furniture	Small	Rural

Figure 2.21   Segment profitabilities reveal where core value is created: business-to-business wholesaler.

Current turnover

Customer groups

Product groups	Core large 'corridor'	Semi-core medium 'corridor'	Non-core large + medium + urban	Non-core small+ rural
Core fast-moving office supplies	12.0	13.2	0.6	0.2
Semi-core slow-moving office supplies	1.0	4.2	0.2	0.2
Furniture	1.6	0.6	2.6	6.6

43.0

(a)

	Current business	Core business
Turnover	43.0	33.4
Gross profit	20.2	15.6
Variable	4.0	3.0
Product handling	4.2	1.6
Customer service	8.8	4.6
Marketing contribution	3.2	6.4
Genuinely fixed	1.6	1.6
PBIT	1.6	4.8
Capital employed	16.4	11.4
ROCE	10%	42%

(b)

Figure 2.22   Constructing an income statement for the core: office products wholesaler (£ million). (a) Most companies have a 'core' ... (b) which is, potentially, highly attractive.

core. For our office products wholesaler, ten depots each with their own salesforce were not ideal for serving the core, and so a medium-term objective of reducing to four depots was appropriate (Figure 2.23). The higher stock turn this promised brought some SKUs back into profitability. The logic also became compelling for increased investment in EDI (electronic data interchange) to allow core customers to place their own orders directly; an excellent example of value being created for customers *and* suppliers by eliminating steps in the chain. Traditional telesales is still required, but only for a minority of business.

The non-core business is the next focus for analysis. What is the right approach for these customer and product segments?

- Perhaps regional 'pocket' depots can be viable, only stocking the fastest moving products and acting as a transhipment point for deliveries from the main depots to more remote conurbations.
- Maybe a purpose-designed furniture operation can add value, with one central store.
- Can we skim the cream from competitors by offering a low-cost bulk service of the top 600 lines – only shipping out quantities of products (not one stapler!) grouped into pallet-sized deliveries?

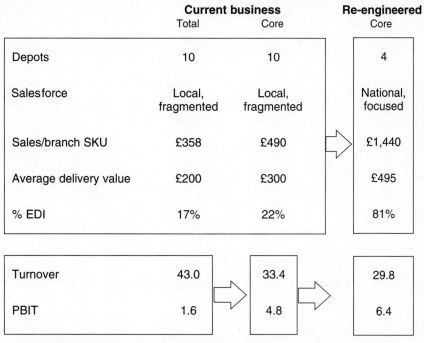

| | Current business | | Re-engineered |
	Total	Core	Core
Depots	10	10	4
Salesforce	Local, fragmented	Local, fragmented	National, focused
Sales/branch SKU	£358	£490	£1,440
Average delivery value	£200	£300	£495
% EDI	17%	22%	81%

Turnover	43.0	33.4	29.8
PBIT	1.6	4.8	6.4

Figure 2.23 Re-engineering to serve the core single-mindedly can radically simplify a business and make it more successful.

Configuring value chains appropriately to the segment is the key. It is much less risky, and probably more profitable, for a business to adopt segment-specific strategies to serve the revenue base it already has, than to launch into some new business area.

Over time a business can be transformed by this approach (Figure 2.24). The core is the focus for growth, progressively displacing the marginal business retained only to soak up short-term 'fixed' costs. Re-engineering to serve the core augments profitability. On top of this comes the 're-entered' non-core business, a drain on profits at the outset, but a significant contributor once the segment-specific value chains are in place.

2.5 Summary

As businesses become more complex – with broadening product ranges serving an increasingly segmented customer base and indirect 'overhead' costs growing faster than directs – knowing what your value chain does well is difficult to identify but is most important in the face of rising competition. Value chain analysis is an excellent means of

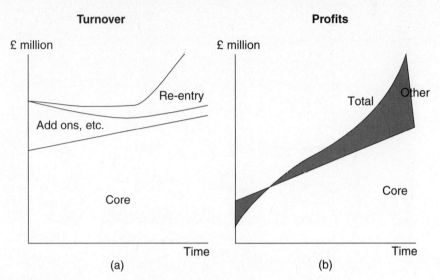

Figure 2.24   *(a) An apparently evolutionary strategy ... (b) can revolutionise performance.*

disentangling the complexities to reveal what is really going on between a company and its market. Once the economics of one's own business are understood, it is relatively easy to model a competitor's too. Getting to grips with the value chains of customers is the next step, to see how well value is created for them. Customers are the ultimate arbiters of what is, or is not, valuable. How much of the value created is captured by the customer, and how much by the supplier?

Even crude approximations can give valuable insights and the author encourages you to try the technique for yourself. It is immensely powerful!

References

(1)   Porter, M.E. (1985). *Competitive Advantage*, New York: The Free Press.
(2)   Gwynne, R. and Hasworth, G. (1993). 'Implementing activity based management at Mercury Communication', *Management Accounting*, December, p. 36.

3

Strategic financial accounting for analysing performance and resources

By Tony Grundy

Editor's introduction

In Section 4.4 of *Exploring Corporate Strategy* the importance of assessing an organisation's position *vis-à-vis* its competitors is discussed. Financial analyses, and financial ratios in particular, are some of the ways for an organisation to compare its performance with other players in its industry. Tony Grundy's chapter details and complements the discussion in *Exploring Corporate Strategy* by explaining how financial statements can be dissected in such a way that financial data can be turned into valuable information when making strategic decisions.

3.1 Introduction

Although most strategy books make some reference to financial ratios, this is primarily in the context of *internal* rather than *external* analysis. Financial ratios are thus seen as being the principal concern of financial analysts and not that of the strategic planner (and more widely, strategic thinkers – which all managers should be).

Yet financial statements offer an untold wealth of combined strategic and financial insights. Financial ratio analysis can be very readily coupled with strategic analysis within a single process of:

Strategic Financial Accounting

Strategic financial accounting (or SFA) emphasises the importance of using strategic vision to explore how value is generated or destroyed both at corporate and business levels. Strategic financial accounting is thus defined as:

> *The process of analysing financial statements and company reports by both financial and strategic techniques. This process creates a more rounded view of business performance, position and potential.*

Financial statements can be used for a variety of strategic purposes, particularly:

- In formulating one's own company's strategy, especially to support and test out the strengths, weaknesses, opportunities and threats (SWOT) analysis.
- In understanding the strategy of key competitors, for instance to pinpoint their strengths and weaknesses, their opportunities and constraints, and likely strategic intent.
- In gaining a deeper understanding of key customers' strategic positions, and their present and future needs.
- In evaluating avenues for corporate development – particularly by acquisition, joint ventures and alliances.
- For targeting breakthrough cost reductions (these being cost reductions well beyond incremental cost management).

Strategic financial accounting is also valuable for understanding and anticipating strategic change in both your own and in other companies. In particular, SFA can be used to assess competence in *implementing* strategic change. This invites key questions during the review of annual reports including, for example:

- What does the corporate report reveal about management's past track record in implementing strategic change?
- What is the potential financial impact (both in terms of upsides and downsides) from current strategic change initiatives – both internal and external?
- *How aware* does senior management appear to be (based on the chairman's and directors' reports, and other commentary) of the problems, constraints and uncertainties which they are likely to face in *future* implementation?
- Where gaps or enormous challenges are apparent, what does top management intend to do about it?

This chapter now explores SFA in depth by explaining the SFA process, through a case study of IBM for the accounting period 1993/94 and by drawing out the key lessons generally.

3.2   *The SFA process*

Analysing financial statements is very much an art and not a science. Many managers do not appreciate this – their prime concern is (a) to get the ratios 'right', and (b) to be able to say immediately whether these ratios indicate 'good' or 'bad' performance.

However life is just not that simple. It is rarely possible to do a mechanistic analysis of a company and then say simplistically that 'because ratios x, y, z, are weak, the company is about to go bust ...' It is only by looking at financial ratios along with some strategic analysis that the underlying performance, position and potential can be effectively dissected.

Figure 3.1 gives us an eleven-stage process for achieving a

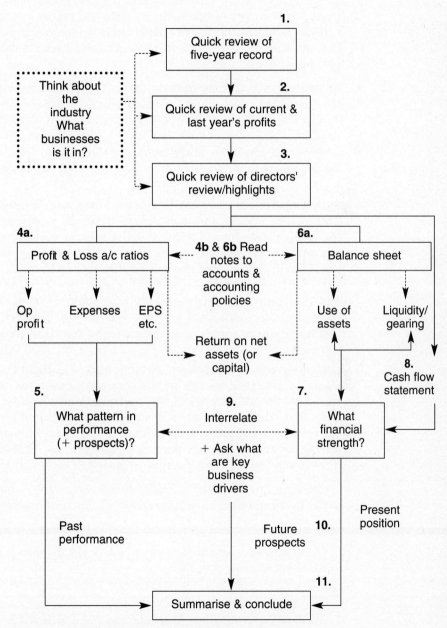

Figure 3.1   A process for interpreting annual reports and accounts.

complete strategic and financial vision of a company. This process combines competitive, financial and organisational analysis.

1   Quick review of the five-year record

It is fruitful to start with the company's five-year review. This is often buried at the back of the company's annual report and allows the analyst to pick up a quick picture of trends before looking at the detail of current trading. This review of longer-term historic trends will help identify, for example:

- an uneven past trading record – implying competitive vulnerability;
- the impact of exceptional (or extraordinary) items – these are often due to major strategic errors of judgement or implementation in the past;
- longer-term trends in margins or operating profit (and costs) – illustrating shifts in both competitive and financial positions.

2   Quick review of current year's and last year's profits

This review involves a quick glance at the current year's profit (and the comparative figure) without doing a lot of detailed ratios. For instance, if expenses are rising faster than turnover then a skilled reader with a numerate eye can readily spot this.

You might also wish to think about the nature of the industry and the company's businesses at this point. How does the current result look in comparison with the industry environment? To answer this may require some ongoing tracking of trends in the sector.

3   Quick review of directors' review and highlights

There is always a wealth of insights (and questions) which can be raised by the statements of the chairman and the chief executive as they also usually contain some key financial highlights. Directors' statements often tell you a lot about the impact of current business strategies and tactics on financial performance. However, you may have to read behind the lines; for instance, a comment such as:

> *'Trading has been difficult with tough competitive conditions which we are responding to by aggressive pricing and marketing'*

may mean

> *'We are locked in a price war which could do the company lasting financial damage.'*

Or

> *'We have refocused our business and have divested non-core activities X and Y'*

may mean

> *'At last we have recognised that a number of acquisitions were ill-thought-through and we are now drip-feeding divestments over a number of accounting periods – with more bad news to come.'*

It is also particularly useful to have a quick look at the directors' backgrounds (if available), and their style and personal drive (revealing the company's capability). In addition, you may need to reflect on the present and future impact of the economic cycle, and whether the market is (or might become) fiercely competitive, or whether management has simply taken on too much (especially when diversifying).

Finally, it may be fruitful to analyse trends in the percentages of different businesses. This may highlight important changes in the mix of businesses which may have come about either through a deliberate strategy or emergent strategy, or more likely a mixture of the two.

4 & 5   Profit and loss account – key ratios

The profit and loss account can seem a little confusing to many managers, but at bottom the profit and loss account is relatively straightforward to understand. The main source of confusion comes from the sheer number of different levels of profit.

In answering the question of 'Which line of operating profit do I take in my comparison?, the answer is:

> *'It depends – if you take the operating profit line before interest then this gives a useful comparison of trading performance irrespective of what financing structure is in place. But where a good deal of working (and longer-term) capital is tied up in the business, then arguably managers should be seen as responsible for profit after interest (both at the business, as well as at group, level).'*

Exceptional items are trickier to interpret. You need to look at what they are – in order to discriminate between recurring and non-recurring items. This may be difficult – especially where management is accident prone. If you are in doubt, just calculate the ratio both ways to see what the result is. Also, conjecture what *further* exceptionals are to come.

It is also fruitful to analyse key expense ratios as a percentage of revenues, but you will probably need to go back to the more detailed notes to the accounts to get sufficiently refined data to work with.

6 & 7   Balance sheet

The balance sheet *must* be read in unison with the notes to the accounts, otherwise you will easily pick up the wrong numbers (for example, assuming that 'debtors' is the same thing as 'trade debtors'). Also, you will need to do a quick skim read of all the detailed notes. For instance, it is easy to miss notes like 'contingent liabilities' simply because they were not relevant to a specific ratio. Contingent liabilities (even in one-line notes) have been known to have subsequently brought major companies to their knees. Notable UK examples include Colorol and Polly Peck.

You will now need to work steadily down through the balance sheet, considering in turn:

- *The company's use of assets*: stocks, debtors, fixed assets relative to turnover. (You can also look at the number of people relative to turnover from the relevant profit and loss account note). You should also look at debtors days relative to turnover.
- *Liquidity*: consider especially the 'quick ratio' or 'acid test', which is the ratio of current assets (less stocks) to current liabilities.
- *Gearing*: or the ratio of borrowings to total risk capital.

Turning first to liquidity, most managers will ask: 'What is a good liquidity ratio?' The answer, again, is: it depends. Usually the quick ratio needs to be looked at relative to the pattern emerging from:

- the level of gearing – both from the balance sheet ratios and comparing the interest per the profit and loss account with profit before interest and tax (or 'interest cover');
- debtors days and the level of stock;
- creditor strain – this can be analysed by looking at how high trade creditors are relative to estimated purchases value;
- the cash flow statement – how cash positive is the company?

Invariably managers now ask: 'What is a good (or bad) gearing ratio?' Not surprisingly, our answer is: 'again, it depends'.

First of all, gearing can be defined in two different ways as:

A   *Longer-term borrowing*, i.e. shareholders' funds plus longer-term borrowings, or
B   *Longer-term borrowing*, i.e. shareholders' funds.

You may often hear a definition of relatively 'high gearing' as being between 50 and 100 per cent on definition B. But on definition A this would be the equivalent of 33–50 per cent.

Some industries, such as non-fashion retailing, can cope with a higher level of gearing than others. These typically have a lower operational gearing – that is, where fixed costs are not so high (and costs are less cyclical). Property or airlines would be examples of industries with more cyclical costs and relatively higher fixed costs, and thus higher *operational* gearing. So the total business gearing of a company can be defined as:

Business gearing = Financial gearing × Operational gearing

An issue is whether to include in 'longer-term borrowings' (as part of the gearing calculation) only those short-term loans which are effectively financing longer-term business investment. A rule of thumb is to include these short-term loans as quasi-long-term 'borrowings' if they appear to be substantially invested in assets which are effectively non-current and longer term. (The analyst will need to look at the assets side of the balance sheet on a case-by-case basis to decide).

If we now turn to measures of accounting return, it is often easier to calculate return on total capital employed, or 'ROCE' (rather than trying to do both ROCE and RONA (return on net assets)). ROCE is defined as:

$$\frac{\text{Profit before interest and tax}}{\text{Net assets + Long-term liabilities}}$$

8　The cash flow statement

The cash flow statement is more amenable to a higher level review than to performing lots of ratios. Some particularly useful tests are:

1　Check that net cash inflow from operating activities is positive, and question whether this is likely to continue.
2　Test if net cash inflows from operating activities exceed (or are on a par with) investing activities. (Unless the company is easily able to raise money externally, then having a low ratio of net operating cash inflows to investment may result in over-dependence on external financing).
3　Compare the actual proportion of net cash inflow from operating activities to the cash flow from financing. Is most of the investment programme being financed from internally generated cash flow or from external sources?

Although, in the example shown in Illustration 3.1, net cash inflow is positive, it is small relative to total investing activities (£5m as against £15m). There is also high dependence on external financing with the bulk of investment being financed by loans of £8m. Together this represents a weak position.

Strategy in action

Illustration 3.1

A quick example

	£
Net cash inflow – operating activities	5
Interest (net) and dividends	(2)
Taxation paid	(1)
Investing activities:	
– acquisitions (2)	
– organic (13)	(15)
Financing – new loans	8
Decrease in cash (overall)	(5) outflow

9   Interrelate financial position and prospects – what are the key business drivers?

Key questions to help us to interrelate financial position and prospects are as follows:

- What overall pattern is revealed about current financial health and business performance?
- Is the company drifting, or has it gone into ill-thought-through ventures?
- Is its financial success based on favourable market and competitive conditions which might now be crumbling, or is it in a sticky and difficult market but succeeding because of astute management?

Answering these questions involves some incisive, strategic thinking, closely interrelated with the financial analysis.

10   Future prospects

A number of key questions will help to identify future prospects from the annual report and accounts:

1   Look at past profit growth. Is this really sustainable (for instance, consider quality of business development, threats to margins, the threat of business opportunities drying up, the impact of product/market lifecycles, or of economic cycles, and so on)?

2   What is revealed about the company's apparent future strategic and financial intent? (Consider statements made by directors, the

company's capital programmes, themes in innovation, and market and product development and so on.)

3   Do management really have the strengths to tackle the task that they have set themselves or is imposed on them, or has the business outgrown them?

11   Summarise and conclude

At this point you should now be readily able to summarise the half-a-dozen key insights and deliver some prognosis for the future, thus bringing the strategic and financial analysis together as an overall 'helicopter view'.

Now that we have explored all eleven steps of SFA, we are well placed to analyse IBM's 1994 annual report and accounts.

IBM, financial and strategic turnaround 1993–1994

IBM is a fascinating case for two reasons. First, IBM experienced a major demise in the late 1980s/early 1990s prior to a rebirth in the mid/late 1990s. Second, IBM's annual report for 1993–1994 contains some relatively transparent insights into the linkages between financial and strategic performance, position and potential.

1   IBM's five-year review

IBM's financial performance from 1990 to 1994 is shown in Illustration 3.2. The review highlights graphically the impact of combined market and competitive pressures on IBM. This IT giant, once regarded as unassailable, was plunged into massive losses during the recession in the early 1990s. This malaise was greatly amplified by IBM's weakening competitive position. IBM's once unassailable position as 'first choice supplier' to many companies was at least partially tarnished, its cost base was too high and its flexibility lacking, particularly to the needs of the newly flourishing personal computer market.

IBM's gearing and losses peaked in 1993 – note that both IBM and the reader are spared the embarrassment of calculating losses as a percentage of stockholders' equity in 1993 (this equity halved in historic value between 1990 and 1993).

2   Quick review of current year's profit and loss account

Illustration 3.3 shows IBM's total revenues and profits/(losses). Evidently IBM had moved from a huge loss (after restructuring costs) to a much healthier profit. This had involved reducing its indirect costs

Strategy in action

Illustration 3.2

Five-year comparison (extracted from IBM's 1994 accounts)
(Dollars are in millions except the share amounts)

	1994 $m	1993 $m	1992 $m	1991 $m	1990 $m
For the year:					
Revenue	64,052	62,716	64,523	64,766	68,931
Net earnings (loss) before					
changes in accounting principles	3,021	(7,987)	(6,865)	(598)	5,967
Per share of common stock	5.02	(14.02)	(12.03)	(1.05)	10.42
Effect of accounting changes	–	(114)	1,900	(2,263)	–
Net earnings (loss)	3,021	(8,101)	(4,965)	(2,861)	5,967
Cash dividends paid per share					
of common stock	1.00	1.58	4.84	4.84	4.84
Investment in plant, rental					
machines and other property	3,078	3,232	4,698	6,502	6,548
Return on stockholders'equity	13.6%	–	–	–	14.8%
At end of year:	$	$	$	$	$
Total assets	81,091	81,113	86,705	92,473	87,568
Total debt	22,118	27,342	29,320	26,947	19,545
Stockholders' equity	23,413	19,738	27,624	36,679	42,553

Strategy in action

Illustration 3.3

IBM's total revenues and profits/(losses)

	1994 $m	1993 $m	Change
Total revenues	64,052	62,716	+2.1%
Gross profit	25,284	24,148	+ 4.7%
Total operating expenses (indirect)	20,279	23,840	−15.0%
Restructuring costs		8,945	
Operating income/(loss)	5,005	(8,637)	
Other income and interest	1,377	1,113	+23.7%
Interest expense	1,227	1,273	−3.7%
Earnings/(loss) before tax	**5,155**	**(8,797)**	

by some 15 per cent of total revenues. This may seem a very large re-duction but may be considerably less than what IBM *could have achieved* or *still needed to achieve*.

Illustration 3.4 highlights the strength of IBM's hardware sales, which were up by 5.7 per cent. This represented both good and bad news. The good news was that IBM was once again making progress in its core hardware business. IBM's first half-year figures for 1995 (not shown here) suggested that this trend was being sustained, resulting in a considerable further improvement in both sales and profit. The bad news in the 1994 results was that IBM was continuing to lose share of the faster growing (and higher margin) software business. This may also suggest a strategic opportunity for IBM – of, for instance, acquiring a major software company (thus making IBM's bid for Lotus in 1995 look a distinctly unsurprising turn of events).

More worrying was the rentals and financing business being 17.8 per cent down (and especially so in view of the associated high margins). Although this decline was halted in the first half of 1995, this trend obviously deprives IBM of one avenue for profitable growth.

If we compare each business area's margins then (except for software and maintenance) there is improvement, but overall the impact is slight (1 per cent contribution to profit). This is because of the adverse change in the business mix (with lower margin areas growing faster than higher margin areas).

IBM *has*, however, achieved a dramatic breakthrough due to its cost base, which had fallen by over 6 per cent of turnover between 1993 and 1994.

3 Directors' review and highlights

Louis V. Gerstner, chairman and CEO of IBM, tells us (page 2, IBM's 1994 report) that the four key priorities for IBM are:

- to be profitable
- to become more competitive
- to increase shareholder value
- to grow.

He also outlines a plan to reduce costs by a further $1.7 billion by mid-1996. Louis Gerstner's view is that the computer industry will resume growth generally. There is, however, little comment in the annual report on *which* particular segments offer the most attractive balance between faster growth *and* sustainably higher margins, *and* which fit IBM's own competitive positioning. So, we are left with only a broad idea as to *how* IBM will strengthen its competitive position.

The section of IBM's report on 'Management Discussion' now highlights a number of important features:

- IBM's personal computer revenue is growing, but at a slower pace than its competitors.
- Mainframe processor revenue is declining – and faster than anticipated.

- Service revenues showed stronger growth but with weaker margins.
- Maintenance revenues and gross margins are being increasingly squeezed by the competition.
- In IBM's wholly owned subsidiaries, employment had dropped 14.7 per cent between 1993 and 1994 (and in 1996 was down 27.1 per cent on 1992 – obviously a very big achievement).

The overall impression is thus one of a company shedding resources at a very fast pace, but only just at a pace sufficient to keep up with the rate of external change and cost pressures. A second challenge now looms apparent. New (and more profitable) business growth now needs to come more to the fore beyond 1995/96 in order to sustain IBM's turnaround.

4   Profit and loss account 1993 and 1994

Illustration 3.4 gives a detailed analysis of revenue percentages, margins and shifts in the expense base for 1993 and 1994. These figures

Strategy in action

Illustration 3.4

IBM Report and Accounts – Financial Ratios 1994

Profit and loss account

Revenue percentages	1994 %	1993 %
Hardware (5.7% up)	50.5	48.8
Software (3.6% up)	17.7	17.5
Services (same)	15.1	15.5
Maintenance (1.1% down)	11.3	11.6
Rentals & financing (17.8% down)	5.4	6.6
(overall 2.1% up)	100.0	100.0

Margins (relative to sales)

Hardware	34.1	32.3
Software	58.7	60.6
Services	20.0	14.7
Maintenance	49.7	51.4
Rentals and financing	59.6	58.3
Average margins	**39.5**	**38.5**

Expenses (relative to sales)

Sales, general, admin.	24.8	29.1
R&D and engineering	6.8	8.9
	31.6	**38.0**

reveal a number of areas where margins are either strengthening or weakening. This highlights areas of intensifying rivalry (particularly in software and maintenance). Note once again that most of IBM's improvement in fortunes came from reduction in its internal cost base.

5, 6 & 7   The balance sheet and cash flow

A number of financial ratios suggest a major improvement in the financial position. For instance, if we look at IBM's liquidity ratios they show some very favourable changes:

$$\text{Current ratio} = \frac{\text{Current assets}}{\text{Current liability}} \quad \overset{1994}{\frac{41{,}338}{29{,}226}} = 1.41 \quad \overset{1993}{\frac{39{,}202}{33{,}150}} = 1.18$$

$$\text{Quick ratio} = \frac{\substack{\text{Current assets} - \\ \text{inventories}}}{\text{Current liability}} \quad \frac{35{,}004}{29{,}226} = 1.20 \; \frac{31{,}637}{33{,}150} = 0.95$$

In 1993 IBM's 'quick ratio' or acid test was just below the financial analysts' rule-of-thumb for the value of liquid current assets to exceed at least the value of current liabilities. However, in 1994 the liquidity position with a quick ratio of $1:2$ was much healthier. A quick ratio significantly below 1.0 (especially around or below 0.5) is potentially very worrying.

It is somewhat harder to assess the number of days' sales tied up in IBM's trade receivables. To calculate this statistic we have excluded rental income from turnover:

$$\overset{1994}{}$$
$$\text{Accounts recoverable as number of days' sales} \quad \frac{14{,}018 \times 365}{(64{,}052 - 3{,}425)} = 84 \text{ days}$$

$$\overset{1993}{}$$
$$\frac{11{,}676 \times 365}{(62{,}716 - 4{,}166)} = 73 \text{ days}$$

This suggests a relatively slow settlement of debtors. The increase of 11 days of days' sales between 1993 and 1994 shows a surprising worsening in efficiency in IBM's collection record. This might also suggest some questions about whether there are significant problems of slower-paying and even of doubtful accounts receivable (debtors).

IBM's effective utilisation of assets also seems to be an area for future improvement. For instance, if we perform a crude comparison of inventories as a percentage of hardware sales we find that:

	1994	*1993*
Inventories as a percentage of hardware sales	$\dfrac{6{,}334 \times 100}{32{,}344} = 19.6\%$	$\dfrac{7{,}565 \times 100}{30{,}591} = 24.7\%$

This suggests that although inventories are falling they still appear rather high. (We would need to adjust the above calculation for mark-up to get a better feel for just how much physical stock relative to physical sales volume IBM is holding).

But does the efficiency of IBM's asset utilisation matter strategically? The answer is again yes, it certainly does. For instance, suppose IBM could reduce its hardware inventory by, say, 40 per cent. This would represent a $2.5 billion saving in net assets, and might reduce interest costs by around $150 million (which is around 12 per cent of the current interest expense). Further, if IBM's hardware levels are materially out of line with competitors, its higher cost base also puts it at a significant competitive disadvantage.

A similar argument could be put for reducing debtors. For example, if IBM could reduce the average period of debtors outstanding to 60 days, the reduction in working capital would be:

$$\frac{(64{,}052 - 3{,}425) \times (84 - 60) \text{ days}}{365} = \$4 \text{ billion}$$

This, in turn, might save $350 million of interest costs.

Having examined IBM's thirst for working capital, let us now turn our attention to its longer-term assets and how efficiently these were being used. If we divide IBM's total turnover by the net book value of its fixed assets we find that there was some marginal improvement:

	1994	*1993*
$\dfrac{\text{Total turnover}}{\text{Net book value}}$ (of fixed assets)	$\dfrac{64{,}052}{16{,}664} = 3.8 \text{ times}$	$\dfrac{62{,}716}{17{,}521} = 3.6 \text{ times}$

This again suggests that IBM had a rather high capital base relative to its turnover (and ultimately to its profit).

Moving next to IBM's gearing (calculated on the earlier Basis B), there had been a dramatic improvement.

	1994	*1993*
IBM's gearing:	$\dfrac{12{,}548}{23{,}413} = 53.6\%$	$\dfrac{15{,}245}{19{,}738} = 77.2\%$

Illustration 3.5 shows IBM's cash flow, which also displays a remarkable improvement. For instance, if we compare IBM's cash flow gener-

Strategy in action

Illustration 3.5

IBM's cash flow statement (extracts)

	1994 $m	1993 $m
Inflows		
Net earnings (loss) – cash flow	3,021	(8,101)
Depreciation	4,197	4,710
Amortisation of software	2,098	1,951
	9,316	(1,440)
Outflows		
Plant investment	3,078	3,154
Disposals	(900)	(793)
Software investment	1,361	1,507
	3,539	3,868

ated from operations with IBM's invested cash flow (to establish how easily investment is financed from internal sources), we see that:

Underlying cash flow from operations (with the exceptional P&L a/c restructuring charges written back), divided by investment cash flow

1994

$$= \frac{(3{,}021+4{,}197+2{,}098)}{(3{,}078-900+1{,}361)}$$

$$= \frac{9{,}316}{3{,}539}$$

$= 2.6$ times

1993

$$= \frac{(-8{,}101+8{,}945^*+4{,}710+19{,}510}{(3{,}154-793+1{,}507)}$$

$$= \frac{7{,}505}{3{,}868}$$

$= 1.9$ times

*Note in 1993 there was an 8,945 ($ million) accounting provision for restructuring charges which led to the overall loss of 8,101 ($ million). As this charge did not directly affect cash flow it is here added back. This presentation also enables us to look at longer-term underlying trends.

This comparison obviously highlights a distinct improvement in IBM's cash flow. Once we have stripped out the rather confusing effect of the restructuring charges, IBM's cash flow for both years does not appear all that bad. (We have taken out the figure for restructuring charges as this is exceptional and confusing in view of lags between accruing these charges and the actual cash outlays.)

Finally, if we now look at return on capital employed (for 1994 only, as 1993 was in a major loss position), IBM's capital structure is as follows:

	1994 $m	1993 $m
Long-term debt	12,548	15,245
Other liabilities (mainly pension)	14,023	11,177
Deferred income tax	1,881	1,803
Total stockholders' equity (equating to net assets)	23,413	19,738

We see that return on capital employed is:

$$\text{ROCE} = \frac{\text{Profit before interest expense and tax}}{\text{Net assets} + \text{long-term liabilities}}$$

$$= \frac{5,005}{23,413 + (12,548+14,023+1,881)} = \frac{5,005}{51,865} = 9.6\%$$

This represents a low rate of return, reflecting both IBM's very substantial asset base (relative to turnover) and the absence of high operating margins overall (and the industry's fierce competitive rivalry). IBM's strategic turnaround was based on reducing cost and protecting sales from further decline, rather than volume and margin growth. The potential of creating a more lean and effective capital base as a means of improving ROCE did not seem, at 1995, to have been exploited to the full.

8 & 9   Business drivers – financial position and prospects

Out of our analysis so far, the key business drivers impacting on IBM's financial and strategic position are therefore:

- The intensifying competitive rivalry in IBM's traditional heartland, mainframe business.
- Whether IBM can introduce and gain dominance in more powerful (and more cost-effective) large systems than its rivals.
- IBM's capacity to adapt its organisational culture (a) to drive cost levels down still further without losing its effectiveness, (b) to accelerate and overtake faster and more responsive companies at the software end of the industry, or (c) to acquire them – like Lotus Corporation, but without destroying their competitive essence.
- IBM's ability and determination to squeeze its investment base further.
- Once these turnaround ingredients are in place, to avoid squandering its cash flow and restored profitability on product/market areas with

which IBM will not easily be able to compete long-term (unless it has genuinely transformed its capability).

10 & 11 Lessons overall

IBM certainly faced a daunting challenge at the end of 1994. Over the 1995–97 period its improvement in business and financial performance was sustained, making IBM a classic turnaround case. The magnitude of the challenge underscores the influence of top management, who, in this case demonstrated great tenacity in tackling the issues highlighted in this case study.

3.3 Summary

The IBM case study highlights how companies' annual reports can be subjected to a combined *strategic and financial* X-ray using SFA. Strategic financial accounting can reveal major and sometimes stark insights into a company's performance, position and potential.

The strategic planner's (and thinker's) arsenal is therefore incomplete without an understanding of financial analysis tools. But we also need to understand the results of financial analysis in a strategic context. By interweaving strategic and financial analysis we are also in a much better position to determine when, how and where we use financial analysis tools rather than see them as secondary and peripheral.

4 *Comparative analysis: benchmarking*

By Geoff Tomlinson

Editor's introduction

Organisations must be able to assess their competences against 'best-in-class' as an important part of sustaining competitive edge – as explained in Section 4.4.3. of *Exploring Corporate Strategy*. In his chapter, Geoff Tomlinson explains how benchmarking can be implemented in practice and highlights how valuable the results of benchmarking can be if the process has been tightly controlled and successfully managed. The reader should find this chapter very practical and useful through the extensive illustrations of benchmarking in practice.

4.1 Introduction

When properly resourced and implemented, benchmarking is a very powerful tool to focus and drive change. It assists the change process by providing objective targets and demonstrated best practice. It can enable the organisation to take a quantum leap in process and bottom-line performance improvements and outstrip competitors.

Undertaking a benchmarking study, however, is not for the faint-hearted. If you have made available significant dedicated resources for the study, including people who will be involved in implementing any best-practice improvements, and you have secured senior management commitment to the study, then you have already taken some important steps towards securing the success of the project. If you have not, then you should seriously review why not, before considering starting a benchmarking project.

The keys to successful benchmarking are a tight scope and detailed planning. To understand the area you wish to benchmark, a process map can be drawn. This also enables you to determine the data that you need to collect. To improve the effectiveness, there is a need to think imaginatively of potential benchmarking partners from whom you can learn. These partners may well come from outside your industry. Once established, data exchange and analysis should be conducted with the benchmarking partners. It is crucial to follow through the benchmarking study with effective implementation.

4.2   *What is benchmarking?*

In dictionaries a 'benchmark' is defined as 'a point of reference from which measurements may be made. Something that serves as a standard by which others may be measured'. Therefore, in general terms, measuring against a benchmark will pinpoint the relative location. From experience, A.T. Kearney* has produced the following definition of company benchmarking:

> *An objective and comparative evaluation of processes using indicators established through direct research among a representative group of similar or competing organisations, which can lead to the implementation of best practice.*

This differs from the dictionary definition in two important respects. Firstly, it focuses on processes (which drive performance) and, secondly, it potentially includes the next stage – that of implementing best practice (Illustration 4.1). The implementation phase is crucial, because only this stage turns any potential improvement in current practices and performance into reality.

Strategy in action

Illustration 4.1
Benchmarking at Xerox

In his book *Benchmarking*, Bob Camp (1), of Xerox describes the benchmarking of a Xerox distribution warehouse. After considering the highly varied nature of the products handled, the team chose a mail-order firm, L.L. Bean which specialised in outdoor pursuits as their key benchmarking partner. By studying how L.L. Bean handled bulky items such as canoes, they identified practices that allowed them to handle large photocopiers more effectively. Bob Camp emphasises that benchmarking was effective only because it was done by the Xerox warehouse operations staff, not some central staff function. In addition, the team had carefully studied their own operations first, so that they shared an understanding of the baseline from which they were working, and the areas in which they needed to focus their examination.

* A.T. Kearney is an international management consultancy with offices in over 40 countries. In the last few years, over 100 major benchmarking studies have been conducted for client organisations world-wide.

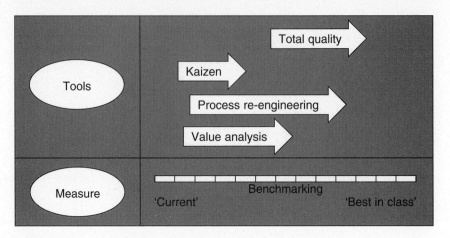

Figure 4.1   Benchmarking complements other tools.

4.2.1   Where does benchmarking fit?

Benchmarking helps to identify relative performance against the selected measures. This understanding of positioning is critical to the business improvement process, and provides input to the application of other improvement tools (Figure 4.1).

Using benchmarks will help identify the size of the gap, and therefore the amount of improvement that is necessary to match and surpass best practice. Once this gap has been ascertained, it allows corrective action.

Benchmarking can complement other tools such as total quality management and process re-engineering because these tools require a mechanism by which to measure the current position, and set objectives for any improvements as a result of the use of the tools.

4.3   The different forms of benchmarking

Benchmarking can take different forms that vary by the amount of resources required and the quality and detail of data (Figure 4.2). They share the common feature that they add structure to the normal 'gossip' that can be collected through a salesforce or similar channels.

In the matrix, moving towards the upper right box increases the quality of the data, but also the resources required for the study. Potential benefits also increase as you move towards the upper right box, as this approach gives the greatest understanding of performance and the practices that drive that performance. It also allows insights

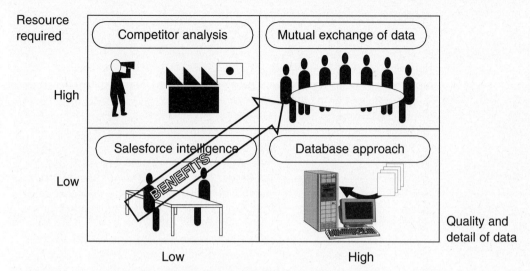

Figure 4.2   *There are several forms of benchmarking.*

into other industries, which are likely to have developed in different ways and therefore have different practices, some of which may be superior to your own industry. It is recommended that at the outset you consider the manner in which you will be using the benchmarking output, the resources you will be able to commit to the exercise and, therefore, the form of benchmarking that will be most appropriate to you. This chapter will focus on the mutual exchange of data as the most complex form of benchmarking but which also has the potential to provide the greatest benefits.

4.4   *Choosing an area to benchmark*

Benchmarking requires detailed (and resource-consuming) data-gathering and analysis, therefore an organisation should concentrate its resources on benchmarking areas that are considered key to itself (core competences) and/or key to its customers (competitive advantage) (Illustration 4.2). Obviously these may change over time, so each must be reassessed periodically to determine if it is still in line with the strategic direction of the organisation.

Another consideration is the organisation's previous experience of benchmarking. If this is the first benchmarking project that the organisation has undertaken, then it is important that the project succeeds. Therefore, the first study should be short, focused, likely to be successful and demonstrate significant learning value and high impact within the area studied. It is also important that the project is seen to have top management support and involvement.

Strategy in action

Illustration 4.2

The ethical pharmaceutical industry

In the ethical pharmaceutical industry, competitive advantage is largely driven by having a stream of researched and patented products that are well marketed. Profitability of many of the largest pharmaceutical companies depends on just a handful of products. Critical to future performance is the availability of future blockbuster products in the 'product development pipeline'. When choosing an area to benchmark, therefore, R&D and sales and marketing are two priority areas because of the impact that any performance improvements can have on the business. In addition, they are also two of the largest components in the cost chain (2), making even a small percentage reduction in costs a significant saving.

Of course, there may also be large improvements to be made in other areas such as manufacturing, and these should not be ignored. It is useful to prioritise all the opportunities in terms of overall business impact, and degree of importance to the company.

Many benchmarking studies fail because the focus is too broad. It is essential that the focus of the study is determined by the importance of the project to your customers and to your organisation. A good area to benchmark is one in which you feel you are competitively disadvantaged. If you have areas in which you already have ideas on improvement, and/or the staff believe they can implement these ideas effectively, then this is probably not an area to benchmark unless the improvement targets are unclear.

4.5 The benchmarking process

The benchmarking process has four phases, as shown in Figure 4.3.

4.5.1 Planning: who, which data and practices?

Thinking of a business in terms of processes is important for the understanding of current practices and, therefore, future process im-

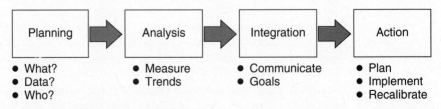

Figure 4.3 Benchmarking has four phases.

provements. Figure 4.4 shows an example below of a section of a procurement process. The ability to understand and map the processes you wish to benchmark within your organisation is critical to the success of the project. Actions and ways of doing things can be mapped as a process (Illustration 4.3), irrespective of whether it is an auto-part being produced or a service being provided.

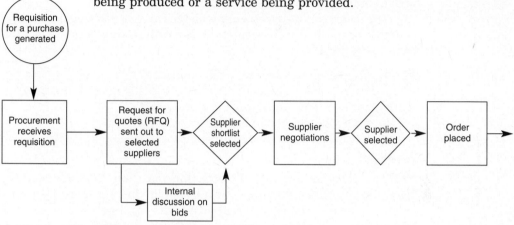

Figure 4.4   Part of a procurement process.

Strategy in action

Illustration 4.3

The Ritz-Carlton Hotel company

Horst Schulze, President of the Ritz-Carlton Hotel company, made the following statement (3):

'Although we were voted the best hotel company in America in 1987 for the second time, we knew we were not good enough because we were not satisfying all of our customers. We thought we were the hotel experts, and that we should know what a customer wants. We thought that the guest comment card was a good measure, but it wasn't.

We looked at companies like Xerox and Motorola, and saw that they had a "process" approach. We studied it carefully and learned that they design quality into the product at the start. Slowly we realised that this was not just for manufacturing. A process is a process.

Not only do we now study how the process can provide what the customer wants, we study how we can deliver the product so it costs us less.

Over the last four years, customer satisfaction increased from the low 80s into the high 90s, and employee satisfaction soared from the high 70s to the low 90s. So, customer satisfaction went up; employee satisfaction went up; and efficiency improved dramatically – all because we managed a process. Our basic values have not changed. Only now we have the processes to ensure that we live our values.'

An understanding of the process you are benchmarking enables you to determine the data to collect. The process should be mapped to include both inputs (inputs from whom, in which form, how often) and outputs (output to whom, in which form, how reliably). The process should also include details of who conducts each stage, with which resources, and to what standards.

The sources of data can vary widely. There is a variety of publicly available data. Before the search, it is worth asking yourself the following questions:

- Who is recognised as a leader in this industry?
- Who is recognised as the leader in this process in other industries?
- Is any data available on relative performance?
- Are there any indications of best practice?
- Are there third parties who may have information on any of the above questions?

Data searches should include both internal and external sources. Examples of external sources include public domain material (news articles, journals, market research reports, on-line databases) and field experts (previous successful practitioners, professional associations, academics, consultants). Internal sources include intelligence gathered through normal business (e.g. from customers, suppliers, competitor information) and your own personnel who may have worked in other companies in the past.

In some cases it may be necessary to commission original research, such as customer feedback or market research. This should only be conducted after it has been established that the material is not available by other means, as it can be time consuming and costly.

Benchmark selection

When selecting whom to benchmark against there are four categories:

- Internal
- Competitive
- Functional
- Generic

Internal (against similar internal units)

This has high credibility, and normally provides easy access to the data. In addition, there are rarely issues with confidentiality. This is particularly useful where there is little previous experience of benchmarking because of the ease of access, and the opportunity to make mistakes in private. This method can often work effectively where there are a number of similar locations or units that are currently operating inconsistently. The limitation of this method is that your benchmark is internal, and therefore you are not bringing new learning to the organisation, but only maximising the current knowledge and practices of the firm. This can, however, still provide substantial benefits.

Competitive (against competitor organisations)

Competitive benchmarking normally has the highest credibility within the organisation, but it has some major disadvantages: confidentiality of data may be a problem, and any best practice incorporated will only allow you to catch up with competitors, not gain an advantage over them.

Functional (against organisations known for best practice in that function)

This type of benchmarking can allow you to leap-frog over the competition as you can choose to benchmark against a functional leader who may not be in your industry – for example, a recognised leader in marketing from another industry. Good benchmarking disciplines are essential to focus the project, bridge the different terminology and situations in different industries and translate the applicable best practices to your own situation.

Generic (against conceptually similar processes)

Generic benchmarking consists of 'stepping back' from the process you are trying to benchmark and comparing it with a conceptually similar process; for example, manufacturing companies who have benchmarked against pit crews of Formula One motor racing teams. The manufacturers were interested in this comparison because their manufacturing process included change-overs of production processes between products, and minimising machine downtime was critical to manufacturing economics. Similarly, a motor racing pit crew needs to minimise the 'downtime' of the car being in the pits. This type of benchmarking is the greatest challenge because of the requirement for thinking of organisations with broadly similar processes, and then being able to extract the best practices that could improve your own process. Because the potential improvement is limited only by your creativity, real breakthroughs can be achieved. It is recommended that this type of benchmarking is for high performers who feel that step change improvements are not possible using the other forms of benchmarking.

Once you have selected the type of benchmarking you wish to pursue (Illustration 4.4), you then need to develop candidate selection criteria, and draw up a candidate list.

Strategy in action

Illustration 4.4

Four types of benchmarking for a rail operator

A rail operator found that while passengers valued rail as a method of transport based on cost and convenience, the highest proportion of passenger complaints concerned the cleanliness of the trains. The operator wanted to look at someone against whom it could benchmark to reach best practice.

Table 4.1 *A rail operator's four types of benchmarking*

	Type	Process	Examples
Increasing difficulty and potential benefits	Internal	Train hygiene	• Between intercity routes • With regional express routes • With regional rail services
	Competitive	Public transportation hygiene	• Motorway service stations • Airports • Coach stations
	Functional	High usage facility hygiene	• Fast food chains • Office/factory services
	Generic	High usage, high standard facility hygiene	• Milking parlours • Food factories

Table 4.1 indicates the four types of benchmarking that were considered. As you move down the list the potential 'leaps forward' in improvement increase, but difficulties in the benchmarking project increase because, at one end of the scale, you have an in-house benchmarking exercise that can deliver improvements through increasing consistency of similar processes, while at the other end you have the generic approach, which has the challenge of thinking very creatively, potentially yielding radical and innovative process improvements, but which requires a good understanding of processes and how they can relate to your situation.

Table 4.2 *There are ethical issues to consider*

Legality	Avoid areas that may imply a restraint of trade
Mutuality	Provide the same level of information that you request
Confidentiality	Do not pass information to a third party without permission
Information use	Use information only for the purpose of improvement
One contact point	Use the designated benchmarking contact

4.5.2   Analysis: data collection, measurement and trend identification

Before you consider the exchange of data there are a number of ethical issues to consider (Table 4.2) because of the potential involvement of third party organisations.

It is obviously critical that the measures you are using are comparable, and there are various ways of ensuring that you will be comparing 'apples with apples':

- jointly develop the questionnaire.
- agree definition of terms.
- agree qualitative and quantitative measures.
- involve the people who will implement the procedure.

It is also important to have an appreciation of the time that the benchmarking study will take, where best practice is currently, and where it will be by the time you have completed implementation.

For site visits the team should be fully prepared and briefed before the event. Roles should be defined as to who will take the lead in asking the questions and who will record the information. It is always preferable to observe the operation at first hand, and to arrange for a follow-up meeting if time is limited. It is also good practice to complete a trip report soon after the visit, following a team debrief, where consensus should be gained on what was seen by the team.

4.5.3   Integration: results communication and goal setting

Communication of the results can be a great way to get buy-in from senior management, and to agree the gap between current performance and best practice with the rest of the organisation. This ensures agreement about the extent of the gap, and is of enormous help in goal setting. Setting best practice goals should (a) be a combination of targets that are independent of historic and current performance, (b) have a realistic timescale, and (c) be genuine stretch targets, i.e. significantly better than is currently believed possible. They should be based on the 'best of the best' performances found (Illustration 4.5), and not on a single company.

Strategy in action

Illustration 4.5

A UK food manufacturer

For a major UK food manufacturer, A.T. Kearney looked at the manufacturing cost chain of internal factories, other food industry participants, and the 'best of the best' to reduce costs while improving processes. The range of cost reduction targets to aim for was set in two ways:

- The 'best of the best' costs were modified to be able to compare them with internal costs, and then the internal cost chain was reconstructed as if they were at the 'best of the best' levels. This showed that costs could potentially be reduced by over 40 per cent.
- Using a database of manufacturing costs from other industry participants, and modifying for specific factors within the food manufacturer, indicated that cost reductions of up to 30 per cent were achievable over a two-year timescale.

Both of these methods were used to set 'stretch' targets that were realistic, but also challenging. In addition, senior management expectations were framed on what was possible, based on 'best of the best' and industry experience.

4.5.4 Action: plan, implement and recalibrate

The three elements of the action phase are the planning, implementation and recalibration of the benchmarking improvements.

There are two key aspects to the action-planning stage. The first is structuring the activities by detailing the tasks that need to be completed, who will complete what, over which time period and how it will be accomplished. Consideration should also be given to the sequencing of tasks relative to each other. The second aspect is change management, i.e. gaining acceptance and support from the rest of the organisation – some key pointers on this are given in Section 4.6. The action plan covering both of these issues should also include a specification of desired results, and a means to monitor the implementation.

The actual implementation team can be structured in a variety of ways:

- *Line management.* The advantages include the high level of commitment the line managers should have, as they will directly benefit from the improvements. The main disadvantage is the line managers' potential time commitment needed to implement successfully, as this may impact on the day-to-day operations.
- *Project management.* This is a separate, dedicated team and so is often used in large and complex projects, although line management is still needed to gain expertise in the new practices to be able to follow them successfully.

- *Appointment of a 'process champion'.*   This person is a senior manager who accepts responsibility for the designated process. By having senior backing of the process improvements on a daily basis, obstacles to change can often be removed more easily, although only critical business processes are designated for process champions, due to the high level of senior management involvement.
- *Cross-functional team.*   This is a team comprising of individuals from different parts of the process (and therefore often from different functional areas) which has the advantage of support right through the business process from those who will be performing the improved process. This method can be extremely effective as their early input can avoid costly problems, but it requires high commitment from all team members (and functional heads) to make the necessary time available for the project.

Which team structures are chosen (it may be a blend of several) depends on specific factors such as the complexity of the project, the resources and the perceived importance of the process. During implementation the benchmarking project needs to become an integral part of the normal planning, management and financial processes of the organisation.

The purpose of recalibration is to understand the point to which competitive and industry best practice has progressed, and to help assess whether a repeat study should be undertaken enabling a con-

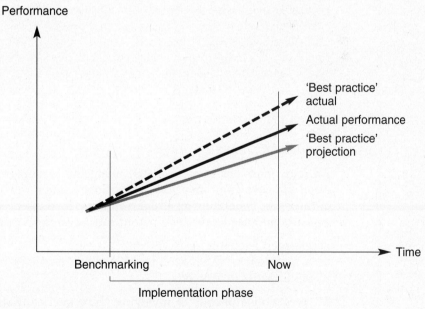

Figure 4.5   Recalibration aids continuous improvement.

tinuous process of improvement. An integral part of this is understanding the external changes in best practice that have taken place
since the start of the project, as well as to assess internal factors, including attitudes to a further benchmarking study and updated benchmarking data.

By the time the implementation phase is completed, actual performance has normally improved on the original best practice performance projection. However, the actual best practice is also likely to
have increased in that period, requiring recalibration (Illustration 4.6)
and new target setting (Figure 4.5).

Strategy in action

Illustration 4.6

Motorola Inc.

Motorola Inc. first embarked on its 'Six Sigma' quality programme in manufacturing in the 1960s. Six Sigma is a statistical term attached to the concept of
achieving approximately zero defects. By the 1980s, Motorola had included distribution, marketing and customer service in the target areas, using benchmarking to improve its services. For example, as a result of the benchmarking
process, customer satisfaction surveys are conducted and senior management
customer-visit programmes and computerised customer response systems
have been introduced.

Within the customer ordering process, the results to date show a simul-
taneous 70 per cent improvement in both quality and cycle time. The most significant improvement was the time taken to process a customer's order. This
was reduced from 15 days in 1988 to three hours by 1993. But Motorola has not
stopped there – it constantly monitors how far off 'Six Sigma' quality it is, constantly benchmarking and recalibrating to find the next opportunity (4).

4.5.5   Use of third parties

All four phases can be conducted using the resources of the organisation. However, you may wish to consider using a third party for some
of the work, depending on circumstances. Third parties, including consultants and academics, can potentially be useful by providing:

- accelerated learning
- data confidentiality between benchmarking partners
- added impetus to a project.

There are also pitfalls in involving third parties. Experienced users
warn not to hand over the whole process to third parties for two

reasons. You are the experts in your own process and should remain so, firstly, to maximise the effectiveness of any improvements and secondly, to develop know-how within the company (Illustration 4.7). Many practitioners recommend that if you are going to use third parties a suitable role would be as facilitators of the process (5).

Strategy in action

Illustration 4.7

The use of third parties

An illustration of where consultants or academics can be used to overcome confidentiality issues is in a multi-client study which involves potential competitors. In 1992 an A.T. Kearney multi-client study was conducted in purchasing and procurement practices in 25 large FMCG and discrete manufacturing companies across Europe, North America and Japan, who were competing in some products and markets. The study arose because of wide recognition that purchasing was a key process, and that relationships with suppliers were changing, but there was uncertainty about what the best practices were. Five areas of leadership practice were included in the study: organisation, supplier management, performance measurement, information systems and managing the process. Three forms of data collection were used:

- process mapping in each company
- desk research and field interviews (in which participating companies were actively involved) to obtain information in the public domain and check best practice companies
- quantitative questionnaire.

A.T. Kearney then analysed and summarised the data and processes, and fed the results back to the participants. This was initially conducted at an all-client workshop where no individual company positions were disclosed, and then to each company separately, where the position of that company relative to the others in the study was disclosed.

In this instance the use of a third party assured confidentiality of commercially sensitive information while allowing each company to identify its relative areas of weakness and competence. The participating companies effectively outsourced the project management and analysis to the consultants.

4.6 Implementation and the change process

No discussion of benchmarking and how it can improve an organisation would be complete without serious consideration of the change process. It is a huge area in itself, and therefore cannot be covered effectively in this chapter; however, there are at least some key pointers that need consideration.

4.6.1   *Action by senior management*

Benchmarking projects often require the implementation of step changes in process improvements. This commonly transcends functional boundaries and requires full commitment of senior management to sanction the changes.

4.6.2   *Managing the change process*

The change process must be managed correctly. Change that is implemented too slowly or too quickly can damage the organisation. The correct speed for change should be determined based on the culture of the organisation and the size of the step change required. There are many barriers to change, including:

- defending the status quo: 'Our business is different'
- lack of credible team: delegated or inadequate resources
- 'culture' change only: no focus on results
- changing business priorities and unclear objectives.

4.7   Is benchmarking right for my organisation?

Less that 20 per cent per cent of all 'Total Quality' programmes succeed, as measured by sustained improved actions or bottom-line business benefits.

4.7.1   *The value of benchmarking*

Benchmarking can benefit the organisation in three ways (Illustration 4.8):

1 Gap identification and objective target setting:
   (a) providing credible and unarguable targets
   (b) proactively targeting improvement
   (c) providing an opportunity to become industry leader.
2 New insights and improved practices:
   (a) objective evaluation of customer requirements
   (b) providing many options for improvement
   (c) generation of superior performance.
3 Overcoming barriers and providing a motivation for change:
   (a) concrete understanding of competitor position
   (b) high commitment for change.

Strategy in action

Illustration 4.8

The benefits of benchmarking

The following examples are typical results from recent benchmarking projects (6):

Area	Example	Results
Customer services	Feedback mechanism	Improved response time by over 50%
Finance	Finance practices	Reduced costs by 15–20% and process time
Information management	Order process/fulfilment	Raised customer service levels from 30% to 90% in 12 months, reduced costs by 15%
Manufacturing	Production optimisation	Reduced quality defects by over 50%, facility utilisation increased from 62% to over 90%
Marketing	Packaging development	30% reduction in new packaging development time
New product development	Development process	Reduced time to market by 30%, defined a two-year vision of new product launches
Sales	Salesforce effectiveness	Improved productivity by 25–30%

4.8 Summary

Benchmarking is a valuable tool for comparisons, and a very logical step for setting objective targets and enhancing performance measurement. It can often be the first step in creating the recognition that change and improvement are required.

As a final word of caution, benchmarking does not provide all the answers to all questions. It is best used if it is focused and controlled correctly. It is also not black and white. Many issues are subject to interpretation and are likely to provoke conflict, therefore the results should be used judiciously. However, if used correctly it can be a powerful improvement weapon.

Notes and references

(1) Camp, R. (1988). *Benchmarking, the Search for Industry Best Practices that Lead to Superior Performance*, ASQC Quality Press. This is the 'original' guide to benchmarking, that takes you through the methodology. It is useful as a reference guide.

(2) *UK Health & Household Company Spreadsheets* (1992), BZW Research Ltd, April.

(3)   Extracts from 'Excellence in progress' (1995), *Executive Excellence*, **12** (2), 9–10.

(4)   'Benchmarking success at Motorola' (1993). *CMA-Magazine*, **67** (2), 32–33.

(5)   Ransley, D.L. (1993). 'Training managers to benchmark', *Planning Review*, January/February.

(6)   Examples of various A.T. Kearney Benchmarking Projects, 1990–1995.

Further reading

Leibfried, K. and McNair, C. (1994). *Benchmarking: a Tool for Continuous Improvement*. Harper Collins. This is a good introduction to benchmarking that includes many practical examples across many industries and business functions.

Planning Review (1993). 'Strategic benchmarking: how to pick the right target', January/February. This is a collection of articles and case studies written by practitioners. It provides a realistic view of the pros and cons of benchmarking.

The Benchmarking Centre Ltd is a commercial organisation set up to establish links between companies for networking and communications. It is affiliated to similar organisations in the USA and Sweden, and is particularly useful if you are considering benchmarking as a major future organisational tool.

5

A 'patient focus review' of surgical services*

Business process re-engineering in health care

By Stuart D. Francis and Patrick G. Alley

Editors' introduction

Chapters 4 and 10 of *Exploring Corporate Strategy* emphasise that the strategic capability of an organisation goes beyond the resources which are available and is concerned with how those resources are deployed and controlled. Business Process Re-Engineering (BPR) is concerned with dramatic performance improvements by reconfiguring the resources and activities of an organisation, as described in Section 10.2.3 of *Exploring Corporate Strategy*. In this chapter, Stuart Francis and Patrick Alley describe a BPR process in the department of surgery in a hospital in Auckland, New Zealand. The aim, as in many service organisations, was to create a much more 'customer' focused service for patients. Patient focus teams analysed internal processes and proposed radical changes.

5.1 Introduction

This chapter describes a business process re-engineering project in the Department of Surgery of a publicly-funded hospital in Auckland, New Zealand. Waitemata Health Limited (WHL), the parent organisation in this article, has existed as a Crown-owned company now for almost two years. Formerly a part of an Auckland-wide purchaser/provider government organisation, the present organisation is now responsible for the provision of secondary medical and surgical services to approximately 375,000 of Auckland's population.

Since 1984 New Zealand society has undergone fundamental change. The traditional social welfare state is being challenged seriously by a competitive market-orientated environment of user

*First published in *Business Process Re-engineering & Management Journal*, Vol. 2 No. 1, 1996, pp. 48–62. © MCB University Press, 1355–2503

pays and state sell-offs. Delivery of health care has not been immune from these challenges. The problems confronting WHL started in 1984 with the opening of a new hospital which however had been designed in the early 1960s. Costs plus funding and resource constraints made for only limited provision of services from this hospital. A strong bureaucratic tradition has meant that staff attitudes and work practices have not changed since that time.

The new health system has separated the role of the purchaser from the provider. This separation has been modelled on the reorganisation of the British National Health Service. However, unlike the British system, the purchasing is done largely by regional health authorities (RHAs) rather than by budget-holding general practices. Provision of services, particularly secondary services, is done by Crown health enterprises (CHEs). These organisations mirror the function of trust hospitals in the UK. These reforms were initiated in 1992, costs and benefits have not yet been clearly identified. Both CHEs and RHAs battle to develop adequate contracting processes. It is difficult for many CHEs to operate within the revenue 'allocated' by the RHAs (despite the new role, many RHAs still have difficulty being 'purchasers' and not 'funders').

Eleven CHEs have been labelled 'work-out' CHEs (where there is no agreed business plan, showing a pathway to break even, between the treasury and the board of directors) requiring the continuation of a Crown-appointed observer until the completion of the 'work-out' process. Effective information, particularly about service mix, remain the largest challenge for many CHEs. BPR is another avenue that some CHEs are taking to simplify and introduce clarity into their operations. BPR is achieving wide acceptance in health care settings as pressure increases on health care providers to improve quality and cost effectiveness (1–3).

5.2   *Business process re-engineering*

Michael Hammer and James Champy's seminal article 'Reengineering work: don't automate, obliterate' (4), is potentially the single most quoted source about business process re-engineering. It is an enlightening look into the benefits for organisations redesigning their work processes to reflect better the circumstances of modern business. Their article proposes that, as new models of products are designed to suit our changing times, then so too should we redesign the organisations that produce those same products.

Others suggest that BPR should precede major investments in technology. Venkatraman's central thesis is that 'the benefits from Information Technology (IT) deployment are marginal if only superimposed on existing organisational conditions' (5). He suggests this is why organisations have failed to achieve the significant cost improvements championed for so long by IT. One interpretation is that perhaps BPR is management's response to the organisational change that IT has been driving with the introduction of new technology. Bergman emphasises the importance of the need to couple IT development with re-engineered business processes, citing health care examples that failed to achieve the potential benefit from BPR (1). Essentially, IT departments need to be intimately involved with the BPR so that they can implement what BPR discovers.

BPR is especially appropriate in health care (6). In a special look at re-engineering in health care, Bergman (1) states:

> 'Applied broadly across the spectrum of patient care procedures, business practices and strategic planning initiatives, reengineering has the potential to recreate organizations to improve quality and customer responsiveness, reduce costs and streamline business operations.'

5.2.1   Key premisses of re-engineering

According to Hammer, BPR is the 'fundamental rethinking and radical redesign of business processes to achieve dramatic improvements in critical measures of performance'. This does not imply downsizing, restructuring or automating which primarily are designed to shed cost. BPR deals with increasing productivity, capacity and profitability. Indeed, it has been suggested that an overtly cost-reducing focus for BPR is less likely to succeed. Like total quality management (TQM), it is process oriented, focusing on core value-added processes that impact on the customer's experience. Unlike the incremental improvements in process suggested by TQM, BPR calls for the radical redesign of those processes (7). However like TQM, the majority of implementations of BPR seem to have failed (8–13).

There are many benefits that BPR offers to organisations if they can manage to 'do it right':

- stronger alignment of core processes to business strategy
- the creation of customer value as a driver for all activity
- business architecture is optimised for efficient cross-functional performance
- benchmarking is used to accelerate learning and stimulate change
- enhanced capability and performance lead to increased ambition and conviction (14).

5.2.2   Potential pitfalls and requirements

- Failure to understand what BPR is and is not (15, 16).
- The decision to re-engineer is a strategic business decision; doing re-engineering is operational (15, 17).
- Poor project management that does not establish a strategy for change (11, 15).
- Under-resourcing, under-empowering, under-funding (9, 15).
- Passionate leadership, visible sponsorship (9, 15).
- Communicate, communicate, communicate (9, 18).
- IT is an enabler, not a driver of fundamental change – look for the win–win (1, 19).

The challenge for organisations then is twofold. First, the planning and implementation of BPR must be timely and methodical. Second, the ever-present reality of failure must be guarded against. The principal reason for the failure of such a simple methodology is that, despite all the efforts of academics and consultants, today's managers resist and are unable to manage *change*.

5.2.3   A new approach to change

One of the first tasks of the project team was to explain why we were taking so long to effect change. For some managers and clinicians, even when convinced of the need for change, it was a case of 'Slow down! We don't want this to fail like other things that have been rushed into'. The expectation that change is 'short and sharp', and that it fails seems paradoxical. Figure 5.1 shows different approaches to change. The critical difference between the traditional mental model of change (the dotted line) and the patient focus review model of change (the solid line) was one of the central messages of the early communication efforts. In Figure 5.1, the dotted line typifies how some might approach any given problem. Identification, analysis, redesign and implementation require increasing amounts of time and effort.

An alternative strategy is depicted by the solid line. Identification of the problem includes establishing root causes. Analysis examines the root causes, including questioning whether we need a cure or a plaster to cover the problem. Consequently, with the research completed, redesign and implementation are more a matter of course, than an expression of chaos.

This was a point that was emphasised heavily and repeatedly in communications to the staff at WHL. It was important first to differentiate our change from less popular and less effective previous changes and, second, to explain why unilateral and radical change had not already occurred. The temptation of a 'quick win' in order to gain credibility from some sectors of the workforce was resisted more com-

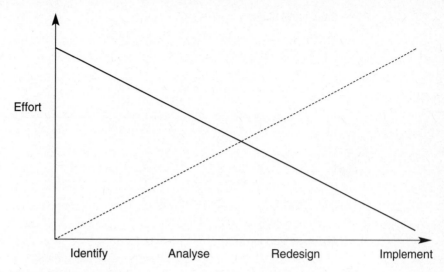

Figure 5.1   *Approaches to change.*

fortably in the light of Figure 5.1. Some minor early beneficial changes took place largely by asking the reason for some practices which at first sight seemed unnecessary or repetitive. However, the focus remained firmly on problems, not solutions.

A second quality management tool that the patient focus review teams utilised in both process analysis and, more importantly, in the communications efforts, are the cause-and-effect diagrams (also known as Ishikawa or fishbone diagrams). In addition to drawing attention to the contributing causes to even a simple problem, by reversing the direction of the fishbone we were able to illustrate the obvious complexities of change. It stands to reason that if a large number of factors contribute to causing a problem, then a solution to that problem is likely to have a return effect on those same factors.

Figure 5.2 depicts the two uses of the cause-and-effect diagrams. A topical 'problem' (an introduction of a new dictating system that had significant teething problems) was discussed in reference to the two diagrams. How the reverse fishbone might have been employed in determining whether the system would have been implemented, or indeed solved the perceived problem in the first instance, was discussed openly.

5.2.4   Change as a clinical initiative

It is crucial that the staff of the organisation accept the reason for change and this meant 'distancing' the patient focus review from being

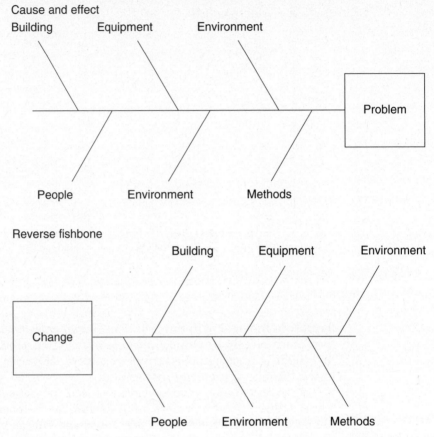

Figure 5.2   Fishbone diagrams.

seen as another management change doomed for poor planning and execution. The high level of clinical involvement and the total commitment by those clinicians sent a strong message to staff. The roles of the project leader, the coordinator and the consultants were labelled clearly as 'support' members.

5.2.5   'Let's not change for the sake of change'

While it was an easy task to demonstrate the complexity of current processes and develop an environment for change, it was made clear that staff were unwilling to change for the sake of change. It is important that staff are committed to the project objectives, and that the project team communicate their findings so that all staff are able to judge the need for change for themselves.

5.3   *Aims of the patient focus review*

It has commonly been advanced that clinicians will only accept change if it is slow and incremental. The hazard of this approach is that the *status quo* is always close to the intended change and thus there is a strong tendency to revert to the old ways. By making change more radical and well thought out, the temptation to slip back to the *status quo* is diminished.

The surgical service of Waitemata Health Ltd has been set up on the traditional British model of secondary health care delivery. Three teams of two surgeons sharing several registrars (residents) and a variable number of house surgeons (interns) work from two 32-bed wards where nursing services are overseen by a charge nurse. The workforce of each ward is about 20 full-time equivalent staff nurses. Each ward and each team of surgeons take turns on acute duty. Surgeons are often performing elective surgery when they are on call. Acute cases are referred by general practitioners and a preliminary telephone call to the admitting registrar is usual to discuss the case. On arrival the case is assessed by a large number of health professionals and investigations and treatments are initiated. The senior surgeon on call may be unaware of the existence of the case until next morning if the registrar is unconcerned about the case.

Elective surgical cases are seen in outpatient clinics on referral mainly from general practitioners. Patients are assigned priority on the basis of the information in the referral letter. If surgery is deemed suitable the patient is added to a waiting list of variable length. Surgeons and registrars see patients together in these clinics. Case records are under the jurisdiction of a medical information department which is physically separate from the clinical areas.

Since inception in 1984 the workload in surgery has risen about 250 per cent. The reasons for this increase include an expanding population and a change in the demography so that there is an increasing number of elderly patients presenting to the surgical service. The mean age of general surgical patients is 74 years. Elective but not acute orthopaedic surgery is practised in WHL; this particular speciality is practised from two institutions so that patients are seen initially for assessment in another facility some considerable distance from WHL.

Early in the process it was agreed that the progress of the patient focus review (PFR) team would be communicated to the workforce by a series of 'roadshows'. These were presentations lasting about 20 minutes that were repeated at different times of the day in different venues a total of about 20 times. Audiences varied from two or three nightstaff in a ward staffroom at 7 a.m. to 20 or 30 people in a conference room at lunchtime.

Clarity of aim is an important message portrayed by the road-show team. It had to be both practical and 'sellable'. The three key objectives of the review and redesign of the surgical process within Waitemata Health were:

1   *Improve the patient experience.* This must be the paramount concern of any improvement efforts in a health care organisation. The desire was not only to improve overall satisfaction levels, but also to reduce the amount of variation in satisfaction levels.
2   *Reduce waste in the process so as to reduce the cost per case.* The focus of this measure is to reduce the cost on surgical services through the reduction of waste. Repetition, duplication and other activities which add little or no value to the process are to be eliminated thereby reducing cost per case.
3   *Increase the overall productivity of the surgical processes.* The focus of this objective is to increase the volume of work done within the existing level of resources.

The last two, although disturbing for many staff, were presented as an ethical issue: 'The health dollar is scarce – it should not be wasted.' The combination of these two ideas, both very similar in meaning, suggests that by reducing waste, more patients would be able to be seen within present resources. It was made very clear that the agenda of the review did not include 'job slashing'. This point was emphasised repeatedly to engender a positive environment for change and to maximise staff participation.

Alongside the three key objectives, there were a number of principles which would direct our efforts:

•   minimise steps in the process
•   minimise faces that a patient has to see and deal with
•   minimise 'hand-offs', where responsibility for the process is passed on to another
•   bring the service to the patient, not the reverse
•   integrate primary care providers with our secondary services.

5.4   Leading from the top

An interdisciplinary steering committee was selected by the group manager of surgical services and the CEO of Waitemata Health. The committee included senior managers of business services, information systems, community health, a consultant general surgeon, as well as the manager of surgical services, the business analyst of surgical services and the CEO. The general surgeon chairs the steering committee.

The manager of surgical services was chosen by the steering committee to act as team leader for the project team and the business analyst as the team coordinator. Other members are the general surgeon, an anaesthetic consultant, charge nurse of a general surgery ward, charge nurse of the theatre complex, customer services officer (formerly a practising midwife), a community services manager (formerly a district nurse) and an information services representative. The team leader committed a minimum of one day a week to the project, and the team coordinator committed at least four days a week to the project team.

Six of the eight members of the project team are clinicians. It was important to establish firmly the patient focus review as being clinician driven for four reasons:

1   Without clinical support, the change will be doomed to failure
2   Commitment to patients is the primary motivator for everyone in the organisation
3   'Management' does not have a faultless track record of change making
4   The management–clinician interface is, historically at least, characterised by a climate of suspicion and animosity, particularly in times of resource scarcity.

As the review progressed, spoke teams developed from the project team to examine in detail different processes identified by the project team. This enabled increased staff participation and made available specialist knowledge of the processes of different departments. External consultants were selected to manage the project infrastructure and to assist in the training of all those involved in the project.

5.5   Flowcharting patient experience

An enlightening process at the best of times, the degree of revelation proved embarrassing even to most of the project team who had not realised the departmental complexity through which our customers journeyed. Few were aware of the full patient experience of repeated questions, pointless waiting and delayed decision making. It was apparent that the present system has had problems plugged, checks initiated, and improvements made with little reference to other departments.

The patient experience was separated into eight subprocesses for study (Figure 5.3). Initial analysis centred on the first two of these: pre-admission and admission. Two teams were established to examine the acute admitting process and priority 'A' bookings. It was thought initially that there would be several 'quick win' opportunities – these very quickly grew more complicated as the analysis progressed. As much of the work was focused on the support functions, not part of surgical services, we found that we were limited as our communications team had yet to begin the education of other departments. Further to

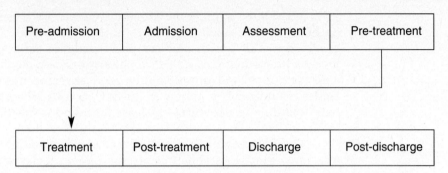

Figure 5.3   *The eight subprocesses of the patient experience.*

this, we needed to prepare a plan for the active involvement of those directly involved in the process, without presupposing any possible outcomes of our analysis.

5.6   *Baselining present performance*

Evaluation of any resource commitment is an essential component of the management process. Unfortunately consultant-led development is often the least evaluated of any investment organisations make. An early problem with which the project team grappled was defining baselines for each of the three project aims so that progress could be measured. Unfortunately each aim is an 'elephant-sized' problem with which most CHEs in New Zealand are presently grappling.

There are measures that will result from the redesign of particular processes, such as the number of steps in the process, the number of people involved, and total time taken. In addition to these, it was decided to focus on a few key indicators that relate to the three objectives and are expected to change as a result of the project. These key indicators are:

- patient satisfaction
- surgery time to theatre time
- activity measures (bed turnover, length of stay, day surgery to in-patient surgery)
- average laboratory tests per patient
- staff satisfaction
- unnecessary utilisation of staff time.

A literature review was performed which assisted the project team in understanding that they were headed in the right direction. It highlighted many of the potential causes of failure in process re-engineering efforts.

5.7   A methodology for change

The first few months of the project were spent developing the project team. As a project team, our confidence in our skills as facilitators of analysis and change is at the point where we must now develop more fully the involvement of other staff in relevant spoke teams. Each spoke team has a member of the project team to facilitate, train and coordinate the team. Other members are drawn from relevant departments, with the majority being clinical staff.

Four spoke teams were established some four or five months after the initial project team meeting. Some are 'major' in that their scope is large and that the process is a core process. Others are 'minor' in that they have a restricted scope and are 'digging' for information about potential problems. The spoke teams are:

- *The admission process* – from the moment of referral (by the patient or the general practitioner) until the decision to admit is made.
- *The discharge process* – until the end of the patient's WHL episode.
- *Theatre utilisation* – from the moment the call is made for the patient to be delivered until the patient departs from the theatre complex.
- *The orthopaedic admission process* (a joint-venture with another CHE) – as for the admission team.

Given a history of poorly managed and poorly planned organisational change, it was important to establish a number of key messages that the project team presented.

5.7.1   The admission process

The admission team began to untangle the complexities of how patients are actually admitted to WHL inpatient facilities. There are four broad categories that describe how patients are admitted:

1 presentation in the emergency department
2 presentation in the acute assessment ward after GP has obtained permission for an acute admission
3 admission that is arranged at the time of an outpatient visit
4 a patient is selected off an inpatient waiting list and is required to attend a pre-admission clinic.

Each process was mapped through until the decision was made to either admit, discharge, or transfer to another facility. Table 5.1 shows several measures that were made of the processes.

Table 5.1   *Different routes of admission*

Admission via	Steps	Doctors	Faces (employees with whom) the patient interacts)	Forms
Emergency department	63	4	8–15	21
Acute assessments	55	4	15	21
Clinics	106	3	15	35
Orthopaedic waiting list	98	5	33	50

Interestingly, several issues cropped up once the teams began to 'dig down' into the affairs of the organisation:

- Discovering the 'seen but not admitted register', kept in triplicate, but without anyone appreciating why it existed. Two days after its unearthing, it stopped being maintained.
- A traditional gate-keeping role of registrars is for GPs who must obtain permission to admit acute patients. A survey that revealed that 92 per cent of the time the patient was accepted, while the remaining 8 per cent were declined due to that type of service being unavailable at WHL, questions whether that requirement is always necessary.
- The perceived problem with acute assessment ward staff not being able to obtain a surgical registrar was seemingly obvious once it was established that the 'on-call' registrar was only actually available for 'on-call' work for 38 per cent of their four-week roster.
- All outpatients are directed to a revenue officer in the main entrance rather than direct to outpatients so that their name and address and welfare card number can be recorded, in order to apply a user part-charge that costs WHL more to collect than the actual revenue obtained.

After a period of several months it became apparent that any desire to 'quick fix' the current operations was a poor use of team energy and time. As will be explained shortly, this perceived inactivity was something that the team had to manage. It was strongly felt that the role of the re-engineering effort had to be towards defining why processes had to exist, and then redesigning the organisations to deliver them. The next section explains the methodology employed by Waitemata Health.

5.8   *The patient focus review as a process of re-engineering*

5.8.1   *Identify 'what is now'*

Activities included in understanding current processes: process mapping, measuring, time/motion, fishbone diagrams, brainstorming, affinity diagrams and modelling. Out of this analysis the re-engineering team develops an improved understanding of what actually happens. Issues become clearer and are described quantitatively. Non-value adding components of current processes are identified as many problems and issues 'fall out' of the analysis.

Some problems may appear as potential 'quick win' solutions that can be implemented without a great deal of effort. Several things need to be considered before any change is made. First, consider the likely consequences of the change. One tool for this is a reverse fishbone diagram depicting the consequent effects on the different limbs of the diagram. Second, be mindful that later re-engineering may redesign the improvement out of the process completely. Often, the simple 'quick win' does not appear as easy after preliminary investigation. The re-engineers were careful not to have a 'quick fix' that failed, thus creating implementation problems later in the project.

5.8.2   Clarify why the process exists

The solution concept is all about distilling the most basic elements of why a particular process exists. To do so, it is important to 'break free' from existing constraints, and to think about what the process might achieve in a perfect world. It is important to maintain the customer's perspective of what it is they expect from the process, not what the organisation expects.

Key considerations are:

- Why do we perform these tasks?
- What is it meant to achieve?
- If we did not do this, what would happen?
- What are the critical outcomes of the process? (Ignore completely what the current situation is like, focusing instead on the core elements of what actually needs to be done.)

This step is of particular importance in a health care organisation as a clinician's perspective of why an admission process exists is very different from why administration officers believe a process must exist. It is important to resist viewing the process from how it will be administered. First build a concept that satisfies the needs of patients and clinicians, as this is where the most fundamental change can occur.

5.8.3   Develop the solution concept

Once those involved in the re-engineering efforts have a clear understanding of why the process exists, these core objectives need to be tested by the staff involved in the process. Simultaneously, the team needs to break free from their current perceptions of how the organisation achieves those objectives. Typically there is much debate about how to achieve these objectives as each participant tries to break free from convention.

In one meeting by the admission team, over one hour was spent trying to arrive at a common understanding of the needs of the different types of patients currently seen. Convention makes us label them as 'emergency department', 'acute assessment', 'outpatient clinic' or 'waiting list' patients. The revelation to the team was that the patient needs in all of these categories are exactly the same, and it was the inequity of how the organisation provided services to each of the different types that was responsible for many of the problems of the system. By segmenting the provision of services across the different departments and locations, appropriate resources were being stretched beyond their capacity, and inappropriate resources were being spent administering the segmenting.

5.8.4   How to enable the solution concept

Organisational change is complex in any industry; several idiosyncrasies existing in health care often lead health-care managers to contend that organisational change in health care is even more complex. Once clinicians have determined critical elements of the new processes, it is time to begin exploring how the solutions will be enabled. This includes:

- *Information technology solutions*. Many IT solutions have the potential to improve information flows radically within, and external to, the organisation. The re-engineering efforts must work in conjunction with this so that the business processes correspond so that the potential gains are realised.
- *Human resources*. Re-engineered processes are very likely to change what work is done where it is done, and who does it. Changing people is often regarded as the most difficult component of any organisational change. BPR projects have introduced case management, multi-skilling, flatter hierarchies and, although not often in health care, lower headcounts.
- *Physical space*. It is often difficult to conceptualise process changes as people are not conditioned to picturing how something will work without a visual picture of where the new processes will work. Careful attention is required at this point to ensure that critical details are not overlooked. In particular, clinicians have the opportunity to participate in the design of their facilities.

There are four areas of which we are mindful as we begin the redesign of some processes and exploratory analysis of others:

1   *Communication*. The project team spent the first two months develop-

ing their own skills and carrying out the first level of analysis. Towards the end of this time, murmurs were beginning to be heard regarding what outsiders perceived the patient focus review to be. A presentation by a visiting group from a pilot site in the UK enabled us to begin an intensive road show-style education programme based around a 20-minute presentation. To date, 18 or so presentations have been made, in a variety of locations at a variety of times, for audiences of between 4 and 25.

2   *Involvement*. Involvement of staff directly involved in the process in question is important as typically they have little understanding of the present process beyond their strict departmental tasks, and very often even less of an idea about how a redesigned process might look cross-functionally. With an opportunity to participate in the analysis and redesign process, staff are far more likely to develop a wider understanding of the process in its entirety and its impact on the customer.

3   *Position on jobs*. BPR programmes frequently incur a headcount reduction as the redesigned process simply does not need as many people. However, many health care organisations have been explicit in stating that no one will lose their job as a result of the BPR effort. This was flagged as an issue that may need clarification. Obviously if the level of staff attrition and organisational growth are sufficiently large then such assurances are more likely to achieve positive contributions from staff.

4   *More time for the project team*. One of the clear messages from the literature is that BPR efforts that lack strong time commitment from the CEO and senior manager are very likely to fail. We felt that we had to take more responsibility for team members to spend more time on the PFR. There was an overall enthusiastic reaction from staff for the call for participation, and it was made clear that we were prepared to meet necessary costs of overtime or replacement staff.

This chapter summarises progress made to date. While future reports will carry further information about what was done and how effective it was, this chapter has presented the preliminary steps about how a medium-sized hospital sets about a process re-engineering project.

Notes and references

(1)   Bergman, R. (1994). 'Reengineering health care', *Hospitals & Health Networks*, **68** (3), 28–36.
(2)   McManis, G.L. (1993). 'Re-inventing the system', *Hospitals & Health Networks*, **67** (19), 42–8.
(3)   Bard, M.R. (1994). 'Reinventing health care delivery', *Hospital & Health Service Administration*, **39** (3), 397–402.
(4)   Hammer, M. and Champy, J. (1990). 'Reengineering work: don't automate, obliterate', *Harvard Business Review*, July–August.

(5) Venkatraman, N. (1994). 'IT-enabled business transformation: from automation to business scope redefinition', *Sloan Management Review*, **35** (2), 73–87.

(6) A survey cited in Pierson, D.A. and Williams, J.B. (1994). 'Remaking the rules: hospitals attempt work transformation', *Hospitals & Health Networks*, **68** (17), 30, found that over 60 per cent of health-care institutions surveyed were doing, or had done re-engineering.

(7) See Allender, H.D. (1994). 'Is reengineering compatible with total quality management?', *Industrial Engineering*, **26** (9), 41–44, for a further discussion on this relationship.

(8) Hammer, M. and Champy, J. (1994). *Reengineering the Corporation: a Manifesto for Business Revolution*, Allen & Unwin, St Leonards, Australia, is the most commonly cited reference for high failure rates.

(9) Hall, G., Rosenthal, J. and Wade, J. (1993). 'How to make re-engineering really work', *Harvard Business Review*, **71** (6), 119–31, present the findings of research with over 100 companies.

(10) Manganelli, R.L. (1993). 'It's not a silver bullet', *Journal of Business Strategy*, **14** (6), 45.

(11) Anonymous (1994). 'Poor planning leads to high failure rate in business re-engineering', *Personnel Management*, **26** (8), 6.

(12) Sorohan, E.G. (1994) 'Executives: get real about reengineering', *Training & Development*, **48** (3), 11–12.

(13) Chang, R.Y. (1994) 'Improve processes, reengineer them, or both?', *Training & Development*, **48** (3), 54–58.

(14) Talwar, R. (1993). 'Business re-engineering – a strategy-driven approach', *Long Range Planning*, **26** (6), 22–40.

(15) One study found that only 49 per cent of senior executives claiming to be doing reengineering could successfully define BPR as process redesign: Klein, M.M. (1994) 'The most fatal reengineering mistakes', *Information Strategy: The Executive's Journal*, **10** (4), 21–28.

(16) Hequet, M. (1994). 'The people squeeze in health care', *Training*, **31** (7), 35–39, illustrates this by blurring the distinctions between: 'patient-focused care', 'total quality management', 're-engineering', 'cutting costs', 'transformation', 'streamlining work processes' and 'cross-training'. Hequet likens these together in the space of four sentences.

(17) Leth, S.A. (1994). 'Critical success factors for reengineering business processes', *National Productivity Review*, **13** (4), 557–568.

(18) William Waldegrave, Permanent Under-Secretary for Health for the Thatcher government in *The Nation's Health*, 1992 said, 'Change that does not take into consideration those who will implement the change is doomed to failure.'

(19) 'Many of the most successful BPR projects have been ones in which new technology was delayed to later phases' (Hall *et al.*, 1993).

Further reading

Anonymous (1994). '10 rules of thumb for reengineering', *HR Focus*, **71** (1), 18.

Anonymous (1994). 'Hospitals increase satisfaction and reduce costs by re-designing around patients', *Health Care Strategic Management*, **12** (6), 18.

Anonymous (1994). 'The perils of inadequate leadership', *Harvard Business Review*, **72** (5), 137.

Bashein, B.J., Markus, M.L. and Riley, P. (1994). 'Preconditions for BPR success', *Information Systems Management*, **11** (2), 7–13.

Beckmam, J.D. (1993). 'The longest wave', *Healthcare Forum Journal*, November/December, 78–82.

Boston, C. and Vestal, K. (1994). 'Work transformation (why the new healthcare imperative must focus on both people and processes)', *Hospitals and Health Networks*, 5 April, 50–54.

Burdett, J.O. (1994). 'TQM and re-engineering', *TQM Magazine*, **6** (2), 7–13.

Dunbar, C. (1994). 'MultiCare health system saves millions of dollars through redesigned care', *Health Management Technology* (July), 22–29.

Manganelli, R.L. and Klein, M.M. (1994). 'Your reengineering toolkit', *Management Review*, **83** (8), 26–30.

Moss, M. (1994). 'From reengineering to service integration', *Nursing Management*, **25** (8), 80E–F.

Patching, D. (1994). 'Business process re-engineering', *Management Services*, **38** (6), 10–13.

Sherer, J.L. (1994). 'Medical center gets facility face-lift, attitude adjust-ment', *Hospitals & Health Networks*, **68** (2), 58.

Smith, B. (1994). 'Business process reengineering: more than a buzzword', *HR Focus*, **71** (1), 17–18.

Vitiello, J. (1993). 'Reengineering: it's totally radical', *Journal of Business Strategy*, **14** (6), 44–47.

Voss, B. Vitiello, J., Johnson, C. and Winslow, C.D. (1993). 'Setting a course for radical change', *Journal of Business Strategy*, **14** (6), 52–57.

Wachel, W. (1994). 'Beyond incremental change', *Healthcare Executive*, **9** (4), 18–21.

Part II
The business environment

6
*Scenarios made easy**

By David Mercer

Editor's introduction

One of the main themes of Chapter 3 of *Exploring Corporate Strategy* is how managers can analyse and understand their external environment: in particular, what they can do to better deal with its uncertainty. Section 3.3.3, 'The use of scenarios', presents scenario planning as a tool that can help managers to audit the environment and, in particular, to envision the long-term future. This process allows managers to question the taken-for-granted assumptions they hold about their environment, its constituents and its evolution. The section stresses that the main aim of scenario planning is to generate an alternative 'picture' of what the future could be, and in this way it is also a basis for testing strategic options (see Section 8.2.2, 'Screening options', of *Exploring Corporate Strategy*). While the core principles of scenario planning were introduced in *Exploring Corporate Strategy*, in his chapter David Mercer shows how managers can painlessly approach scenario planning. He describes how scenarios can easily be written using a six-step process that he has developed on the basis of his practical experience. He also highlights how the process can help broaden managers' perspectives.

6.1 Background

Though the concept was first introduced as 'La Prospective', by Berger (1) in 1964 and the word 'scenario' itself was reportedly first used by Herman Kahn in 1967 (2), the theoretical foundations of scenario forecasting were mainly developed in the 1970s, especially by Godet (between 1974 and 1979) (3). By the early 1980s these approaches had developed into a sophisticated forecasting technique which was primarily recommended for the integration of the output from other sophisticated (qualitative) approaches to long-range forecasting. Although

* First published in *Long Range Planning*, Vol. 28, No. 4, pp. 81–86, 1995.

it was inevitably based upon judgemental forecasts, its use typically revolved around forecasting techniques which brought together groups of experts in order to reduce the risk involved. The techniques included Delphi and, especially in the context of scenarios, Cross-Impact Matrices, which were popular at that time.

Possibly as a result of these very sophisticated approaches, and of the difficult techniques they employed (which usually demanded the resources of a central planning staff), scenarios earned a reputation for difficulty (and cost) in use. Even so, the theoretical importance of the use of alternative scenarios, to help address the uncertainty implicit in long-range forecasts, was dramatically underlined by the widespread confusion which followed the Oil Shock of 1973. As a result many of the larger organisations started to use the technique in one form or another. Indeed, just ten years later, in 1983 Diffenbach (4) reported that 'alternate scenarios' were the third most popular technique for long-range forecasting – used by 68 per cent of the large organisations he surveyed.

Practical development of scenario forecasting, to guide strategy rather than for the more limited academic uses to which it had previously been put, was initiated by Wack (5) in 1971 at the Royal Dutch Shell group of companies (hereafter, for simplicity, referred to as 'Shell') which has since led the commercial world in the use of such scenarios – and in the development of more practical techniques to support these.

As most of the work reported to date, especially that undertaken by Shell, has mainly focused on improving the effectiveness of the techniques involved we have concentrated our own efforts on making the scenario planning process as a whole easier to use; making it more accessible to a wider range of organisations. More important, perhaps, these developments make the technique available for use by almost all managers – across the organisation – who might want to use it as one *part* of their overall planning processes, without the need for extended involvement of outside experts, or corporate staff specialists.

Thus, experience in the Open Business School, using the simpler approaches we have developed, indicates that it can be implemented with relative ease in most organisations. Indeed, in addition to its use by commercial organisations, we have implemented it in a county council and a health authority – and even in parts of government in the developing world. Its use in dealing with uncertainty, arising from alternative futures, which was the original reason it entered into management theory, still holds true – and usefully *complements* more traditional forms of planning. In our experience, however, its greatest virtue – especially in the simplified form – is that its use naturally (and painlessly) widens managers' viewpoints and helps to extend their planning horizons beyond the short term.

The form of scenarios we chose as the main vehicle to link the various elements of our distance-taught MBA course was the widest-ranging possible; that of 'environmental scenarios' (sometimes referred to as 'industry scenarios' to distinguish them from 'global scenarios' undertaken by governments). These examine the total external environment for the whole industry within which the organisation operates.

In order to meet the needs of managers who are not experts in long-range planning, it was found necessary not just to introduce students to other people's material, but to develop our own simpler approach to the subject; albeit that this builds upon the work of others (especially that of Shell, much of it unpublished). In creating this easier-to-use form of scenario forecasting, we have in turn built upon the experience of more than 1,000 students who have taken the course over this time – and who have, between them, written more than 4,000 full length scenarios.

In particular, permission was received from 213 of the students taking the course in 1993 for their work to be used as a basis for statistical analyses. Of these projects, 165 were found to be suitable for further (content) analysis. These were analysed, in the context of this chapter, to see how they used the techniques they had been taught.

6.2   Simple scenarios

The most important message is that scenarios *can* be simple: and, in our experience, the simpler they are – and the simpler the process used to derive them – the more powerful they tend to be, not least because those using them are able to understand how they work. Indeed, our students in general used the technique quite specifically as a simple one, eschewing the more sophisticated elements. For instance, despite having been introduced to the technique on the course, only 3 per cent of the students made any use of the cross-impact matrices which were almost mandatory in the scenarios of earlier times. In addition, none of the organisations, in either the commercial or public sectors, with which we have worked has used this technique or, indeed, *any* of the other sophisticated techniques which used to be required for the development of scenarios.

In fact, the basic concepts of the process are simple. In terms of the overall approach to forecasting, they can be divided into three progressive groups of activities (which are, generally speaking, common to all long range forecasting processes):

- environmental analysis
- scenario planning
- corporate strategy.

The first of these groups comprises environmental analysis. The central part represents the specific techniques which differentiate the scenario forecasting process from the others in long-range planning; and it is, not surprisingly, this which will take up most of the rest of the chapter. The final group represents all the subsequent processes which go towards producing the corporate strategies and plans.

6.3 *Environmental analysis*

Scenarios can only be as good as the information they are based upon. For this reason, the analysis must be of as high a quality as possible. The practical advice we give our students is to cultivate a deep curiosity about the external environment and to maintain maximum exposure to the widest range of media. Beyond this, they are also recommended to develop an informed viewpoint which will improve their chances of recognising early signs of change, no matter from what direction they are coming.

In practice, 72 per cent of students in the survey used general reading as the main source of their analysis, combined with the information they received from the industry and specialist press which they read as a normal part of their work. A further 18 per cent did not even extend their search beyond general reading! A small proportion, 7 per cent, undertook a wider search, covering a range of sources as scenario theory would recommend, but there was no obvious major gain in final quality from this. Less than 1 per cent used any form of database even though these students were required to make extensive use of remote computer services as part of the course. Indeed, it has to be noted that the type of information which is required for environmental scenarios is most probably that which the participants have already assimilated from their general (and specialist) reading. In the case of the largest group of participants in the United Kingdom, provided by Surrey County Council (SCC), none of the nearly 80 councillors and officers involved had undertaken *any* previous environmental analysis.

In addition, there seems to be no special expertise involved in detecting these shifts. Indeed, perhaps the best advice is to analyse the external environment as a team. If nothing else, this extends the coverage of the scanning; but it also seems to go much further, to develop resonances as the team interact with each other, inevitably comparing notes as the process develops, and amplify the early signs of change. Our experience indicates that the most effective team size is between five and seven members. In the case of SCC, for example, this was achieved by splitting the participants into four separate sessions of 20 to 30 individuals each; and, within these, into four teams, each of six or seven people.

The subsequent analysis needs more academic rigour. The key here is that the process is one of education for the team, by total immersion in the facts which define the environment they are studying. When the scenario development finally gets under way it is not the material available on paper that is productive, it is what is in the team's heads. Indeed, the first stage of scenario forecasting – the choice of the assumptions – is embedded in this supposedly earlier process of environmental analysis. It is inevitable that, as the team works together on the analysis, it will start to develop ideas as to what the assumptions might be and will probably have spent a considerable time – over the weeks, and perhaps months, that the environmental analysis should take – arguing about what these mean.

6.4 Scenario planning

Even this part of the process is, at its most basic level, relatively simple and requires just six steps:

- Decide drivers for change
- Bring drivers together into a viable framework
- Produce initial (7–9) mini-scenarios
- Reduce to 2–3 scenarios
- Write the scenarios
- Identify issues arising.

6.4.1 Step 1 – Decide drivers for change

The first stage is to examine the results of the environmental analysis to determine which are the most important factors that will decide the nature of the future environment within which the organisation operates. These factors are sometimes called 'variables' (because they will vary over the time being investigated), but we prefer the term 'drivers' (for change) since this terminology is not laden with quasi-scientific connotations and reinforces the participant's commitment to search for those forces which will act to change the future.

In the ideal approach, the first action should be carefully to decide the broad assumptions on which the scenarios will be based. Only then, as a second stage, should the various drivers be specifically defined. Participants, though, seem to have problems in separating these stages, and indeed only 40 per cent of those in our survey made any attempt to spell out the assumptions separately. Despite this, most still managed to discover the drivers, without any obvious deterioration in quality; so having separate stages is not essential to the process and we no longer emphasise this separation in our own use of the technique.

Perhaps the most difficult aspect, though, is freeing the participants from the preconceptions they take into the process with them. In particular, in our experience most participants will want to look no further than the medium term, five to ten years ahead (36 per cent of those in our survey did so, and indeed, a further 42 per cent wrote about periods less than five years ahead), rather than the required longer-term, ten or more years ahead (which only 22 per cent addressed). This may not seem a problem when nine years is a very long time in many areas of commercial activity, but we have found that a time horizon of anything less than ten years often leads participants to extrapolate from present trends, rather than consider the alternatives which might face them. When, however, they are asked to consider timescales in excess of ten years they almost all seem to accept the logic of the scenario planning process, and no longer fall back on that of extrapolation. Indeed, in our own work with outside organisations, we now ask them to project their 'industry sector' scenarios 15 years into the future. In the case of the SCC exercise this produced drivers ranging from the effects of 'increased longevity for individuals' to 'changes in the power of the global trading blocs'.

There is a similar problem with expanding participants' horizons to include the whole external environment. Only 22 per cent of the scenarios in our survey could be considered as being totally externally oriented. The largest category, 42 per cent, took in some of the external environment but mixed it with internal factors. Despite the thrust of our teaching, a relatively high proportion, 36 per cent, wrote what amounted to corporate scenarios (which describe the future of the organisation itself, largely on the basis of internal factors). On the other hand, the results indicated that if participants can be persuaded to address the ten-year horizon, perhaps an easier task, this also tends to make them look further out in terms of the external environment. With the longer timescales, this has not proved a problem for our work with other organisations.

Brainstorming

In any case, the brainstorming which should then take place to ensure that the list is complete may extend their viewpoint and unearth more variables – and, in particular, the combination of factors may suggest yet others.

Almost any form of brainstorming seems to work, but our own internal usage has revolved around the use of flip-charts, mainly because that has been the available medium and is often prescribed for creative decision-making sessions. In our more recent work with organisations in the public sector, for example, we have tended to use

Post-It-Notes placed on a wall by team members, since this enhances the flexibility of the process; and hence encourages creativity.

Important and uncertain

This step is, though, also one of selection – since only the most important factors will justify a place in the scenarios. The 80:20 Rule here means that, at the end of the process, management's attention must be focused on a limited number of the most important issues. Experience has proved that offering a wider range of topics merely allows them to select those few which interest them and not necessarily those which are most important to the organisation.

In addition, as scenarios are a technique for presenting alternative futures, the factors to be included must be genuinely 'variable'. They should be subject to significant alternative outcomes. Factors whose outcome is predictable but important should be spelled out in the introduction to the scenarios (since they cannot be ignored).

At this point it is also worth pointing out that a great virtue of scenarios is that they can accommodate the input from any other form of forecasting. They may use figures, diagrams or words in any combination.

6.4.2   Step 2 – Bring drivers together into a viable framework

The next step is to link these drivers together to provide a meaningful framework. The theoretical approach adopted by the course encouraged students to first of all build 'event strings' by linking together the various drivers and developing them to see the links between them as well as their onward progressions over time. The great majority, 74 per cent, of scenarios in the survey claimed to include this step, but inspection indicated that there was actually relatively little development – they merely restated the drivers in different combinations. It might seem, therefore, that the basic requirement at this stage is to group the drivers into combinations that are meaningful to the participants. Once again, we now use this simpler approach for our own planning processes. Indeed, following our later work with other organisations, we now only ask for the 'drivers' – and do not mention 'event strings'.

This is probably the most (conceptually) difficult step. It is where managers' 'intuition' – their ability to make sense of complex patterns of 'soft' data which more rigorous analysis would be unable to handle – plays an important role. Even so, the SCC teams found it relatively easy to cluster around factors such as 'fragmentation of disadvantaged communities' and 'links with Europe'.

Again, in our own planning we tend to use flip-charts to organise the drivers into meaningful patterns. The whole process appears to flow very naturally once the participants accept the simple principles behind it.

6.4.3   Step 3 – Produce initial mini-scenarios

The outcome of the previous step is usually between seven and nine logical groupings of drivers. In our experience this is surprisingly easy to achieve.

Having placed the factors in these groups, the next action is to work out, very approximately at this stage, what is the connection between them. What does each group of factors represent?

6.4.4   Step 4 – Reduce scenarios

The main action, at this next stage, is to reduce the seven to nine mini-scenarios/groupings detected at the previous stage to two or three larger scenarios. The challenge in practice seems to come down to finding just two or three 'containers' into which all the topics can be sensibly fitted. This usually requires a considerable amount of debate but usually produces fundamental insights into what are the really important (perhaps life and death) issues affecting the organisation.

There is no theoretical reason for reducing to just two or three scenarios, only a practical one. It has been found that the managers who will be asked to use the final scenarios can only cope effectively with a maximum of three versions! Shell started, more than two decades ago, by building half a dozen or more scenarios but found that the outcome was that their managers selected just one of these to concentrate on. As a result the planners there progressively reduced the number to two, which is the number we also now recommend.

Complementary scenarios

As used by Shell, these two scenarios are *complementary* since this helps managers avoid choosing just one 'preferred' scenario and lapsing once more into single-track forecasting (negating the benefits of using 'alternative' scenarios to allow for alternative, uncertain futures). This is, however, a potentially difficult concept to grasp, where managers are used to looking for opposites: a good and a bad scenario, say, or an optimistic one versus a pessimistic one. In practice, we found that this requirement posed few problems for the great majority, 84 per cent, of those in the survey who easily produced 'balanced' scenarios. The remaining 16 per cent fell into the expected trap of 'good versus bad'. At the beginning of the 1990s, for example, Shell's two complementary scenarios were 'Global Mercantilism' and 'Sustainable World'; which, by the mid-1990s, transformed into 'Just-Do-IT' (focusing on the effects of liberalisation) and 'Big Me' (reflecting community cohesion).

Testing

Having grouped the factors into these two scenarios, the next step is to test them, again, for viability. Do they make sense to the participants? If the scenarios do not intuitively 'hang together', why not? The usual problem is that one or more of the assumptions turns out to be unrealistic in terms of how the participants see their world. If this is the case then you need to return to the first step – the whole scenario planning process is above all an iterative one. Where there is a larger number of participants, the 'stability' of the scenarios can also be tested by comparing the sets of scenarios produced by the separate groups. In practice, we have found that these usually tend to converge, even where, as was the case with SCC, there were a dozen separate groups; in that case, they tended to cluster around decentralised options, such as 'democracy', or centralised ones, including 'giants learn to dance'.

6.4.5   *Step 5 – Write the scenarios*

The scenarios are then 'written up' in the most suitable form. The flexibility of this step often confuses participants, for they are used to forecasting processes which have a fixed format. The rule, though, is that you should produce the scenarios in the form most suitable for use by the managers who are going to base their strategy on them. This is essentially a 'marketing' decision, since it will be necessary to 'sell' the final results to the users. On the other hand, the best way may be to use the form the author also finds most comfortable.

Most scenarios will, perhaps, be written in word form (as a series of alternative essays about the future); especially where they will almost inevitably be qualitative. Nearly half (47 per cent) of those in our survey chose to use the normal business report format – hardly surprising when they, and their audience, would probably use this in their day-to-day communications. A further 13 per cent reduced the material to something closer to an expanded series of lists. Just over a quarter (28 per cent) enlivened their reports by adding some fictional 'character' to the material – perhaps taking literally the idea that they are stories about the future – though it was still clearly intended to be factual. On the other hand, they may include numeric data and/ or diagrams as Shell's scenarios do (and in the process gain by the acid test of more measurable 'predictions') though less than 1 per cent of our students did so. Finally, 9 per cent of the students took some delight in using a fictional form, as they were entitled to, assuming the character of a leader writer of the *Financial Times* in the year 2010, for instance.

6.4.6   Step 6 – Identify issues arising

The final stage of the process is to examine these scenarios to determine what are the most critical outcomes; the 'branching points' relating to the issues which will have the greatest impact (potentially generating 'crises') on the future of the organisation.

6.5   Use of scenarios

It is important to note that these final scenarios may be used in a number of ways:

6.5.1   Containers for the drivers/event strings

Essentially, they are a logical device, an artificial framework for presenting the individual factors/topics (or coherent groups of these) so that they are made easily available for managers' use – as useful ideas about future developments in their own right – without reference to the rest of the scenario. It should be stressed that *no* factors should be dropped, or even given lower priority, as a result of producing the scenarios. In this context, which scenario contains which topic (driver) or issue about the future is irrelevant.

6.5.2   Tests for consistency

At every stage it is necessary to iterate, to check that the contents are viable and make any necessary changes to ensure that they are; here the main test is to see if the scenarios seem to be internally consistent – if they are not then the writer must loop back to earlier stages to correct the problem.

6.5.3   Positive perspectives

Perhaps the main benefit deriving from scenarios, however, comes from the alternative 'flavours' of the future their different perspectives offer. It is a common experience, when the scenarios finally emerge, for the participants to be startled by the insight they offer as to what the general shape of the future might be. At this stage it is no longer a theoretical exercise but becomes a genuine framework (or rather set of alternative frameworks) for dealing with that future. As we see in the more detailed example presented in Illustration 6.1, the (scenario) frameworks adopted by the OUBS were 'Edutainment' and 'The Club'.

Strategy in action

Illustration 6.1

Scenarios: an example

We have now used this approach with several thousand students, working in teams and as individuals, and the results described above summarise our experience with these. In terms of a specific example, however, the most directly practical perhaps was the one we undertook, as the management team of the Open University Business School (OUBS), in late 1994 – as part of our overall planning process.

This activity represented the first day of a two-day residential meeting, off-site at a hotel, where a key requirement of such sessions is that participants are not disturbed. The management team, of 30 or so individuals, was split into three separate teams – each in a separate room – with an even balance of experience (academics alongside administrators) in each. They had not undertaken any preparation, in terms of formal environmental analysis (though they would have prepared for the annual planning process which was taking place in parallel), but – like most of the managers who participate in our sessions – they had a sound understanding of the (higher education) 'sector'.

The morning session concentrated on steps 1 and 2, essentially those of deciding what were the key drivers for change, for the 'sector' ten years or more ahead, and organising them into meaningful patterns. The medium used was simply that of flip-charts. As has been our experience with other groups, they had few problems describing the key drivers, even some of those – such as the significant shift in MBA content – we might have thought were less obvious.

The 20 or so drivers surfaced by each group at the first stage typically included cryptic statements such as: accredited learning, life-time membership, use of IT, growth of distance learning, changing expectations of managers, requirements of multinationals, social marketing, short courses, doctoral programmes, modular approaches. The pattern at this stage looked very much like the output of a brainstorming session, except that they were more focused. Like most other groups we have worked with, however, they did not formalise their workings and, in particular, they did not produce 'event strings' (patterns of development over time).

At the second stage these were reduced to around eight main groups of-

6.6 Corporate strategy

Scenarios are, of course, only a means to an end. They identify the long-term forces, and consequent events, which the organisation's conventional long-range planning must address. The next step, therefore, starts by matching the organisation's limited internal resources to the essentially unlimited external challenges which may face it. The special contribution of scenario planning in this context is to allow, and indeed encourage, the development of a robust set of strategies.

Illustration 6.1 continued

drivers, including such elements as: ongoing education, partnerships, changing corporate needs, research versus training, changing expectations of students. In particular, they discussed at some length drivers which included the potential demise of the MBA as the mainstream business school offering, with a switch to social marketing approach which could be closer to the traditional social science curriculum, and the emergence of non-traditional suppliers, such as the software and entertainment groups.

The afternoon started with step 3, the 'mini-scenarios', but – again as is usually the case – these had already been largely decided by the previous step. Most of the afternoon was, therefore, taken up with step 4, that of deciding the scenarios. The debate at this stage, and indeed throughout, was as important as the output – allowing the participants to come to a consensus view which informed later work in OUBS. This was summarised (step 5) in the form of flip-chart presentations, which were given to the whole group – and discussed by them, when there was a plenary session at the end of the day – to decide the overall consensus view.

There was, indeed, a surprising degree of consensus between the groups; all of them (as an especially useful form of testing) agreeing on one out of the two scenarios, and two of them agreeing on the other one:

1 *Edutainment* – the first of these described a future in which computer delivered education was used for the most popular courses. These products would be more comparable with the markets for feature films – costing tens of millions of dollars to produce and selling for only a few tens of dollars each, so demanding 'audiences' of millions of users – resulting in the providers coming from the media owners or the major software vendors.

2 *The Club* – on the other hand, there was the provision of ongoing (higher) education to small groups, who would develop links with the establishments – typically the existing HE institutions – providing this; more in a club atmosphere than a classroom.

Interestingly, this debate did not have a direct impact on the annual plan discussed on the second day – it seems that the radical ideas brought forward at such sessions need time to be assimilated – but it has significantly influenced long-term developments in the School since that time.

These will not necessarily result in an optimal outcome for a specific situation but should offer the possibility of achieving the best overall outcome. In particular, they should protect as far as possible against all the major threats potentially facing the organisation and then exploit the most important opportunities open to it.

The use of scenarios, therefore, should help ensure that as many as possible of the long-term threats and opportunities facing the organisation are identified and addressed. Shell (5–7) has demonstrated a number of times how such an awareness of the alternatives facing it has enabled it not simply to handle changed market conditions, but to capitalise on them. At the beginning of the 1970s, when it first adopted its scenario planning approach, it was probably the weakest of the major oil multinationals. Two decades later it has become the strongest of them. These facts are not necessarily connected, but Shell's senior management is convinced that its dedication to scenario planning has at the very least made a significant contribution to this dramatic improvement in performance.

Scenarios do, however, still demand some considerable investment of time, often of scarce senior management time, so if they are to be justified they must earn their keep. In essence this means that they must be genuinely useful, and used, as the (external) basis for corporate strategy. Thus it is recognised by all those who are actively involved in the scenario planning process that persuading line managers to make use of the scenarios produced is by far the most difficult part of the whole process. It is no accident that the large corporate planning department at Shell spend at least half their time promoting their scenarios.

Indeed, the whole process of scenario forecasting must be imbued, from the very start, with the objective of positively influencing the strategy of the organisation. This means that, on the one hand, the scenarios must be carefully balanced between stretching the imagination of the management and being believable. On the other, it requires a significant investment in the education of the senior management. The marketing of the scenarios needs to be every bit as sophisticated as the writing of them. The introduction of the process should be seen as a long-term project. It can take a number of years before senior managers really trust scenarios sufficiently to put their faith in the strategies which are developed from them.

The cultural problems facing those who wish their organisations to take scenarios seriously should not, therefore, be underestimated. As the final part of the course, our own students subsequently went on to produce a corporate strategy based on the scenarios they had developed for their industry – or at least that was the brief. Based on the anecdotal reports of their tutors, backed by the 32 cases tracked, we found that in practice, despite all the teaching and very explicit instructions we had given, almost all of the students lapsed into producing 'traditional' strategies which almost entirely addressed short-term internal factors, ignoring the external long-term trends. Only 13 per cent delivered strategies which effectively addressed the outcomes of their scenarios!

This failure to have an immediate impact on published strategy should not, however, discourage those considering use of the technique. Our own experience, and that of Shell, was that the first scenarios produced *are* relatively neglected in the subsequent planning. It may take literally years for the process to deliver all its benefits.

Even so, our observation is that the participants do obtain major benefits from the process – even in the short term. On the other hand, the main benefit is much less direct than that usually claimed, and indeed is often not even obvious to the participants themselves. It is the enduring change in viewpoint of all those participating, extending their perspectives to include the wider environment and the longer term. In view of the 'short-termism' exhibited by so many managers, this shift in attitude must in itself be invaluable. Above all, therefore, scenario planning should be seen as a process of learning.

Acknowledgement

The author is grateful to the many academics and students who have contributed to this work, and to the corporate planning group at Shell, particularly Graham Galer, for their invaluable help.

References

(1)   Berger, G. (1964). *Phénoménologies du Temps et Prospectives*, Paris: Presse Universitaires de France.

(2)   Kahn, H. (1967). *The Year 2000*, Calman-Levy.

(3)   Godet, M. (1987). *Scenarios and Strategic Management*, London: Butterworth.

(4)   Diffenbach, J. (1983). 'Corporate environmental analysis in large US corporations', *Long Range Planning*, **16** (3), 107.

(5)   Wack, P. (1985). 'Scenarios: uncharted waters ahead', *Harvard Business Review*, September–October.

(6)   Wack, P. (1985). 'Scenarios: shooting the rapids', *Harvard Business Review*, November–December.

(7)   Kahane, A. (1992). 'Scenarios for energy: sustainable world vs global mercantilism', *Long Range Planning*, **25** (4), 38.

7

Competitor analysis

By Gerry Johnson, Cliff Bowman and Peter Rudd

Editors' introduction

There is no prescribed 'correct' way of undertaking competitor analysis. However, many of the techniques introduced in *Exploring Corporate Strategy* can be used to analyse competitors and the competitive position of an organisation. Figure 3.13 in Chapter 3 of *Exploring Corporate Strategy* summarises the range of techniques that might be appropriate. This chapter shows how a set of such techniques might be used together to provide an understanding of the competitive position of an organisation and provide guidelines as to its future strategy. It does this by drawing together the results of a PEST and Five Forces analysis by means of impact analysis, examining competitive standing in the context of market segments, analysing customer and manager perception of value and the consideration of all these in relation to different positions of competitors in relation to the Strategy Clock. The strategic implications of this series of analyses are then discussed. This is done by using a practical example of the application of such techniques by the executives of an industrial goods company.

7.1 Introduction

In Chapter 3 of *Exploring Corporate Strategy*, Figure 3.13 sets out numerous ways in which competitors can be analysed using techniques explained in the book. The purpose of this chapter is to show how four of these can be employed in such a way as to:

- identify the competitive position of a firm in relation to its competitors
- contribute to the criteria by which the strategic options open to a firm can be evaluated.

The techniques are all outlined in *Exploring Corporate Strategy* and, in turn, follow the bases of analysis suggested in *The Essence of Competitive Strategy* (1). They are used here in the context of a case example in order to show how, used together, they build on one another as a means of understanding the competitor position of a firm.

7.2   *The case context*

The case example used here is that of a highly competitive industrial market. The distribution of electrical power around industrial and commercial premises can involve complex systems analogous to the fuse boxes used in domestic situations. Typically these take the form of switchboards which comprise electrical components and protective devices. This equipment is intended to protect both people and plant in the event of a fault developing somewhere in the power distribution network. The market for such distribution systems in the UK is highly fragmented, with some estimates placing as many as 2,000 companies active in the industry. Given this, it is difficult to ascertain the total size of the market, and figures ranging from £60m per annum are quoted. The sector is closely linked with the construction industry, and as such business cycles vary according to building activity, it is often the first to go into recession and the last to come out. Overall, however, the market has reached maturity and is growing slowly at best.

In these circumstances a company competing in the market must be very clear of its strategic position in relation to competitors and of its own competitive strategy. How might this be done?

In this case example the executives concerned with one manufacturer of switchboards – we will call it Alpha – asked the following questions:

- To what extent have changes in the industry affected us differently from competitors? How has this yielded opportunities and posed threats differentially between competitors?
- How do competitors' positions differ by market segment?
- To what extent do different competitors meet the needs of customers in different segments do a greater or lesser extent than their rivals?
- What does this tell us about the different positions in terms of competitive strategies adopted by competition?
- What does all this suggest about the strategy we should follow?

To do this the executives focused on a number of competitors:

- Beta was a subsidiary of one of the component manufacturers, a multi-national group. It was a relatively new entrant into the industry, having been started by the component supplier.
- Gamma was also a subsidiary of a multinational component supplier, but had been acquired by the parent group rather than being a start-up. The company was an established business of many years standing.
- Delta was a collective set of competitors which were often called 'panel

builders'; these were typically small businesses, owner controlled, with limited overheads and probably limited facilities. However, they needed very few significant orders each year to keep in business and they were able to produce basic products very cheaply.

7.2.1   Stage 1: Impact analysis

There had been significant changes in the market for switchboards from the early 1980s onwards. PEST and Five Forces analyses identified a number of key changes, notably:

- As previously explained, *economic cycles* affecting the industry had a pronounced effect on this sector. In times of recession orders fell dramatically, in good times orders rose substantially. This was an industry subject to *boom and bust*.
- There had been major *technological* changes associated with developments in electrical engineering and electronics which meant that the traditional components that were used in switchboards had been greatly reduced in size and made more user-friendly. However, these were less commonly made by the switchboard builders themselves than in the past; rather they were usually manufactured by firms from overseas, notably France and Japan. *Specialist component* manufacturers had therefore entered the market.
- This in turn had encouraged the *growth of panel builders*. Previously they had not been a major force in the market, which had been dominated by integrated manufacturers of components and switchboards. However, access to cheaper imported components meant that it was relatively easy to set up in business to manufacture switchboards. The result was an increase in *competitive intensity* and this contributed to a driving down of margins.
- Triggered by the recession of the early 1980s, but continuing through that decade, the pressure on companies that were purchasers of switchboards to reduce costs meant that many of them reduced their engineering department staffing levels and outsourced the buying and project management of engineering projects. In effect, this meant that *contractors* began to become *powerful buyers* much more strongly than hitherto.

These key factors had major influences on the industry. But to what extent did they have variable impacts according to competitors? Impact analysis was able to help assess this. Table 7.1 shows how the executives rated each of the environmental impacts according to the impact on themselves and the three other competitors.

- All those involved in the market were negatively affected by economic conditions. What distinguished the competitors was their capacity to respond to market and technological conditions.

Table 7.1   *Impact analysis*

	Alpha	Beta	Gamma	Delta
Boom and bust	−1	0	−1	−2
Technological change	−1	+1	−1	+2
Entry of component manufacturers	0	+1	−1	+2
Growth of panel builders	−2	0	−2	+1
Contractor buying power	−1	0	−2	+1
Competitive intensity/reduced margins	−1	0	−1	+2
Totals	−6	+2	−8	+6

Scoring system

+2, Very positive impact; +1, Positive impact; 0, Neutral;

−1, Negative impact; −2, Very negative impact

- The differences between Beta and Gamma showed the different importance attached to the sector by the two parent groups. They also highlight the importance of market perception, since the two companies had very different profiles with customers.
- Most of the driving changes within the market had been to the benefit of the panel builders, some driven by them and some by component manufacturers.
- Alpha clearly had to try to place itself in a better position to respond to market changes.
- Given the structure of the panel builders, both in terms of size and cost, it was clear that none of the established manufacturers would be able to compete on a least-price strategy. There was a need for identifying a clear strategy based on differentiation and enhanced added value.

7.2.2   Stage 2: Competitor analysis by segment

As the nature of the market for switchboards changed, different forms of buying had evolved, in particular as between direct buying by end users and buying (and project management) by contractors. There were then changes in the segmentation of the market. Understanding the current and historic relative positions of competitors in different segments was therefore important. The three segments the executives were specially concerned about were:

1   The segment of the market dominated by contractors who had, in effect, taken over the control of buying of switchboards for many companies.

2   The segment of the market still strongly influenced directly by the

Table 7.2 · *Competitive standing by market segment*

	Alpha	Beta	Gamma	Delta
End-user market	+1	0	0	−1
Contractor market	0	+1	−1	+2
Consultants	−1	+2	−2	−1

Scoring system
Strength in market segment:
+2, Very strong; +1, Strong;
0, Neutral; −1, Weak; −2, Very weak

end-user buyers and particularly by engineers working for those companies.

3 The segment employing specialist consultants to design systems.

It is not always possible to quantify market strength by market segment. However, even if this is not possible, understanding relative positions from a qualitative point of view may be possible. This is what the executives were able to do for a number of the competitors in the market. Table 7.2 summarises their findings for themselves versus Beta, Gamma and Delta.

They concluded that the end-user segment was not particularly well covered, and presented a more attractive target than the others, especially given Alpha's traditional strengths there. The ongoing analysis therefore concentrated on this segment.

7.2.3 Stage 3: Understanding perceived added value (or perceived use value)

Section 3.5.3 of Chapter 3 in *Exploring Corporate Strategy* stresses the importance of understanding how customers stand in relation to the perceived value offered by the products or services of competitors. This requires analysis of perceived customer needs to be undertaken by market segment, which is what the executives of Alpha did with reference to the end-user segment.

The first step was to identify the characteristics of the products and services offered by switchboard builders most valued by buyers in the segment. The executives had carried out market research which showed this, and their findings are summarised in Table 7.3. This research had also given some clues as to the relative weighting of these different characteristics. Although this had, in the end, to be a matter of judgement by those doing the research, it was possible to get a quantified view of their relative importance; and these are also shown in

Table 7.3   *End-user segment weighting of value adding characteristics*

Characteristics	Weighting (%)
1. Reputation for reliability	30
2. Post-sales support	23
3. Delivery	18
4. Ability to supply test certificates	15
5. Technical and manufacturing quality	14

Table 7.3. Reputation with regard to reliability and post-sales support emerged as key characteristics. The weightings as shown in Table 7.3 are also shown graphically as the solid line in Figure 7.1.

The next step in the exercise was to consider how other executives in the firm viewed Alpha in comparison with the findings of the research. These executives were also asked to rank Alpha's performance against the key characteristics established in the research. Their weightings are shown as the dotted line in Figure 7.1. The differences are evident. While agreeing about the importance of reputation for reliability, the executives viewed Alpha's advantages in terms of aspects of technical performance rather than 'service' type characteristics such as post-sales support valued in the marketplace.

This situation gave further cause for concern when the positioning of competitors was considered in similar ways. The market re-

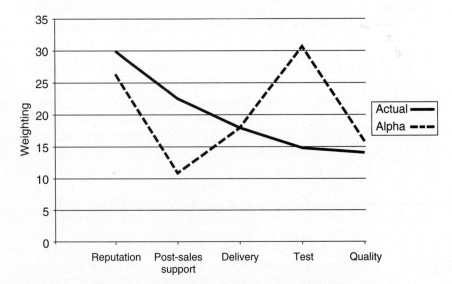

Figure 7.1   *Value adding characteristics: user versus executive perceptions.*

Table 7.4   *Relative competitive standing of competitors in the end-user segment**

	Alpha	Beta	Gamma	Delta
Reputation	30×0.45=13.4	30×0.6=18	30×0.17=5	30×0.17=5
PSS	23×0.2=4.6	23×0.8=18.4	23×0.2=4.6	23×0.2=4.6
Delivery	18×0.5=9	18×0.8=14.4	18×0.4=7.2	18×0.8=14.4
Test	15×0.9=13.5	15×0.4=6	15×0.4=6	15×0.2=3
Quality	14×0.75=10.5	14×0.6=8.4	14×0.6=8.4	14×0.4=5.6
Total	51	65.2	31.2	32.6

* During the market research, scores out of 5 were awarded to each company according to performance in the different areas. The average scores were converted to a score out of 1 so that the total weighting taking into account the five characteristics gives a score out of 100 for each competitor.

search had also established relative 'scores' for competitors against the various characteristics. This was done by taking each of the weightings of characteristics in Table 7.3 and applying these to the score for each competitor against each of the characteristics. This is shown in Table 7.4, which amounts to a quantified view of the competitive standing of the different competitors in the end-user segment.

7.2.4   Stage 4: Relative competitive strategies

Drawing together stages 2 and 3, it was possible to see how the different competitors were positioned in terms of their competitive strategies in the different markets segments. This was done by using the framework of the Strategy Clock, explained in Chapter 6 of *Exploring Corporate Strategy*. This required the executives to rate the competitors on two dimensions, perceived price and perceived added (or use) value.

Perceived price can be informed by the actual knowledge of price quoted by competitors, and in this case the executives had a good idea about this because much of it was known through the tendering procedures that took place in the industry. However, it was also important to qualify price in terms of *perceived* price. This again was informed by asking customers how they perceived the relative pricing of competitors. So objective assessment of price levels was also informed by subjective views of customers of the relative pricing positions of the competitors. The relative positions in terms of price of the four competitive groups is then shown on the horizontal axis in Figure 7.2 using an index of 0–100.

Perceived added (or use) value can be informed by the evidence provided in stage 3. The vertical axis therefore represents the weighted aggregate scores of the four different competitors in terms of contributing to perceived added (or use) value, as shown in Table 7.4.

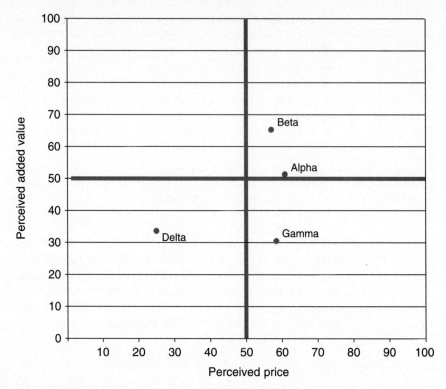

Figure 7.2   Competitive positions on the 'Strategy Clock'.

Of course there were more competitors to be taken into account than is shown on this table and illustrated in this exercise; and the executives did, in fact, include these in the analysis. But the position that emerged was similar to that shown in Table 7.4. Alpha's competitive position was seen by customers as being relatively high priced but other competitors were perceived as offering higher value; and this was in the more attractive market segment for Alpha. The analysis helped clarify the reasons for this. Alpha had an undoubted reputation for quality, but in terms of technical aspects of its operations linked to its product. While technical quality was recognised as important by customers, it was not weighted as highly as the service aspect; and other competitors were seen as better than Alpha in this regard.

7.3   *Strategic implications*

The Alpha executives reached a number of key conclusions as a result of these analyses. First, they should, indeed, place more focus on the end-user segment than the contractor segment. Alpha's position here was historically stronger and it had a reputation for reliability which was seen as centrally important by the users. In any case it had emerged in their analysis that the contractor segment placed a much greater emphasis on price, and it was unlikely that Alpha would be able to achieve competitive advantage in this respect, particularly with regard to the panel builders.

The emphasis, therefore, had to be on differentiation, building on a historic perception of reliability. However, it had to be recognised that this was not just a technical issue; it was a matter of addressing the perceived needs of customers in the end-user segment, and the analysis had identified that, in this regard, reliability was much more to do with wider aspects of service than it was to do with technical aspects of the product.

In turn this raised an internal issue in Alpha. The evidence from the exercise suggested that the executives themselves, while recognising Alpha's traditional reputation for reliability, did indeed attribute this essentially to technical aspects related to the product and to the engineering of that product. So there was a difficult issue to do with rearranging cultural change that had to be addressed internally if Alpha was to improve its competitive positioning.

7.4 Summary

This chapter has used a case example of how different ways of undertaking competitor analysis can contribute to an understanding of the competitive standing of a firm. There are, of course, other ways of undertaking competitor analysis, as suggested in Figure 3.13 in *Exploring Corporate Strategy*. However, whatever approaches are used, the overall aim should be to achieve more than a description of competitors; it should be to understand the reasons for the positioning of one firm in relation to another. In so doing, competitor analysis can provide a basis for considering future strategic direction and the opportunities and problems associated with achieving competitive advantage.

Reference

(1)   Faulkner, D. and Bowman, C. (1995). *The Essence of Competitive Strategy*, Hemel Hempstead: Prentice Hall.

8

Strengths, weaknesses, opportunities and threats (SWOT) analysis

By Tony Jacobs, Jill Shepherd and Gerry Johnson

Editors' introduction

Strengths, Weaknesses, Opportunities and Threats (SWOT) analysis has become a popular analytical tool used by managers and students. It has the merits of being straightforward to employ. However, there are problems associated with it, not least in its subjectivity and in drawing out any implications from the exercise. In *Exploring Corporate Strategy* the technique is used at the end of Chapter 4 to show how the impact of issues identified in Chapters 3 and 4 can be considered together and in terms of their impact on each other. This is the departure point for this chapter, which goes on to show how SWOT analysis can be used more specifically both for the analysis of strategic issues and the evaluation of strategies. The chapter argues that SWOT analysis can be undertaken more rigorously and provide more direct links to application by employing scoring mechanisms which, while often subjectively based, require managers to discuss and debate the grounds for such scoring. The chapter uses a worked example from the pharmaceutical industry to show the application of the techniques it develops and, this respect, can usefully be read in conjunction with the case study on the pharmaceutical industry in *Exploring Corporate Strategy*.

8.1 Introduction

SWOT analysis is a popular tool used by managers as an organising framework for intuitive information and as a means of summarising and integrating more formal analyses about the external operating environment and an organisation's current resources and capabilities. However, care has to be taken to avoid several potential pitfalls, some of which can also be applied to other frameworks and tools of analysis:

- A SWOT analysis can result in long lists of observations which provide little overall insight or clarity about required action. This chapter suggests ways of avoiding this.
- There are no formal mechanisms to ensure that managers challenge their own frames of reference or their organisation's paradigm; indeed SWOT can be used by managers to 'ride their own hobby-horses'. However, if such a challenge can be achieved, this is where useful analysis rests, and this chapter suggests ways in which this can be done.
- A further danger is that managers might conceive of strengths and weaknesses in terms of the strategy they aim to implement rather than that which currently exists. In this sense it is important that the strengths and weaknesses are considered in terms of current realised strategy rather than just future intended strategy.
- There is also evidence that there is a tendency for managers to see environmental changes as threats rather than opportunities. Such negative perceptions of change may hinder the identification of opportunities. Again this chapter suggests ways of overcoming this.

The purpose of this chapter is to show how SWOT analysis can be used more effectively than is often the case by demonstrating how it can integrate and enhance other frameworks of strategic analysis, and contribute to the evaluation of strategic options.

SWOT stands for strengths, weaknesses, opportunities and threats; the strengths and weaknesses are statements of the internal capabilities of an organisation. A strength, therefore, would be an internal resource which would enable an organisation to deal effectively with its business environment – for example, close and good links with customers. An internal weakness would leave opportunities poorly accounted for, or not addressed at all. For example, a weak distribution system might hinder sales of a popular and fast-moving product.

Opportunities and threats exist outside of the organisation in many different areas; examples might include competitor moves, government legislation, technological advances and changing customer needs. Typically the environmental opportunities and threats presented in a market are the same for all competitors; the issue that will vary will be their ability to capitalise on them.

The aim of SWOT analysis is to match likely external environmental changes with internal capabilities, to test these out and challenge how an organisation can capitalise on new opportunities, or defend itself against future threats. The exercise, therefore, seeks to challenge the robustness of an organisation's current strategy and highlight areas that might need to change in order to sustain or develop its competitive position.

8.2   Steps in SWOT analysis

There is no one 'right way' of undertaking SWOT analysis. The approach taken here is to apply the idea of identifying strengths, weaknesses, opportunities and threats to contribute to strategic analysis and strategy evaluation. The chapter uses a worked example from the pharmaceutical industry and shows how the series of steps followed can progressively add insight and value to the manager's thinking about strategic issues.

8.2.1   Identification of strengths, weaknesses, opportunities and threats

There is first a need to identify what might be the key external forces which constitute opportunities and threats, and the key capabilities or competences (or lack of them) which constitute strengths and weaknesses. This identification might be done by using some of the analytical techniques suggested in Chapters 3 and 4 of *Exploring Corporate Strategy* (4th edition). It is not the role of this chapter to repeat these techniques, but their relevance and application to the steps which follow can be illustrated with reference to a pharmaceutical company.

Opportunities and threats

A pharmaceutical company employing frameworks such as PEST and Five Forces analysis in the late 1990s would be likely to identify a number of key changes in its environment:

- Increasing globalisation of the industry
- Entrance of new technologies such as biotechnology and genetics
- Healthcare rationing as governments find themselves unable to fund increasing costs of healthcare
- A more complex and sophisticated customer base. In the UK, for example, regional health authorities (RHAs) are now customers, as well as general practitioners (GPs). Additionally, GPs are now able to manage their own funds and can retain up to 50 per cent of money saved from their annual budgets
- Threat of new diseases and antibiotic-resistant strains of illnesses.

Strengths and weaknesses

Similarly, the resource profile and competences – the strategic capability – of an organisation can be assessed. The internal strengths and weaknesses are related to the available resources, the competence of the organisation in undertaking its activities and the balance of its resources and mix of activities. The tools available for this are detailed in Chapter 4 of *Exploring Corporate Strategy* (4th edition) and notably in Figure 4.1 of that chapter.

Again, using the pharmaceutical industry as an example, analyses of the current capabilities of Company A, an established player predominantly of the European market, identified the following strengths and weaknesses:

Strengths

• large and effective salesforce targeted at GPs
• leading edge research facilities
• global recognition of Company A's leading product
• good current and historic profit margins.

Weaknesses

• no current competences in biotechnology/genetics
• no imminent product launches
• lack of global coordination of research activities
• over-reliance on leading product.

While SWOT analysis itself will not identify such key factors, it does require that they be identified. In this way it can promote thoughtful analytical questioning and the integration of findings which emerge from this.

8.2.2   Challenging managers' mindsets

Of course, the labelling of strengths, weaknesses, opportunities and threats can, itself, give rise to problems. For example, typically managers tend to view environmental changes as threats. SWOT can be a useful tool to challenge managers' mindsets in this regard by switching the labelling of environmental influences from threats to opportunities; in a sense, this is just being able to see external change from different angles.

In our example from the pharmaceutical industry, healthcare rationing was labelled as a threat. However, the development of an innovative new drug, perhaps through the use of biotechnology – the advent of which was also labelled as a threat – could create an opportunity if it decreased overall healthcare expense by reducing the number of costly operations performed or the time patients spent in intensive care hospital wards.

Similarly, managers might assume that their organisation's current strengths will remain as strengths as the environment changes; but this is not necessarily so. For example, managers might view their organisation's brand name as a strength. However, if the organisation is trying to increase sales from outside its traditional customer base, the image conjured up by the brand may be a weakness when viewed from the new market segment.

8.3   A basic SWOT analysis

Assessing the impact of environmental changes on the current strengths and weaknesses of an organisation can help managers to understand the changing environment in such a way that will allow them to identify opportunities, or to recognise threats which are especially important – the key issues. This is how SWOT analysis is used at the end of Chapter 4 in *Exploring Corporate Strategy* (4th edition). It is used here as a basis of showing how such an approach can be further extended both for analytic and evaluative purposes.

The identified strengths, weaknesses, opportunities and threats are collated into a matrix. A scoring mechanism is also used as an aid to provide clarity to the analysis and as a means of getting managers to assess:

- the environmental changes that are most critical
- the internal strengths that will remain as strengths or become weaknesses in the changing environment
- the internal element that is most influenced by each external change.

In our example of the pharmaceutical industry, it might appear as shown in Table 8.1. The scoring system employed is very straightforward:

- A positive (+) score denotes that a strength that a company possesses would help it take advantage of, or counteract, a problem arising from an environmental change or a weakness that would be offset by the environmental change
- A negative (−) score denotes that a strength would be reduced by the environmental change or a weakness would prevent the organisation from overcoming the problems associated with an environmental change or be accentuated by the change
- A zero (0) score indicates that current strength or weakness would not be affected by an environmental change.

Scoring can be a lengthy process, because any matrix of average size will not only generate a large number of impacts to be considered, but will also highlight differences in opinions between managers.

Using our pharmaceutical company (and Table 8.1) as an example, analysis of the company's existing strengths shows that the majority have remained as strengths and will help the company react to the environmental changes. However, the large salesforce, currently targeted at the GPs, is likely to lose its effectiveness as regional health

Table 8.1 *Impact analysis for Company A*

Environmental change (opportunities and threats)	Increasing globalisation of industry	Entrance of new technology	Health care rationing	RHAs now customers as well as GPs	New diseases and resistance to antibiotics	+	−
Strengths							
Large and effective GP salesforce	0	+1	+1	−3	0	+2	−3
Leading edge research facilities	+1	+2	−1	0	+2	+5	−1
Global recognition of leading product	+2	+1	+1	+1	0	+5	0
Good profit margins	0	+1	+1	+1	+1	+4	0
Weaknesses							
No current competences in biotechnology or genetics	−1	−3	−1	0	−2	0	−7
No imminent product launches	−2	−2	−1	−1	−1	0	−7
No global coordination of research activities	−2	−2	0	0	−2	0	−6
Over-reliance on leading product	0	−1	−1	0	0	0	−2
Environmental impact scores	+3 −5	+5 −8	+3 −4	+2 −4	+3 −5		

authorities begin to influence healthcare spending. Fundholding status for GPs will also have the effect of making them more cost conscious and, more importantly, less brand loyal. Thus, what had been a major strength historically can now be seen as less of a strength, even inappropriate, to the changed environment.

Company A's weaknesses have remained as weaknesses. In particular, Table 8.1 suggests that not only is the company's R&D department not 'coming up with the goods' in terms of new products, but the company is not taking advantage of the global brand recognition of their leading product by capitalising on this to generate sales of their other products.

An overall indication of the company's position, given the changes it faces, is shown by the 'environmental impact score' at the foot of the table, in these terms the future does not look very good, with an aggregated negative score against each of the likely environmental changes. This suggests that existing strengths are likely to be offset by existing weaknesses unless action is taken.

8.4 Competitor analysis

Assessing the impact of environmental change on a company's strengths and weaknesses can be augmented by analysis of how environmental changes might affect its competitors.

This assessment can in practice be difficult, not only because of

Table 8.2 *Impact analysis for Company A and major competitors*

	Increasing globalisation of industry	Entrance of new technology	Health care rationing	RHAs now customers as well as GPs	New diseases and resistance to antibiotics	Overall impact
Company A	−2 No global coordination of research but leading product has global recognition	−3 No current competences in this field	−1 Little experience in USA where rationing is already in place	−2 Salesforce still interfacing only with GPs	−2 Current research directed towards traditional diseases	−10
Competitor W	−2 No commercial products; currently a research institution	+5 Leading competences and intellectual property	−4 No experience in sales; drugs in development likely to be costly	−4 No experience; would need to be able to justify high prices to practitioners	+5 All research in new therapeutic areas	0
Competitor X	+2 Very large American-owned global company	+3 Established network of alliances with biotech companies	+2 Strong health economics department	+3 Experience with purchasing organisations in US	+1 Promising products in development but yet to launch any	+11
Competitor Y	−5 European firm with small percentage of sales outside home market	−3 Poor research facilities with no investment in emerging technologies; no financial ability to redress this	+2 Experience gained through facing tough cost-containment measures in own country	−1 Own market still GP based: no experience with dealing with RHAs or equivalent	+2 Promising drug in co-development with multi-national	−5
Competitor Z	+1 Company has over-the-counter (OTC) line with strong global branding	−2 All current research using traditional technologies	+1 Marketing OTC products – a useful competence	+2 Salesforce work as team, interfacing with decision-making units	+3 Reputation for investing in difficult-to-treat therapeutic areas	+5

the difficulties of obtaining enough information to make reasoned judgements, but also because the boundaries of an industry can be unclear and are not likely to provide any precise delineation of competition especially if, as in the case of the pharmaceutical industry, the industry is becoming increasingly global. However, despite the difficulties, attempting to understand how the competition may be affected by environmental change, and how they might be able to capitalise on their own strengths or be restrained by their weaknesses, can be useful to an organisation in developing and pursuing its own strategy.

In our example of the pharmaceutical industry, analysis of Company A's competitors might appear as shown in Table 8.2. Company A's scores, taken from Table 8.1, have been aggregated to allow a comparison with its competitors.

This analysis suggests that Company A, with an overall impact score of −10, is in a poor position, when compared to its major competitors, to take advantage of the changing environment. Competitor X is well positioned with positive scores against all the environmental changes and an overall score of +11. Competitor Z, with its score of +5, is in a relatively good position but its only negative score (−2) is against the environmental change identified as having the greatest impact: the entrance of new technologies. Competitor Y is in a weak position (−5), scoring badly in terms of the predicted globalisation of the industry and new technology and Competitor W's overall position is neutral (0); its weaknesses prevent it from capitalising on its strengths in biotechnology and new disease research.

8.5 Suitability analysis

So far this chapter has shown how SWOT analysis can be used to contribute to *strategic analysis*. However, it can be taken further to help inform the evaluation of strategies by providing a basis for screening options rather like the ranking technique described in Section 8.2.2 of *Exploring Corporate Strategy*. This is now explained and again illustrated with reference to the pharmaceutical company.

The analyses shown in Sections 8.3 and 8.4 above should help managers to generate some strategic options which match organisational capabilities with likely environmental changes; and address competitive strengths and weaknesses. For example, strategies might include moving into new product areas or new markets, vertical integration, company acquisition and so on; these, and other options, are detailed in Chapter 7 of *Exploring Corporate Strategy* (4th edition).

A matrix can be constructed to show the strategic options set against, in this case, *both* environmental changes and strengths and weaknesses. Systematically managers should discuss the likely impact of each environmental change on the alternative strategies, scoring

Table 8.3   *Suitability of strategic options for Company A*

Strategic options	External changes					Strengths				Weaknesses				Aggregate scores	
	Increasing globalisation of industry	Entrance of new technology	Health care rationing	RHAs now customers as well as GPs	New diseases and resistance to antibiotics	Large and effective GP sales force	Leading edge research facilities	Global recognition of leading product	Good profit margins	No current competences in bio-technology or genetics	No imminent product launches	No global co-ordination of research activities	Over-reliance on leading product	+	−
Strategy A*	+1	+3	+1	0	+1	0	+1	+1	0	+2	−1	−3	+1	+11	−4
Strategy B†	+3	+1	+1	0	+1	0	+1	+2	+1	−1	+1	−3	+1	+12	−4
Strategy C‡	0	+3	+1	0	+2	0	+2	0	+1	−2	+3	−1	+2	+14	−3
Strategy D§	0	−1	+3	+3	−3	0	+1	+1	+2	0	0	0	−1	+10	−5

* Strategy A: Form **alliances** with biotechnology companies (to broaden product base)
† Strategy B: Enhance **global coordination** of research activities
‡ Strategy C: Develop own biotechnology capability
§ Strategy D: Consolidate/improve on past strengths and reduce costs

the positive and negative impacts. By aggregating the scores the organisation will be able to see:

- which strategies will capitalise on environmental changes, build on strengths and overcome weaknesses and which will not;
- which strategy, in relation to others, is therefore likely to offer the best way forward.

In the example of the pharmaceutical industry, Company A might produce the matrix shown in Table 8.3.

Strategy D, one of consolidation around past strengths, may appear attractive, as it requires no great change in terms of strategy or organisational culture. It does go some way towards helping the company address a more cost-conscious environment but does nothing to counter the emergence of new technologies and increasing globalisation of the industry, which is seen to have major impacts. In the short term it appears to be a strategy which could be helpful; in the long term it is unlikely to be especially beneficial.

Strategies A and B give similar overall scores. Alliances would possibly give rapid access to new technologies and new products to help re-supply the company's product pipeline. If managed well, that could boost the company's internal R&D, though they might also lead to a further degradation of internal drug discovery effort. And, if the company cannot manage its own research well, how will it manage a network of global alliances? While this strategy has certain advantages, there also appear to be some problems. Strategy B, the restructuring of research effort, could allow the benefit of economies of scale, investment and intellectual capital to be realised in terms of:

- coordinating access and use of expensive high-tech equipment (e.g. robotics) which must be applied across research areas to be economically viable
- increasing the sharing of knowledge and capital across the research function and between research and other functions
- ensuring that contacts with academia and opinion leaders are better managed across the world.

Moreover, it does appear to address some of the key external changes taking place in the industry. The problem is, of course, that the company has no track record in biotechnology or global coordination of research.

Strategy C could conceivably combine the benefits of A and B. New blood, and therefore new skills and experience, would need to be brought into the company to enhance internal resources. In time the salesforce would be presented with innovative products that might themselves reduce spending on certain diseases. In addition, current strengths would be built on to some extent; though again there is a question mark over the company's past capabilities in this field. However, this appears to be the most attractive strategy.

8.5.1   Weighted suitability analysis

The susceptibility of each strategy to environmental change can also be tested by questioning the relative importance of each environmental change on the matrix and weighting them accordingly. The aggregate scores from this process may very well change the attractiveness or appropriateness of the alternative strategies. For example, if the managers felt that increasing globalisation was the most significant external change likely to face the industry in the next few years, then, arguably, it would affect at least three of the columns in the suitability analysis. This is reflected in Table 8.4, where the scores for these three columns have been given additional weightings, thus affecting the aggregate scores. There is little effect on the evaluation of strategy D but the effects on strategy A, and to some extent B, are clear. Strategy A and particularly B address the globalisation issue and, arguably, might build on the existing global reputation of the leading product, but the concern is whether the organisation has the experience and capabilities to manage on a global scale.

Of course, in fact, the real benefit of this approach is to facilitate management debate in the evaluation. Managers have to discuss what is most important and what is not; and what the effects could be. In the case of this company it would, for example, be likely to focus discussion on the capacity of the organisation to manage on a global basis. It might also raise questions about reliance on a single strategy. Perhaps the pursuit of both strategies B and C might make sense.

Table 8.4   *Suitability of strategic options for Company A – weighted analysis*

Strategic options	External changes					Strengths				Weaknesses				Aggregate scores	
	Increasing globalisation of industry	Entrance of new technology	Health care rationing	RHAs now customers as well as GPs	New diseases and resistance to antibiotics	Large and effective GP sales force	Leading edge research facilities	Global recognition of leading product	Good profit margins	No current competences in bio-technology or genetics	No imminent product launches	No global co-ordination of research activities	Over-reliance on leading product	+	−
	×3							×2				×3			
Strategy A*	+3	+3	+1	0	+1	0	+1	+2	0	+2	−1	−9	+1	+14	−10
Strategy B†	+9	+1	+1	0	+1	0	+1	+4	+1	−1	+1	−9	+1	+20	−10
Strategy C‡	0	+3	+1	0	+2	0	+2	0	+1	−2	+3	−3	+2	+14	−5
Strategy D§	0	−1	+3	+3	−3	0	+1	+2	+2	0	0	0	−1	+11	−5

* Strategy A: Form **alliances** with biotechnology companies (to broaden product base)
† Strategy B: Enhance **global coordination** of research activities
‡ Strategy C: Develop own biotechnology capability
§ Strategy D: Consolidate/improve on past strengths and reduce costs

8.6   *Sensitivity analysis*

In some circumstances environmental change might be relatively predictable. Other environmental changes are more difficult to predict or be confident about and, as suggested in Section 8.3.1 of *Exploring Corporate Strategy*, it can therefore be useful to test and challenge the assumptions underlying an organisation's strategic alternatives through sensitivity testing. The results of this might affect the acceptability of the various strategic options.

In the pharmaceutical industry Company A had placed a good deal of emphasis on the likely development of new technologies giving rise to new treatments, especially through the advent of biotechnology. Other industry observers have suggested that this expectation may be misplaced. Let us assume that it was. This can be tested by removing all the factors specifically concerned. At its most extreme, this might suggest taking two of the strategies (A and C) and at least two of the factors (entrance of new technology and competences in biotechnology management) out of the evaluation. Table 8.5 show the resulting evaluation.

Here the evaluation of strategies B and D show that there is little to choose between them in terms of scores. It does nevertheless show that, in making their choice, the managers might need to consider very seriously whether the real issue is increasing globalisation (which would suggest the choice of strategy B) or the restructuring and cost consciousness of the industry (which would suggest strategy D).

The process can of course be repeated for the other environmental changes. For example, Company A identified that the industry in

Table 8.5   *Suitability of alternative strategies for Company A*

| Strategic options | Environmental change | | | | | | | | | | | Aggregate scores | |
	Increasing globalisation of industry	Health care rationing	RHAs now customers as well as GPs	New diseases and resistance to antibiotics	Large and effective GP sales force	Leading edge research facilities	Global recognition of leading product	Good profit margins	No imminent product launches	No global co-ordination of research activities	Over-reliance on leading product	+	−
Strategy B*	+3	+1	0	+1	0	+1	+2	+1	+1	−3	+1	+11	−3
Strategy D†	0	+3	+3	−3	0	+1	+1	+2	0	0	−1	+10	−4

* Strategy B: Enhance **global coordination** of research activities
† Strategy D: Consolidate/improve on past strengths and reduce costs

which it operates was becoming increasingly global: how sensitive are the various strategic options to this? What would the effect be if globalisation did not occur or came about over a much longer timescale than was initially envisaged?

8.7   Summary

SWOT analysis is a popular and well-known framework which is best used by managers with an understanding and knowledge of the day-to-day aspects of an organisation. It can be used either as an organising framework for intuitive information or as part of a more formal process of analysis.

This chapter concentrates on the latter – the more formal process of analysis – and challenges readers to use the SWOT framework in a more constructive and effective way than is often the case, by utilising the basic idea of SWOT analysis in conjunction with other approaches to strategic analysis and strategy evaluation introduced and discussed in *Exploring Corporate Strategy* (4th edition). This approach enhances the benefits of the framework, in particular by:

- thinking through when future changes might occur and the resultant opportunity or threat
- challenging managers' mindsets about when an environmental change is an opportunity or a threat
- matching external changes with internal repercussions, and attempting to gauge the size of the internal impact and identify key priorities for strategic attention
- providing a format for thinking about competitive positioning by comparing the impact of changes on the organisation with that on competitors.

Part III
Organisational culture and stakeholders

9 Mapping and re-mapping organisational culture

By Gerry Johnson

Editor's introduction

Running throughout *Exploring Corporate Strategy* is the argument that strategy has to be considered within the cultural and political context of organisations and, further, that it needs to be translated into day-to-day aspects of the organisation in order to ensure effective implementation. The concept of the cultural web was originally developed by Gerry Johnson in the late 1980s (1) and is explained in Chapter 2 of *Exploring Corporate Strategy*. Chapters 2 and 5 of *Exploring Corporate Strategy* suggest that it can be used as a descriptive and analytical device to understand the relationship between strategy and organisational culture and Chapter 11 shows how it can be used to consider the management of strategic change. In particular, Chapter 11 suggests that comparing an existing cultural web with a desired cultural web can both help flag up potential problems of implementing strategy and stimulate thinking about means of implementation. This chapter provides specific guidelines on how this re-webbing might be carried out, the role that a facilitator of such an exercise might play, and the sort of lessons that might be drawn from such an exercise. If the chapter is being used as a basis for considering the management of strategic change, it is important that it is read in conjunction with an understanding of other aspects of strategic change discussed in Part 4 of *Exploring Corporate Strategy*, including the importance of organisational structure, control systems, political systems and symbolic systems.

9.1 Introduction

One of the main problems organisations face in managing strategic change is effecting changes in organisational culture. Chapter 2 in *Exploring Corporate Strategy* shows how there is a tendency for organisations' strategies to persist because they are configured within that which is taken for granted in the organisation – assumptions about the nature of the organisation, its environment and the way things are done in the organisation. Even when a strategy is formulated, perhaps based on sound rational argument, organisations often find that achieving significant change to current strategy is difficult.

This chapter builds on the idea of the cultural web (1) to show how mapping culture can provide an understanding of barriers to change; and how re-mapping on the basis of the culture needed to deliver the strategy can help identify means of managing strategic change. A case example is used to illustrate this process.

9.2   *The concept of culture and cultural web*

Culture is often explained as that which is taken for granted in a society or organisation. At its most basic, this might be assumptions about what the organisation is there to do, or the reasons for its success historically. Culture can also be thought of as the 'artefacts' of the organisation – such as organisational routines, systems and structures. Again these are likely to be taken for granted as the 'way we do things around here'. These are the components of the cultural web (see Figure 9.1).

This 'taken for grantedness' tends to act as a 'filter' by which members of the organisation make sense of their world internally and

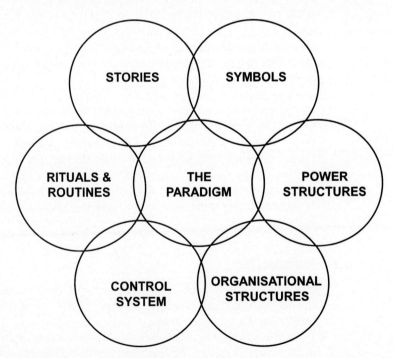

Figure 9.1   The cultural web of an organisation

externally. This can be very helpful for at least two reasons. First, it provides a 'shorthand' way of understanding often complex situations; second, it may be the basis of the organisation's success, providing competitive advantage because the culture itself is difficult to imitate. However, it can also be problematic for two reasons. First, because information, opinions and new ideas may be 'filtered out' and, second, because the culture is likely to be very difficult to change, particularly if the success of the organisation has been based upon it in the past. For a fuller explanation of the role of culture in strategy development, readers should see Chapter 2 of *Exploring Corporate Strategy* (4th edition).

9.3   The value of culture mapping

There are a number of purposes to mapping organisational culture:

- Surfacing that which is taken for granted can be a useful way of questioning what is normally rarely questioned. If no one ever questions what is taken for granted then, inevitably, change will be difficult
- By mapping aspects of organisational culture it may be possible to see where barriers to change exist
- It may also be possible to see where there are linkages in the aspects of organisational culture which are especially resistant to change
- A map of organisational culture can also provide a basis for examining the changes that need to occur to deliver a new strategy
- This, in turn, can be used to consider whether such changes can be managed. In this way practical ideas for implementing strategic change can be developed.

9.4   How to map organisational culture

The cultural web can be used as a device for mapping organisational culture. It has been used effectively in many management workshops (2). How this is done is now described.

- *The aim.* The aim is to generate managers' own perceptions of the cultural aspects of their organisations using the cultural web as a tool.
- *The setting.* The setting may vary, but the approach described here has been used most effectively in groups of 12–15 managers from the same organisations. They have usually been part of a workshop discussing strategy development for their organisation; or perhaps the problems of strategic change in their organisation. In any case, the process is most effective when they have a real understanding of the strategic issues faced by the organisation and, ideally, some responsibility for implementing strategy. The managers could, then, be the senior executive team of a division of a business, for example.

9.4.1   Originating a cultural web

It is necessary for those taking part to understand the conceptual basis of the cultural web and its links to strategy development in the organisation. A review of the concepts and issues raised in Chapter 2 of *Exploring Corporate Strategy* is therefore useful. This explanation should reach the point where the importance of organisational culture, as described by the cultural web, is understood and, in particular, how organisational culture can constrain strategy development and impede strategic change.

In explaining the cultural web it is often helpful to use an example. There are, however, also dangers in this since, if the workshop is to be asked to produce their own web for their organisation, they may end up using elements of the example for convenience. This can be overcome as follows.

It is helpful to begin by explaining the elements of the cultural web, as shown in Table 9.1. As this is done, members of the workshop should be asked to note down examples of each of the aspects of the web as they see it for their own organisation. They should be asked to do this noting those aspects that come to their mind readily.

Individuals can usually do this fairly easily for most aspects of the web, though there may be difficulties with routines, symbols and stories coming to mind as easily as other aspects. This is simply because they are so 'everyday'; they are the essence of that which is taken for granted in action. The other aspect of the web which is difficult for managers to conceptualise is the paradigm itself. This is hardly surprising since it is the assumptions that they live with everyday. Most usually these are not regarded as problematic and are hardly ever discussed; indeed, they are self-evident. It is the equivalent of an individual trying to conceptualise what he or she takes for granted – which is not easy. This is probably better done in the group work that follows; and some guidance is given on this.

After the individuals have noted down their views individually the workshop can be split into groups. Three groups of 4 or 5 are usually effective. Here the managers are asked to compare their individual views and discuss the extent to which they are similar or different. Sometimes there will be considerable similarity. Sometimes there will be differences which might reflect the fact that the managers have different experiences or have been with the organisation for different lengths of time. In any case, it cannot be expected that there will be total consensus. The aim is to find a common aspect of organisational culture rather than to expect that everyone will see everything the same. So the task is for the managers to discuss that which is most held in common.

Table 9.1   *Elements of the cultural web*

- The *paradigm* is the set of assumptions about the organisation which is held in common and taken for granted in the organisation.

- The *routine* ways that members of the organisation behave towards each other, and that link different parts of the organisation. These are the 'way we do things around here' which, at their best, lubricate the working of the organisation and may provide a distinctive and beneficial organisational competence. However, they can also represent a taken-for-grantedness about how things should happen which is extremely difficult to change and highly protective of core assumptions in the paradigm.

- The *rituals* of organisational life, such as training programmes, promotion and assessment, point to what is important in the organisation, reinforce 'the way we do things around here' and signal what is especially valued.

- The *stories* told by members of the organisation to each other, to outsiders, to new recruits and so on, embed the present in its organisational history and flag up important events and personalities, as well as mavericks who 'deviate from the norm'.

- Other *symbolic aspects* of organisations such as logos, offices, cars and titles; or the type of language and terminology commonly used: these symbols become a short-hand representation of the nature of the organisation.

- The formalised *control systems*, measurements and reward systems that monitor and therefore emphasise what is important in the organisation, and focus attention and activity.

- *Power structures* are also likely to be associated with the key constructs of the paradigm. The most powerful managerial groupings in the organisation are likely to be the ones most associated with core assumptions and beliefs about what is important.

- In turn the formal *organisational structure*, or the more informal ways in which the organisation works, are likely to reflect power structures and, again, delineate important relationships and emphasise what is important in the organisation.

It is worth noting the following:

- Identification of the paradigm is usually the most difficult task, for the reasons explained above. Managers may try to over-intellectualise this and slip into substituting the notion of strategy for paradigm. They start discussing what the organisation *should* take for granted or what it should do rather than what it *does* take for granted

- Remember that which is taken for granted may be very simple and straightforward. Managers in a newspaper business, for example, tend to take for granted that people value news; managers in banks tend to take for granted the importance of secure lending; professors in universities take for granted the importance of research. None of these is surprising and should not be. The point is that they are likely to be very embedded and changing them, if change is required, is extremely difficult. So the managers should be advised to look for that which is so obvious that they would rarely debate or discuss it

- The managers may also seek for a whole catalogue of constructs to do with the paradigm. This may not be very helpful. It may be that there are very few constructs taken for granted and held in common

- The elements of the cultural web in the outer circles might give clues as to the nature of the paradigm. The managers might, therefore, find it useful to begin with these outer circles and end by considering how they would characterise the paradigm.

The managers should be asked to note down their views on a blank web like the one shown in Figure 9.2. This might be given to them in the form of an acetate so that it can be presented back in plenary session by each of the groups.

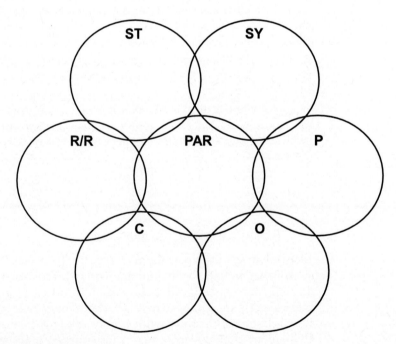

Figure 9.2   A blank cultural web.

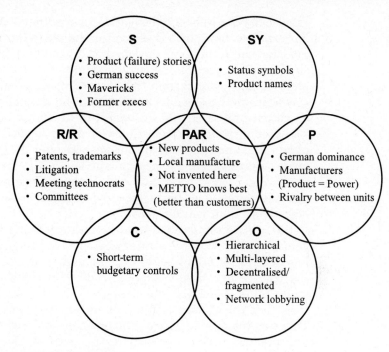

S
- Product (failure) stories
- German success
- Mavericks
- Former execs

SY
- Status symbols
- Product names

R/R
- Patents, trademarks
- Litigation
- Meeting technocrats
- Committees

PAR
- New products
- Local manufacture
- Not invented here
- METTO knows best
  (better than customers)

P
- German dominance
- Manufacturers
  (Product = Power)
- Rivalry between units

C
- Short-term
  budgetary controls

O
- Hierarchical
- Multi-layered
- Decentralised/
  fragmented
- Network lobbying

Figure 9.3   *The cultural web of Metto.*

9.5   *Discussing the cultural webs*

The three groups should then be asked to come back and present their webs to each other. The views of individuals have therefore been discussed in groups and then compared across groups. These presentations can be made by asking someone from each group to talk through the web. At this point it is useful if the managers are encouraged to take a lead in interpreting the web. The session facilitator should avoid the temptation to over-interpret the web as a whole, or parts of it, since he or she cannot be expected to know as much about the organisation as the managers themselves; and very likely the managers will raise aspects of the organisation that may be meaningful to them but not to the facilitator.

Figure 9.3 shows the cultural web drawn up by managers in the European division of a chemicals business (referred to here as 'Metto') and will be used as an example in what follows.

9.5.1   *The role of facilitator*

The role of the facilitator should be to encourage the managers to consider issues such as the following:

1   What does the web say about the organisational culture as a whole? For example, how much is the culture linked to the organisation's heritage; how uniform is it; how long has it been like this; is it a culture of challenge and questioning or constraint and convention? In the case of Metto what emerged from this discussion was the extent to which it was a culture based on technology and the technological fix, a reliance on patent protection and the extent to which the business was organised around powerful regional 'barons' who headed up manufacturing plants and controlled localised research and development. Products not originating from the local production facility were not generally as highly regarded as those that had. It was a culture originating from a piecemeal growth of the business over decades based on product know-how rather than market need.

2   Is the culture compatible with the strategy being followed by the organisation and with the strategy being advocated for the organisation? For example, it might be that the managers see that the strategy and the culture are closely aligned. Indeed in some organisations they might come to see that the strategy is, in effect, a product of the culture; that the culture, not the managers, is 'managing' the strategy. This was the case in Metto. The business suffered from a fragmented and product-driven approach to the market. The top management were endeavouring to identify ways of developing differentiation around an identification of customer need, but the dominance of product solutions prevailed. Furthermore, their attempts at creating greater European integration foundered on the fragmented nature of the organisation and rivalry between units.

3   It is interesting to get managers to consider why organisational cultures are so difficult to change; why they contribute to the continuity and momentum of strategies. Some generalised explanations which have emerged as managers have discussed cultural webs in such workshops are these:

* There exist linkages throughout the web. For example, powerful individuals or groups are closely associated with organisational structures that preserve power bases, with dominant routines which tend to persist, with symbols of hierarchy or authority and with stories about their power or the origins of their power. So it was in Metto. For many years the German factory had been seen as most successful and profitable and, in turn, its senior management most powerful. This was bolstered by stories of German success, the strong brands originating from Germany and the relative failure of products from other areas, and reinforced by the hierarchical but fragmented nature of the organisation

* In some organisations there may be informal linkages throughout the system which are at least as strong as formal systems. For example,

there might exist an informal network of long-standing organisational members with, again, informal rituals of memberships such as social gatherings and symbols and stories embedding their influence. Such linkages may be strongly linked to the paradigm. They both embed that paradigm and take authority or influence from the widely held assumptions within it. In the case of Metto, for example, German hegemony was rooted in their undoubted product success of the past

- These linkages mean that it is difficult to think of the cultural web as discrete elements. The linkages bind the elements together. As one executive in another chemicals firm put it: 'This is one hell of a tight molecule; it is not easy to break apart.

- Elements within the web may compensate one for another. For example, if there are external threats or internal attempts at strategic change giving rise to political conflict or tension, there could be heightened symbolic activity such as story telling of the past which refers organisational members back to core assumptions and defuses the threats. For example, in Metto, although the potentially negative influence of the 'barons' was discussed informally, it was rarely raised in formal management meetings. If it was, the subject might be turned quickly to stories of product successes and failures, a way of emphasising the importance of 'getting this product right' and product innovation – the province of the 'barons' themselves and a core element within the paradigm

- The result is that the organisation as a cultural system can often readily absorb or cope with threats and shocks. It is a coping mechanism which means that existing ways of doing things tend to persist.

4   The cultural web is also a useful way of getting executives to think about the importance of the everyday routines in relation to strategy. Senior executives, in particular, often consider that strategy relates only to decisions made at the top and the management of strategy in their control. What the cultural web often highlights is that it is the more mundane aspects of the organisation that are delivering the strategy; the routines of the organisation, for example. In a workshop with National Health Service (NHS) managers this was put graphically. They used analogies of organisation, concluding that top executives tended to conceive of organisations as pyramids when, in fact, the organisation of the NHS was more like a 'termites' nest' in which everyday routines, mutual adjustments and deference ensured things happened. They went on to observe that many of the more formalised controls and structures which had been introduced in the NHS had been imposed by management on the assumption that they would effect changes; but that this assumed a structure of order which was essentially pyramidal. Within the 'termites' nest' there was a capacity to adjust to such intrusions while carrying on with the routines – the

reality – of organisational life. Whether executives use such imagery or not, it is common to find that the webs prompt discussion and insight about the nature of the organisation as everyday reality, and a clearer understanding that changing that everyday reality becomes crucially important in changing strategy.

Discussion of these sorts of issues, while at a rather generalised level, can help sensitise managers to the need to recognise the importance of cultural aspects of organisations. However, leading on from this, the cultural web can be used in more organisationally specific ways to think about the problems and means of managing change.

9.6   Identifying blockages to change

The cultural web can be used to identify more specific blockages to change. For example, the managers who drew up the cultural web for Metto, as illustrated in Figure 9.3, had all taken part in discussions on required strategy for the organisation and all agreed that what was required was an integrated European operation, building differentiation around high-quality service to customers based on in-depth understanding of customer processes. It was not product technology that would give them competitive advantage, but understanding their customers' businesses and processes better than the competition and tailoring products to that requirement. Intellectually they were all persuaded of this.

However they could also see that the sort of culture described in Figure 9.3 was unlikely to deliver this strategy. Moreover, they could identify some quite specific blockages as to why this would be so. For example, the heritage of technical product dominance was rooted in the emphasis on new product development from a technical point of view, the rivalry between units to develop different products from each other and the obsession with patenting these products and defending them in the courts. This technical obsession was further protected by organisational rituals and symbols: the CEO would always meet with 'technocrats' when he visited factories, he hardly ever met a sales or marketing person. There was a proliferation of technically based product names. The walls of offices were covered with technical illustrations and photographs. Power was also vested in the 'barons' who controlled the important technical processes and products; and they were able to exercise this power through a centralised and hierarchical organisational structure. The most powerful of these barons were those that headed up the German factory, and this power was emphasised through the stories that proliferated about their past success and high-handed attitude.

It might be, of course, that aspects of the culture also facilitate change. In the case of Metto the executives did not highlight many, though they recognised that technical excellence, if appropriately managed, could be a major advantage. However, in other organisations both barriers and opportunities for change have been identified by using the cultural web, and a forcefield analysis such as that described in Section 11.3.2 and Figure 11.4 of *Exploring Corporate Strategy* can be a helpful way of clarifying this.

9.7   The value of re-mapping organisational culture

Conceiving of what the culture would need to look like if a different strategy was being followed is useful and important for the following reasons:

- Conceptually it gives an idea of the extent to which the present culture is an impediment and the extent to which change is required
- Traditional notions of managing strategic change suggest that organisations will change if people can be persuaded to change their views about what makes for success in the organisation. In effect, if they can be persuaded to change their taken-for-granted assumptions – the paradigm. This is a worthy aim, perhaps, but difficult to achieve. An alternative or complementary approach is to develop a work environment and ways of doing things in line with the desired strategy, and in so doing create a context in which people can experience change and see its benefits
- Mapping the sort of structure, systems, routines, rituals and symbols which, desirably, would support a new strategy can give clues to what it might be helpful to change. It can, of course, also give further insights into the difficulties of managing strategic change and therefore give insights into what can and cannot be managed in culture change.

The value of re-mapping the cultural web is discussed further in Chapter 11 of *Exploring Corporate Strategy* (3).

9.8   How to re-map organisational culture

The approach to re-mapping using the cultural web is similar to that described in Section 9.4 above.

- *The aim.* The aim is to re-map the web, but this time to represent how culture would be if the strategy which has been developed was working successfully
- *The setting.* The setting may be the same sort of event as described above: indeed it might be the same group of managers following on from the previous exercise
- *The approach.* The approach is also similar to that described above

The workshop itself may have developed its own strategy for the organisation, or it may be that they or others have done so previously. But the starting point should be a clear statement of the desired strategy for the organisation.

The next step is to ask the managers to repeat the exercise, but this time to see how the organisation would be if the strategy was working effectively. Again, this should be done individually, then in groups and then by the groups reporting back to each other. Figure 9.4 shows what this looked like when done by managers in Metto.

It is likely that the following will be observed:

1   The managers may find it relatively easy to describe the desirable paradigm that would be in place given the new strategy. It is likely to be a reflection of the intended strategy. For example, the managers at Metto recognised there would be a need for a greater emphasis on the customer rather than product technology, much more concern with service to customers and cross-European cooperation.

2   Especially where senior managers are concerned, they are also likely to find it easy to spell out the sorts of structural and systemic aspects of the organisation. Senior managers in particular often see strategy implementation in these terms; change the structure, the measurements and control systems and how people are rewarded and they will

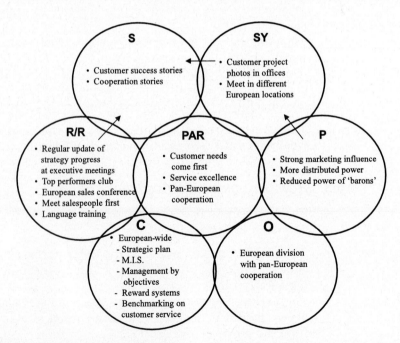

Figure 9.4   The Metto cultural web re-mapped.

behave differently. To some extent the senior management in Metto had already been down this route by setting up a European Division; and they further suggested the importance of a European strategic plan and control and reward systems linked to this. These are, indeed, important aspects of managing change, but they could well be insufficient because they may not address the day-to-day realities of those responsible for 'delivering' the strategy to customers.

3   The bolder managers may also find it relatively easy to identify changes in the political structure and influence systems in the organisation in line with the required strategy. They might identify elements within the organisation that need to be removed or whose power needs to be reduced if the strategy is to work. However, this is likely to be a sensitive area. As the Metto managers considered the re-mapping of the web, there was an explicit recognition that marketing, as a function, had to have more influence and that, generally, power had to be distributed more evenly. The unspoken recognition that the power of the 'barons' militated against the desired strategy developed into an explicit recognition that their power had to be reduced. This was a sensitive but crucial discussion, not least because some of these powerful individuals were among those taking part in the workshop itself. Indeed, this is a good illustration of how the use of the cultural web can help important issues to surface.

4   It is less usual for managers – particularly senior managers – to be able to conceive of the day-to-day aspects of organisational culture and what they would need to be like if the strategy were to be effective. Such day-to-day aspects of culture are more represented by the organisational routines, symbols and stories that exist. If these aspects of culture are not in line with the strategy to be followed, very likely it will be aspects of the existing or past culture that will be drawn upon.

5   The managers at Metto were, however, able to identify several possibilities of changes of a symbolic, ritual or routine nature. They believed it would help if there was more visible attention to updating and monitoring strategy development at the executive on a routine basis. There also needed to be more emphasis on pan-European working and cooperation; and this could be signalled by meeting in different European locations, organising European-wide sales conferences and ensuring that assistance was given to personnel involved in the European operation to develop language skills fully. Much more emphasis needed to be given to recognising the importance of sales and marketing rather than technical personnel, for example, through sales conferences and by a 'top performers club' across Europe for sales people. The suggestion was also made that the CEO should first meet sales personnel rather than technical people on visits to different locations. It was also seen as important that the day-to-day surroundings of offices should reflect a focus on customers. The technical

photographs of products could be replaced by illustrations of projects undertaken for customers, for example. Further, they recognised that stories of change would, themselves, be generated in such ways and passed round the business.

9.9 Managing strategic change

The re-webbing exercise can be especially useful in getting managers to think about what can be managed in effecting change in the culture of the organisation. The managers have two maps: one represents the organisation as it is; the other the organisation as they would wish it to be. Useful questions are:

- *What is the extent of change required?* It could be relatively small scale or very considerable. It is likely that the greater the change, the more there is a need for comprehensive change in aspects of the web. The more fundamental, or transformational, the change, the more likely will it need to be managed by making multiple changes throughout the different aspects of culture described in the web.
- *Which aspects of change are relatively straightforward to manage and which are difficult?* For example, managers may conclude that the ones which are most likely to be straightforward are those to do with structure and systems, and the more difficult are the symbolic and routine aspects of the organisation which are embedded in years of organisational history.
- *Are there any changes which would have particularly high impact?* This might be because they especially symbolise significant change or some aspect of the strategy to be followed. Or it could be that such a change would have a 'knock on' effect. For example, the removal of powerful blockages to change could itself become a story and a symbol of change.

In this discussion amo ng the Metto managers one such change emerged. As debates about the new webs progressed, the issue of historic German dominance and their reluctance to integrate with the rest of Europe eventually came into open debate. The very fact that it was surfaced as an issue seemed to release a determination to resolve the problems, and within a few months of the workshop a number of long-standing German managers had been replaced by others who saw the benefits of European integration and a market focus – a move which came to symbolise change powerfully.

The management of strategic change through the various aspects of organisational culture and systems are described more fully in Chapters 9, 10 and 11 of *Exploring Corporate Strategy* (4th edition).

9.10   Summary

'Culture' is often seen as a barrier to change, the more so because it is difficult to be clear about what is meant by it or if anything can be done to change it. The 'cultural web' has proved to be a useful device for achieving some clarity on what constitutes the culture of an organisation, why this is significant for strategy development, and the ways it might be possible to manage change. In particular, it highlights the importance of that which is taken for granted in an organisation in influencing the persistence of existing strategies, acting to prevent change but, potentially, giving clues as to important levers and mechanisms for achieving change.

Notes and references

(1)   The original development of the cultural web can be found in *Strategic Change and the Management Process*, Oxford: Blackwell, 1987.

(2)   Johnson, G. (1992). 'Managing strategic change: strategy, culture and action', *Long Range Planning*, **25** (1), 28–36, discusses the links between organisational strategy and culture using the cultural web as a basis of explanation.

(3)   For an extended example of the value of a re-webbing exercise, see Heradeous, L. and Langham, B. (1996). 'Strategic change and organisational culture at Hay Management Consultants', *Long Range Planning*, **29** (4), 485–494.

10
Stakeholder mapping: a practical tool for managers

By Kevan Scholes

Editor's Introduction

It should be clear from the discussions in Chapter 2 of *Exploring Corporate Strategy* that, in practice, the processes of formulating and implementing strategies in organisations have a strong political dimension. The need to understand this political dimension of strategy is emphasised throughout *Exploring Corporate Strategy*. It is an issue for strategic analysis (Chapter 5), strategic choice (Chapter 8) and in managing change (Chapter 11). The central tool for analysing the political dimension presented in Section 5.3 of *Exploring Corporate Strategy* is stakeholder mapping. This chapter extends this discussion by providing further practical advice on how to create useful stakeholder maps and how maps can guide political strategies for successful implementation. The chapter concludes with the importance of ethical considerations – particularly the obligations which managers have to their various stakeholders.

10.1 Introduction

The concept of organisational stakeholders is now long established and the implications for strategic management are well understood. In particular, it reminds managers of the following:

- Different stakeholders may have commonality of purpose at a very general level (e.g. 'making profit' or 'providing quality services') but at more detailed levels they would wish to impose different purposes and priorities on an organisation
- Therefore, purposes and priorities emerge from the *political* interplay between different stakeholder groups
- Strategic managers must both understand this political context *in detail* and be able to develop and implement strategies which are politically viable as well as 'rational'.

Stakeholder mapping is one tool to assist managers in understanding this political context and, if undertaken properly, can be of considerable help in developing strategies which are likely to work in practice.

This chapter extends the coverage of stakeholder mapping in *Exploring Corporate Strategy* (Chapter 5, Section 5.3, pp. 195–206).

10.2 The power–interest matrix

Figure 10.1 is a reminder of the basic 'tool' of stakeholder mapping – the power–interest matrix. It is a template on which the 'orientation' of different stakeholder groups can be mapped and through which political priorities can be established.

LEVEL OF INTEREST

	Low	High
Low	A Minimal effort	B Keep informed
POWER		
High	C Keep satisfied	D Key players

Figure 10.1   Stakeholder mapping: power–interest matrix (Source: adapted from A. Mendelow, Proceedings of 2nd International Conference, on Information Systems, Cambridge, MA, 1991).

The broad approaches to stakeholder mapping (as described in *Exploring Corporate Strategy*) are as follows:

- Mapping can be used simply to describe some of the major trends in the political environment. It can be particularly helpful in showing how shifts in one stakeholder group can trigger off changes elsewhere, as shown in Illustration 10.1
- The more common use of mapping (on which this chapter concentrates) is *in relation to a particular strategic development* (such as the launch or withdrawal of a product, the development into new geographical areas or the acquisition (or disposal) of a major asset – perhaps a factory, a hospital or a school)

Strategy in action

Illustration 10.1

Stakeholder mapping to describe the changing political environment

A repositioning of a major stakeholder will trigger a realignment of other stake-holders as priorities and strategies are changed.

The late 1980s in the UK was a major period of local government as the Conservative central government attempted to exert more control and accountability over local authorities, many of which were Labour controlled. Between 1985 and 1990 this produced a significant shift in strategy at local authority level from what had been described as *policy-led* to *finance-led*. In other words, the need to define and deliver strategy within strict financial limits became the dominant consideration for those running local authorities. This change in emphasis caused – and required – some important repositioning to occur among stakeholders, as shown on the stakeholder map below, which illustrates some of the more important shifts which occurred in Sheffield during this period:

A.   Central government decided to be more proactive as discussed above.

B.   The private sector was actively encouraged to play a greater role in the local economy directly (B1), through new agencies such as the Sheffield Development Corporation (B2) and the Training and Enterprise Council (TEC) (B3).

C.   The trade unions became less influential (C) in line with the national trend.

D.   A more executive style of leadership emerged (D1), reducing the power of the Labour group as a whole (D2).

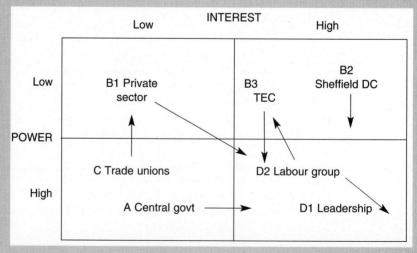

(*Source*: John Darwin, MBA project, Sheffield Business School. First published in *Exploring Corporate Strategy* (3rd edition), 1993.)

- For this new development stakeholders should first be plotted in relation to how they *would line up* – the level and nature (for or against) of their *interest* and the extent of their *power*
- A second map is then plotted showing how you would *need stakeholders to line up* if the development is going to have a good chance of success
- By comparing these two maps, and looking for the *mismatches*, the political priorities can be established
- Political priorities may also be concerned with *maintaining* stakeholders in their current positioning.

Illustration 5.4(a), first published in *Exploring Corporate Strategy* (4th edition, 1997), is reproduced here as Illustration 10.2 to show how these broad steps can be undertaken in practice.

10.3   *Creating stakeholder maps*

Stakeholder mapping can be a powerful and useful tool of analysis but managers using it for the first time often find it a little more difficult than they expected. This section provides advice on how some of these difficulties can be overcome.

10.3.1   *Deciding which stakeholders to plot*

Like most practical tools of analysis, stakeholder mapping is most useful if it strikes a sensible balance between being too simplistic/generic and so detailed that it is difficult to interpret. The following guidelines should be helpful:

- Avoid plotting long lists of stakeholders who 'in principle' or 'potentially' could have an influence on the strategy. This is a particularly important guideline in relation to powerful groups such as 'the ministry', 'the unions' and so on. Remember that the mapping is done in relation to specific strategies, so a judgement must be made as to whether these groups are likely to exercise their power in relation to this particular strategy. This is clearly a matter of judgement of their level of interest, and is discussed below. Groups which certainly will remain indifferent to the strategy could be excluded from the analysis
- Remember that stakeholder groups may need to be subdivided if there are significant differences of 'stance' within the group. This often applies to customers (as in Illustration 10.2) or between different groups of employees. For example, the routinisation of some aspects of professional service organisations by the use of IT and 'non-professional' staff (e.g. in insurance, legal services) has clearly been viewed differently by different staff groups.

Strategy in action

Illustration 10.2

Stakeholder mapping at Tallman plc

Due to falling sales, Tallman plc is having to rationalise its operations. It is proposing to close down its poorly performing operations in Toulouse, and increase production capabilities at its more efficient Frankfurt plant.

Two power–interest maps have been drawn up by company officials to establish likely stakeholder reactions to the proposed closure of the Toulouse plant. While Map A represents the most likely situation, Map B represents the company's most preferred situation, where support for the proposal is regarded as sufficient to ensure success.

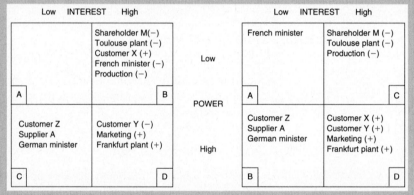

Map A: The likely situation   Map B: The preferred situation

Referring to Map A, it can be seen that, with the exception of customer X, the stakeholders in quadrant B will currently contest the closure of the Toulouse plant. If Tallman plc is to have any chance of convincing these stakeholders to change their stance to a more supportive one, the company must address their

10.3.2   Assessing power

Figure 10.2 shows the general list of sources of power and the use of this list to assess the power of stakeholders in Illustration 10.3. (Both have been reproduced from *Exploring Corporate Strategy*, Figure 5.6 and Illustration 5.4(b)).

Again, some practical advice on using these assessments when deciding where to plot stakeholders on a map are important:

1   There is a tendency to plot too many stakeholders in the bottom half of the map (i.e. to conclude that they have more power than is actually the case).

Illustration 10.2 continued

questions and, where possible, alleviate their fears. If such fears are overcome, these people may become important allies in influencing the more powerful stakeholders in quadrants C and D. The supportive attitude of customer X could be usefully harnessed in this quest.

The relationships Tallman plc has with the stakeholders in quadrant C are the most difficult to manage, since while they are considered to be relatively passive, largely due to their indifference to the proposed strategy, a disastrous situation could arise if their level of interest was underrated. For example, if the German minister were replaced, his successor might be opposed to the strategy and actively seek to stop the plant closure. In this case he would shift to quadrant D.

The acceptability of the proposed strategy to the current players in quadrant D is a key consideration. Of particular concern is customer Y, who is considered to be opposed to the closure of the Toulouse plant, and may have the power to prevent it from happening. The company clearly needs to have open discussions with this stakeholder.

Comparing the position of stakeholders in Map A and Map B, and identifying any changes/mismatches, Tallman plc establishes a number of strategies that may be pursued to change the stance of certain stakeholders to a more positive one and to increase the power of certain stakeholders. For example, customer X could be encouraged to champion the proposed strategy and assist Tallman plc by providing media access.

Tallman plc could also seek to dissuade or prevent powerful stakeholders from changing their stance to a negative one. For example, unless direct action is taken, the German minister's level of interest may well be raised by lobbying from his French counterpart. This has implications for how the company handles the situation in France. Thus, time would be effectively spent talking the strategy through with the French minister and also customer Y, so as to try and shift them away from opposition at least to indifference, if not support.

(Prepared by Sara Martin, Cranfield School of Management.)

2   It is therefore important to revisit the initial mapping with a 'test' question such as: 'If I were to pursue this strategy with disregard to the views of this particular stakeholder, could/would they stop me?'

3   This question sharpens up the political assessment in several important respects:

- It is a reminder that the analysis relates to a particular strategy – not a generalised view of the power of the stakeholder
- The implementation of some strategies may be entirely within the approved discretion of a department or division. For example, the required investments may not need 'central' approval. As many

---

SOURCES OF POWER

(a) Within organisations
- Hierarchy (formal power),
  e.g. autocratic decision making
- Influence (informal power),
  e.g. charismatic leadership
- Control of strategic resources,
  e.g. strategic products
- Possession of knowledge/skills,
  e.g. computer specialists
- Control of environment,
  e.g. negotiating skills
- Involvement in strategy
  implementation,
  e.g. by exercising discretion

(b) For external stakeholders
- Control of strategic resources,
  e.g. materials, labour, money
- Involvement in strategy
  implementation,
  e.g. distribution outlets, agents
- Possession of knowledge (skills),
  e.g. subcontractors
- Through internal links,
  e.g. informal influence

INDICATORS OF POWER

(a) Within organisations
- Status
- Claim on resources
- Representation
- Symbols

(b) For external stakeholders
- Status
- Resource dependence
- Negotiating arrangements
- Symbols

Figure 10.2   Sources and indicators of power.

organisations move to more devolved structures, this is becoming more common. In these circumstances plotting 'The Board' or 'Head Office' as powerful would be incorrect

- Even if a stakeholder could block the strategy, they may choose not to exercise that power. This may be because of lack of interest (see below) but it may be because of the wider political context. For example, major service providers such as Royal Mail or British Telecom 'tolerate' activities of small competitors (some of which may, in fact, be illegal such as breaching the £1 monopoly of Royal Mail) on the grounds that in the 1990s the government or the regulator or public opinion are largely unimpressed by defensive behaviour among near-monopoly providers

4   So sharp political instinct (brinkmanship) is important in stakeholder mapping as well as 'objective' assessment of power.

10.3.3   Assessing interest

This is probably more difficult than the assessment of power. Certainly many managers have learnt the hard way that public

Strategy in action

Illustration 10.3

Assessment of power

Internal stakeholders

Indicators of power	Marketing dept	Production	Frankfurt plant	Toulouse plant
Status				
Position in hierarchy (closeness to board)	H	L	H	M
Salary of top manager	H	L	H	L
Average grade of staff	H	M	H	L
Claim on resources				
Number of staff	M	H	M	M
Size of similar company	H	L	H	L
Budget as % of total	H	M	H	L
Representation				
Number of directors	H	None	M	None
Most influential directors	H	None	M	None
Symbols				
Quality of accommodation	H	L	M	M
Support services	H	L	H	L

External stakeholders

Indicators of power	Supplier A	Customer Y	Shareholder M
Status	H	H	L
Resource dependence	L	H	H
Negotiating arrangements	M	H	L
Symbols	H	H	L

H = high   M = medium   L = low

The marketing department is seen as powerful by all measures, and the production department universally weak. Equally, the Frankfurt plan is particularly powerful in relation to the Toulouse plant. This analysis provides important data in the process of stakeholder mapping, since the strategic importance of power is also related to whether individuals or groups are likely to exercise their power. This assessment thus helped in deciding where to locate the stakeholders on the power–interest maps.

Combining the results of this analysis with the stakeholder mapping exercise, it can be seen that Toulouse's only real hope is to encourage supplier A to reposition by raising its level of interest in opposition to the closure. Perhaps shareholder M could be helpful in this process through lobbying the supplier.

(Prepared by Sara Martin, Cranfield School of Management.)

expressions of interest (support) often cannot be relied upon. Even worse, some stakeholders will express support but, in fact, work quietly to oppose or, at least, delay the implementation of a strategy.

So it is important to assess the likely actions of stakeholders. Practical guidelines are as follows:

- Ensure that a *variety* of sources of information about stakeholder interest are used (in the same way as when assessing power). It is particularly important to use both *formal* (e.g. surveys, reports, etc.) and *informal* (e.g. stories) assessments of interest
- Interest should be categorised as for (+), against (−) or neutral (0) in relation to the particular strategy
- As with the assessment of power, it is useful to revisit the initial mapping with a 'test' question regarding level of interest, such as: *'How high is this strategy on their priorities – are they likely to actively support or oppose this strategy?'*

This sharpens up the analysis in a number of ways:

- Many potentially powerful supporters/opponents of a strategy will in the event not act to support or oppose the strategy. If this is the case they should be plotted on the left-hand side of the map.
- Sometimes the level of interest of a stakeholder group is very dependent on the personal zeal of an individual (a manager, a politician, etc.), so the judgement of interest becomes, in fact, *very personal* to that individual. If they move position or responsibilities, the map may not be valid. It is important to make this additional 'test' in relation to some individuals. For example: 'If this particular minister or chief executive changed, how would the political landscape change?'
- This is a reminder that the political priorities which emerge from stakeholder mapping must be robust in relation to potential changes in the future (particularly prior to implementation of a strategy).

10.4   *Establishing political priorities*

Mapping stakeholders into the four boxes and undertaking the process of identifying 'mismatches' between how stakeholders are *likely to line up* and *would need to line up* (see above) can help in establishing the broad political priorities. This section looks in more detail at the implications of an analysis to the management of stakeholder relationships and also presents a series of commonly occurring maps (situations) and the typical political priorities and actions they would require.

10.4.1 Managing stakeholder relationships

A useful link can be made between the four boxes in the power–interest matrix and styles for managing change (Table 10.1) as described in *Exploring Corporate Strategy*. The following practical conclusions/advice can be drawn:

- It will probably be both necessary and desirable to adopt differing 'styles' for different stakeholder groups even for the same strategy
- *Key players* (box D in Figure 10.1) are both powerful and interested in the particular strategy. This could mean that a style of *participation* would be appropriate for stakeholders who are supportive of the

Table 10.1 *Styles of managing strategic change*

Style	Means/context	Benefits	Problems	Circumstances of effectiveness
Education and communication	Mutual trust/respect; small group briefings	Overcoming lack of (or mis-) information	Time consuming; direction or progress may be unclear	Incremental change or long time horizontal transformational change
Participation	Small group/ taskforce involvement	Increasing ownership of a decision or process; may improve quality of decisions	Time consuming; solutions/outcome within existing paradigm	
Intervention/ manipulation	Change agent retains coordination/control: delegates aspects of change	Process is guided/ controlled, but involvement takes place	Risk of perceived manipulation	Incremental or non-crisis transformational change
Direction	Use of authority to set direction and means of change	Clarity and speed	Risk of lack of acceptance and ill-conceived strategy	Transformational change
Coercion/edict	Exploit use of power through edict or imposition of change	May be successful in crises or state of confusion	Least successful unless crisis	Crisis, rapid transformational change or change in established autocratic cultures

Source: *Exploring Corporate Strategy* (4th edition), 1997, p. 465.

strategy. This could be important in gaining and maintaining their ownership of the strategy. Opponents of the strategy are more problematic – although their *participation* could be important too. Often this would need to be preceded by *education/communication* as a means of gaining their support. In some circumstances the priority could be to 'reposition' opponents to box C (or box B). This is discussed in Section 10.4.2 below

- *Stakeholders* in box C of Figure 10.1 are potentially powerful supporters or opponents of the strategy, but not very interested. Assuming that the priority is to keep them in box C, the most appropriate style is often *intervention* where the 'change agent' drives and controls the strategy while the threshold requirements of the stakeholder are met – i.e. they are *kept satisfied*. An example would be the need to gain all proper approvals from head office and to ensure that company procedures are followed

- *Stakeholders* in box B of Figure 10.1 are very interested in supporting or opposing the strategy, but have little direct power. None the less, the way in which they are managed is important. For supporters of the strategy a style of *education/communication* is usually appropriate. This makes sense both in terms of the expectations of these stakeholders and also because well-informed supporters may gather wider support for the strategy through their actions. For example, they may *lobby* stakeholders in boxes C or D

  Opponents of the strategy may be responsive to persuasion by good-quality communication. However, determined opponents may need to be bypassed through a style of *direction*. There are dangers in this – namely, unfavourable lobbying of stakeholders in boxes C and D. This has sometimes been disastrous, as was seen in the case of Fisons and their dismissive attitude to environmental groups protesting about peat-digging (see the *Fisons* case study in *Exploring Corporate Strategy*)

- *Stakeholders* in box A of Figure 10.1 are both disinterested and have little power, So, in general, the appropriate style is *direction*. Again care needs to be taken that this process is handled appropriately to avoid the dangers of unfavourable lobbying by disaffected stakeholders. This is less of a problem in box A than in box B.

Clearly these general 'prescriptions' need to be treated with some caution in two particular respects:

1   The above must not become a 'creed'. A judgement must be made about the most successful style in relation to the specific stakeholder group, the particular circumstances and the specific strategy.

2   Political priorities are often concerned with repositioning of stakeholders. So the appropriate style usually relates to the box in which you would wish/need the stakeholder to be – not the one they are in

currently. For example, powerful stakeholders who are currently dis-interested in the strategy (box C) are only likely to reposition to become key players (box D) thorough a process of *education/com-munication* (to raise their interest) possibly followed by *participation* to increase their ownership of the strategy.

10.4.2 Typical maps and how to respond

The general advice in Section 10.4.1 can be developed further by look-ing at commonly occurring situations/maps and the political priorities and dangers involved. Nine typical maps are shown in Figure 10.3 and the priorities and dangers are listed in Table 10.2 together with the political mechanisms which might be most appropriate in these cir-cumstances. This section will briefly summarise each of these nine typical maps. Care needs to be taken when using these *stereotype* maps. They are drawn up to show where the *dominant 'weight'* of stakeholder influence lies. For clarity, other boxes are left empty al-though, of course, other stakeholders may be located in these boxes. It

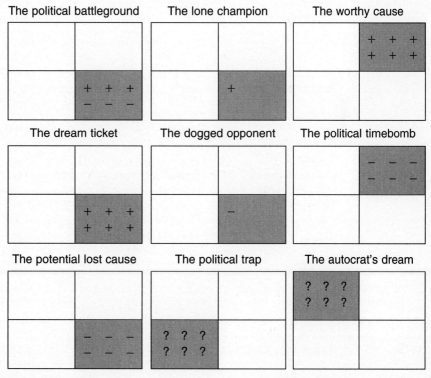

Figure 10.3   Nine typical maps.

Table 10.2   *The nine typical maps: features, dangers, priorities and political mechanisms*

Typical map	Key features of the map	Dangers	Political priorities	Political mechanisms
1. The political battleground	Both strong supporters and opponents of the strategy	'Limbo'	Reduce political risk by: (a) supporter dominates (b) opponents retreat (c) stalemate	Building resource base; overcoming resistance; 'divide-and-rule'
2. The dream ticket	Several champions of strategy; no powerful opponents	Complacency	Keep stakeholders both informed and satisfied	Alliance building and maintenance
3. The potential lost cause	Several powerful opponents of strategy	Progress impossible; other strategies damaged	Change orientation at least of some stakeholders or abandon/modify strategy	Overcoming resistance
4. The lone champion	One powerful champion	Champion is lost	Keep on board; broaden base of support	Maintain participation and/or communication; foster interest and momentum for change of other stakeholders
5. The dogged opponent	One powerful opponent	Opponent prevails	Change orientation; reduce interest; reduce power; find champion	Overcome resistance; side-payments, new priorities; associate strategy with elite; participation/ communication
6. The political trap	Apparent low interest amongst powerful players	Stakeholder 'repositions' and blocks strategy at a late stage	Maintain stakeholders in current position; seek a champion	Keep satisfied; raise their interest through participation/ communication
7. The worthy cause	Supportive stakeholders – all with little power; no key players	No levers for adoption	Find a champion from box B	Empower stakeholders: – help them organise – alliance building – communication (for lobbying)
			Find a champion from box C	Raise their interest through participation/ communication
8. The political timebomb	Opponents – all with little power	Arrogance incites action/ lobbying	Maintain in box B	Keep informed; achieve compliance
9. The autocrat's dream	No powerful or interested stakeholders	Complacency	Proceed to implementation	Direction/edict; keep monitoring stakeholder activities

is also likely that in some circumstances there may be a hybrid of these stereotypes in existence (quite often the *worthy cause* and the *political trap* would coincide). So, these maps are to be used only to point up the broad type of situation you have found in your mapping and, hence, provide a bridge into political priorities and actions as indicated below.

The political battleground

Here there are many key players – divided in their support and opposition of the strategy. There are clear dangers that this highly politicised situation freezes commitments and decisions and the strategy is left in limbo. To avoid this situation change agents could proceed in several ways:

- facilitating the dominance of the supporters – perhaps by assisting in building their resource base
- overcoming the resistance of opponents by communication, or reducing their interest (e.g. through higher priority projects)
- creating a stalemate within which the strategy could proceed.

The dream ticket

This is a situation which occurs infrequently. There are several powerful and interested supporters and no powerful opponents. There is an obvious danger of complacency and it is important that these key players are properly participating or, at least, being kept informed and satisfied. The key political mechanism is alliance building and maintenance.

The potential lost cause

This is a difficult situation where ultimately the strategy may need to be abandoned or considerably modified. There is a wider danger that inappropriate handling of these stakeholders may create political difficulties wider than the particular strategy – the change agent may 'foul their patch'. The priority is clearly to change the 'orientation' of at least some stakeholders and hence create a situation of a 'political battleground' (see above) rather than a lost cause. This is concerned with overcoming resistance – perhaps through the involvement of a respected outsider (e.g. a consultant or member of an external 'reference group').

The lone champion

There are many strategies which succeed through the zealous support of a single powerful champion, such as the chairman of the company or the minister of a department. But there are real political dangers, too, in these circumstances as many managers have found to their cost. The problem is the potential loss of the champion, because either their interest declines (other priorities take over) or their power is lost – for example the minister is 'reshuffled' to another department.

In the former case it important to keep a continuing participation and/or communication. The latter risk can be lessened by broadening the base of support by fostering the interest of other stakeholders (from box C), or building the power base of supporters (from box B).

The dogged opponent

The general advice about managing powerful opponents has already been given (the *potential lost cause*). With a few dogged opponents this advice would stand – change their orientation by reducing their resistance. However, in these circumstances there are other possibilities too. It may be possible to reduce their interest (through 'side payments' or other priorities). Their power could be diminished by association of the strategy with an elite (e.g. the Board) or, even better, finding a more powerful champion.

The political trap

This is a situation of apparent low interest among all powerful stakeholders which may tempt managers to conclude that they can simply proceed with the strategy (i.e. a style of direction). Some managers will be familiar with the political dangers of this approach – a powerful stakeholder intervenes and blocks the strategy at a key decision point, even late in the implementation process. Political priorities are designed to avoid this outcome by maintaining stakeholders in their current position through a style of intervention – keeping them satisfied. Alternatively, it may be politically safer to attempt to create a map more like the *lone champion* by participation of one stakeholder as the champion of the strategy.

The worthy cause

Many managers of not-for-profit organisations will be all too familiar with this situation. The frustrating combination of high levels of interest from stakeholders with little power and vice versa. In many cases a strategy may be zealously owned and supported by middle managers who lack the power of implementation. This is often described as the Cinderella strategy. The priority is to find a champion (key player) from either box B or box C.

Supporters from box B may be empowered in several ways:

- Help them to build, organise and/or create alliances
- Provide information which they could use to lobby stakeholders in box C.

For stakeholders in box C it is again an issue of raising their interest through *participation*.

The political timebomb

Here there are several opponents of the strategy – all of whom have little power. The danger is that these stakeholders are disregarded in such a way that they are incited to gain power either by building alliances or by adverse lobbying of stakeholders in box C. The political priorities are usually to maintain the stakeholders in box B. The mechanism might be to keep them informed or to achieve compliance in any of the ways shown in Table 10.3.

The autocrat's dream

The final map is one with stakeholders only in box A. So managers pro-

Table 10.3   *Political mechanisms in organisations*

Activity areas	Mechanisms				Key problems
	Resources	Elites	Subsystems	Symbolic	
Building the power base	Control of resources; acquisition of/ identification with expertise; acquisition of additional resources	Sponsorship by an elite; association with an elite	Alliance building; team building	Building on legitimation	Time required for building; perceived duality of ideals; perceived as threat by existing elites
Overcoming resistance	Withdrawal of resources; use of 'counter-intelligence' information	Breakdown or division of elites; association with change agent; association with respected outsider	Foster momentum for change; sponsorship/ reward of change agents	Attack or remove legitimation; foster confusion, conflict and questioning	Striking from too low a power base; potentially destructive – need for rapid rebuilding
Achieving compliance	Giving resources	Removal of resistant elites; need for visible 'change hero'	Partial implementation and participation; symbolic implantation of 'disciples'; support for 'young Turks'	Applause/reward; reassurance; symbolic confirmation	Converting the body of the organisation; slipping back

Source: *Exploring Corporate Strategy* (4th edition), 1997, Figure 11.8.

ceed with strategy implementation through direction/edict. It is essential to avoid complacency by continual monitoring of stakeholder reactions.

10.5   Ethical considerations

Stakeholder mapping can be a useful tool for managers. However, the 'mechanics' of undertaking the analysis as described in this chapter can often result in managers (accidentally) coming to the view that it is their role to manipulate all other stakeholders in Machiavellian ways to ensure the best possible chances of successful implementation of a strategy.

This is not an ethically sustainable position in most circumstances since managers are meant to be much closer to 'the honest broker' who is able to understand the conflicting expectations of stakeholders and plot an 'acceptable' path through the political landscape. This is rather easier to say than to do, and this is a reminder and an encouragement to managers to consider their analysis and actions against this ethical 'test' too.

One way of doing this is to plot 'ought to be' maps as well as the 'needs to be' maps discussed above. It could be argued that this is particularly important in public sector strategies, but it is also relevant to the private sector too. The extent to which an 'ought to be' map differs from the 'needs to be' map could raise some very important questions such as:

- Whether minimal effort is a satisfactory stance in relation to stakeholders in box A. These may well be disadvantaged or disaffected groups in society for whom, it could be argued, managers – and certainly politicians – have some responsibility in terms of improving their interest and involvement.
- More widely, that promoting the interests of those most affected by a strategy – whether or not they have interest or power – could be regarded as part of the 'honest broker' role of a manager as described above, even if it makes the implementation of a strategy more difficult or even impossible. So managers have a responsibility for the means as well as the ends. These are difficult, but important issues for managers.

10.6.   Summary

Stakeholder mapping is a useful tool for analysing the political context in which strategies are developed; of assessing the political viability of a proposed strategy; and of developing the strategy in a way which improves the chances of successful implementation. The power–interest matrix has been used as the analytical tool to look at these three important ingredients of any strategy which relate to Chapters 5, 8 and 11 respectively in *Exploring Corporate Strategy*.

11 *Corporate responsibility audit*

By David Clutterbuck

Editor's introduction

The purposes of organisations are strongly determined by the cultural and political context, as explained in Chapter 5 of *Exploring Corporate Strategy*. An important aspect of this is the ethical stance of an organisation, which is of fundamental importance in determining which purposes *should* be prioritised and why. David Clutterbuck's chapter provides a practical approach which managers can use to review an organisation's position on issues of corporate social responsibility (CSR), to develop CSR policies and to put in place procedures to make those policies effective.

11.1 Introduction

Not so many years ago, how a company's management team ran the business was regarded as its own affair. Shareholders rarely asked questions, let alone insisted that the board change its policy or practices. If the company got into financial difficulties, they might be vociferous in their complaints and even demand a change in management – but the day-to-day running of the company was not their affair.

However, today the need to manage and to be seen to manage a wide range of social responsibility issues is becoming increasingly urgent. The problem is that the pay-offs will remain largely theoretical and the discussions largely philosophical unless there are practical and adequate management processes for making social responsibility goals happen. The fine words have to be translated into fine deeds, through commitment at the top and innovation and initiative throughout the rest of the organisation. Every company will want to arrange its social responsibility approaches differently, according to its own priorities, but will need, at a minimum:

- A system to generate and review social responsibility policies at the highest level and, in most cases, at individual business level. This system must be capable of helping the companies develop business strategies that lead to competitive advantage through its public reputation

- A system for gathering information about social responsibility trends and about the organisation's performance
- A system for stimulating change and, where necessary, for enforcing it.

In companies which have gone furthest along this road, one can usually trace an evolution along the following lines, where they:

- recognise the existence of different communities of interest
- understand the needs of these communities and their legitimate demands on the organisation
- develop policies to cover each issue, taking into account conflicts of interest between those communities
- establish priorities for action
- design and implement procedures to put the policies into action
- measure and review.

These issues are reviewed below.

11.2   *Recognising the existence of different communities of interest*

Essentially, a community is a grouping of people with common background or interests. The source of their commonality may, for example, be geographical, occupational, religious or to do with a leisure pursuit. From a corporate social responsibility point of view, the key questions are:

- To what extent do the company's activities impact upon these people's lives?
- How does the company benefit from meeting people's needs?
- What do people have a right to expect from the company?

An interesting and different way of looking at the various communities with which a company becomes involved, is as a series of concentric circles. In the centre is the individual employee, a community of one. There isn't much the individual can do to influence community involvement, unless she or he is one of those highly motivated individuals whose enthusiasm captivates and stirs others; or unless she or he is in top management.

The company has a series of responsibilities to this individual, from providing opportunities for personal growth to ensuring that she or he works in a safe environment. She or he may have strong ambitions to advance within the organisation, or may be content with the responsibilities she or he has now. The potential variance in domestic circumstances, education level, personality type, functional discipline and so on is enormous. The challenging task of those responsible for personnel management (including the line manager) is to apply mass approaches while still treating that person as an individual.

The individual employee is part of a larger community, the team. The team will have a common set of objectives set by management, but it will have its own way of doing things and its own culture. The interaction between the motivation levels and behaviour of the team and the individual is substantial and two way. The team is the most important functional unit in both controlling social responsibility processes and motivating employees to undertake community activities. The company's responsibilities towards the team consist in the main of supporting it in supporting the constituent individuals; in practical terms, this usually means providing quality of leadership.

Above the team is the business unit, or company. We can define two distinct layers of responsibility here. One is local, in the sense of the communities that have a frequent, direct link with the organisation. This includes the employees *en masse*, customers, suppliers and the local community. The local environment, while not a community as such, can be considered in the same light, from a responsibility point of view, with the local community as the primary spokesperson. Depending on how close the company wishes to be in its relationships with shareholders, they belong either in this layer or the next.

Beyond this layer is the national community, where relationships with government and national lobbies become important. Outside this are, in turn, the European community (small 'c' to include non-European Union countries) and, finally, the global community. The European dimension is becoming increasingly significant as multinational companies coordinate social responsibility initiatives across borders. The Third World, while generally a low priority for such initiatives, is gaining greater attention under the twin pressures of economic disaster and the need to adopt and spread good environmental practice.

This relatively straightforward model, with all its flaws, permits serious discussion of where to focus corporate attention at the macrolevel. Which areas can we afford to ignore for the present? Which are vital to our future well-being?

11.3 *Understanding the communities and their legitimate demands on the organisation*

Understanding the nature of each community – its aspirations, limitations, hopes and fears – is an important step in designing initiatives towards it. The process of doing so is essentially the same as would be applied by the marketing function to market segments. In essence, it involves:

- defining precisely who the community is
- assessing to what extent it can be segmented even further
- using market research techniques such as surveys, focus groups, advisory panels and so on to explore their perceptions
- developing relationships with key influences within each community
- communicating regularly with them
- gaining their input into initiative design.

Relatively few companies have a structured database of this kind of information, but it is not difficult to develop; nor, for most companies, should it be difficult to develop the kind of dialogue that will provide useful data. A word of warning, however. Just as many employers made the mistake in the 1960s and 1970s of listening solely to trade union officials on matters of employee interests, on the assumption that the officials genuinely represented employee needs and perceptions, so it is very easy to assume that a few, vociferous voices in a community fully understand its needs and aspirations. Although relying on a few sources of information may be relatively cheap, it is often better to have other, more direct, channels to receive feedback from people within a community, rather than to rely solely on the interpretations of a third party.

11.4   *Developing policies to cover each issue, taking into account conflicts of interest*

Policies can be generated in detail at the functional level (human resources, information technology, public affairs) and ratified by top management; or they can be outlined in broad principle by top management and passed down to be worked into detailed guidelines by function managers. In practice, most companies seem to combine both approaches in an iterative process that, at its most successful, integrates the authority of the board with the functional department's day-to-day closeness to the issues.

The solutions companies have adopted for policy development vary widely. Compare, for example, the approaches to community investment policy given in Illustration 11.1.

Whether it retains or delegates policy making, the board has a responsibility to ensure that the organisation has a clear statement of principles. It must also ensure that any subsidiaries and all functional departments adopt those principles and develop their own more detailed guidelines, relevant to the social responsibility issues they face.

The board is also the point at which policies need to be integrated, to make sure that effort is not duplicated and that the efforts in one area are not undermined by problems in another. A graphic illustration of the kind of problems that can occur if functions are al-

Strategy in action

Illustration 11.1

Community investment policies

Marks and Spencer

Marks and Spencer has a general policy set by the main board, to support the communities in which it operates. Beyond this, policy on how to allocate and manage the £5 million annual budget rests with a community involvement committee with five main board directors. Three specialist subcommittees, each chaired by a director, deal with health care, the arts and community services, which includes education, training and secondment.

Allied Dunbar

Annual reports from Allied Dunbar Charitable Trust state: 'Responsibility and accountability for our community affairs activities have been delegated away from the board. Having made the important decisions in respect of principles, general direction, and resources to be made available, directors rely on trustees, in conjunction with professional staff and advisers, to develop and implement appropriate programmes.'

W.H. Smith

W.H. Smith carried out a community involvement policy review in 1992. The initial working party included a number of disciplines, such as personnel, in addition to the community affairs and sponsorship professionals. At time of writing, the review was still taking place. However, the intention was to involve as wide a spectrum of employees as possible in deliberating over the policy before changes were instituted.

lowed to develop policies independently is an airport. The marketing and human resource departments spent heavily, training staff to be polite and helpful to customers and promoting this to the public. Then the security department, anxious to prevent its staff colluding with other people to avoid immigration and customs controls, forbade them to talk to anyone while on duty. Inevitably, this led to staff turning away in embarrassment when passengers asked for directions, undermining the customer service initiative.

Because concern for different areas of social responsibility action has arisen at different times and within different business functions, it is hardly surprising, for example, to find there is little coordination in many companies between purchasing policy and environmental policy. This normally has to be done at functional level rather than at organisational level.

Although chemical and manufacturing companies, for example, often have a board member responsible for coordinating all environmental policies, few companies have a board member responsible for all social responsibility activities.

One of the best ways to organise social responsibility issues is to have regular meetings between function heads, who report to a board member responsible for ensuring that the company activities in this field are documented and publicised.

Part of the responsibility of this gathering must be to ensure that no key issues fall through the cracks. It should ask such questions as: Who takes responsibility for making sure the company's marketing practices are fair and ethical? It should also ensure that every business function does have clear, written guidelines, job descriptions, mission statements and targets; and that they are mutually supportive.

Who participates in these discussions will vary according to how responsibilities are divided. For example, do the company's links with schools and universities come under human resources, public affairs or community affairs? It is critical that responsibilities are clearly defined and that social responsibility issues are not simply 'dumped' on one individual or department.

11.4.1 Checklist

1 Does our business mission deal with a sufficiently broad spectrum of stakeholder interests?
2 What values do we hold/want to hold towards each stakeholder group?
3 Can we encapsulate in no more than one page:
   • the fundamental responsibilities of the company to its main stakeholders?
   • responsibilities by the stakeholders towards the companies?
4 How will we communicate our values?
5 How will we police them?

11.5 Setting priorities

No company has the resources – either financially, or in manpower, or in simple energy – to tackle all the social issues with which it might legitimately become involved. Moreover, dissipating its resources by trying to deal with too wide a range of issues brings little benefit to either the company or its communities.

In setting priorities, it is helpful to follow a reasoning process along the following lines:

1 What are our *legal* responsibilities towards each community? Now? Likely in the next five years?
2 How are we doing against each of these?
3 What are our *moral* obligations towards each community?

4 How are we performing against each of these?

5 Where will the greatest impacts on the *business* (both positive and negative) come from, in dealing with each of these communities of interest?

6 How are we doing in terms of meeting each of those business challenges?

7 What resource do we have that we could apply to these issues?

8 What resources should come from functional budgets (because they are primarily commercial goals) and what from community investment?

There will inevitably be grey areas, demanding discussion and sometimes compromise, but the key is to follow a structured analytical process (such as that presented in Illustration 11.2) that allows decisions on priorities to be made on a rational basis. It also helps to ensure that major issues are not neglected simply because there was no obvious route to bring them up for consideration.

Strategy in action

Illustration 11.2
The Co-op and American Express

The Co-op took an unusual step in establishing its priorities for community action – it surveyed its members. Under the title 'Your opinion matters', it invited members to 'help us by completing our care poll. It will make sure our community action plans focus on the issues that you care about.'
Among questions asked were:

- how important people felt it was to be kept informed on issues such as solvent abuse or diet and health
- what really concerned people about community life
- whether the Co-op was right to refuse to stock irradiated foods, or ban hunting with hounds from its 30,000 acres of farmland, or whether it should provide bottle banks outside the stores, and so on
- which of a list of charitable causes the Co-op should support.

Although the level of response was not as high as hoped for, one positive result was that two-thirds of the Co-op's customers felt that major retailers should get more involved in local issues. The data from the survey was also helpful in allocating priorities for action.

American Express also asked its card members for their opinions on where to focus its community activities. It invited them to write in to nominate a charity they thought the company should support. From the hundreds of nominations, Amex was able to select five for priority attention: AIDS charity AVERT, Help the Aged, The Greenpeace Environmental Trust, Shelter and UNICEF.

11.6   Procedures for putting the policies into action

By and large, the same basic procedures and controls used to implement any other business programme or project can and should be applied towards social responsibility issues. These include:

- having very clear objectives
- a detailed plan of action, with budgets, clearly assigned responsibilities and specific milestones
- communicating both the objective and the plan
- providing training and other forms of support as needed
- having strong, practical feedback mechanisms.

11.7   Measuring and reviewing

The maxim 'What gets measured gets done' applies here as much as to any other form of management activity. The question is: What do we measure?

The clearer the objectives and the more directly implementation is under the company's control, the easier it is to devise realistic measurements that will be useful both to management and to the communities which have a legitimate interest in the issue. For example, Superdrug's avowed intention to increase the proportion of women in middle and senior management posts to 20 per cent by 1997 should have posed relatively few problems in tracking.

Measuring the impact of a specific charitable donation or a sponsorship initiative is often much more difficult. Here, it may be more appropriate to measure changes in public perception of a programme of related activities over a period of time.

Whether measurements are 'hard' or 'soft', they also need to be tied into the organisation's motivational systems. Few if any companies make social responsibility issues a direct and significant aspect of performance appraisal for managers – yet. However, specific targets (for example, minority recruitment) are becoming more common, and so is a general pressure for managers to be seen to set an example in community involvement.

11.8   Summary: delivering results

Ultimately, the success or failure of companies' efforts to manage social responsibility issues as an integral part of executive responsibilities will depend on three factors:

1   The degree of focus they can apply to ensure that efforts are not diluted.
2   The relevance of the initiatives they undertake, both for the company and for the various communities of interest.

3   The commitment, particularly among top management, to developing the kind of climate where socially responsible attitudes and innovation in community involvement can flourish and become a natural part of 'the way we do things here'.

No single company has all the answers to managing social responsibility. However, we have tried to capture some of the experience of a sufficiently broad spread of organisations, to at least point in the right direction (Illustration 11.3).

Strategy in action

Illustration 11.3

IBM UK

IBM internationally has devoted a lot of time and effort over the past 30 years to developing practical management systems for social responsibility.

At IBM's international headquarters in the United States, an ethical sub-committee advises the global board on broad policy issues. The European board interprets these in equally broad terms and monitors the social responsibility performance of each national subsidiary. It may also promote pan-European initiatives. Within each subsidiary, community involvement is part of corporate affairs, which reports to the national board through the personnel director, effectively tying external and internal social responsibility management together at the business policy level. There is a similar structure across the world, in each major country where IBM does business.

Sarah Portway, the UK public affairs manager, has responsibility for external relations, government relations, issues management and community relations. These functions were only brought together four years ago. Her procedure is detailed below.

I recommend the sort of areas we should operate in, the budget we should have and the organisational structure for the department.

We decided to coin the phrase community investment so that the rest of the company could see what we do as a business investment rather than something attached to the chairman's office as a philanthropic activity. We also wanted people externally to see it as something we expected to make a return on. We are working on how to develop measurement processes – it's a very tough problem.

We decided we should invest in areas most important to IBM. It was very important for our public policy agenda to be aligned with areas of our business where critical things were happening:

- industry policy
- education and training
- the environment.

We concluded we could develop meaningful community policies in the last two.

Illustration 11.3 continued

To these we added the issue of disability with an emphasis on IT as a means of alleviating many of the problems people with physical or mental disabilities may have. The products we bring to market can have a real benefit for these people. Also add voluntary sector empowerment – helping them become more effective and efficient.

We started by analysing what strengths we had as a company. One of the conclusions we came to was that we knew how to manage, but that many charities lacked skills in that area. 'Creative management skills' is a programme based on our own management development course and has been going for six years, just being replaced with an updated version: 'Creative management in a changing environment.'

Under the same banner we set up a fund for community computing. It came about because we were involved in a study by the Community Development Committee into how voluntary organisations used computer equipment. The study found that they didn't use it efficiently because they didn't invest in training. So we instituted small grants of £1,000 to buy computer training for them.

Another important form of voluntary sector empowerment for us is through secondment – lending people. It makes better use of the skills and resources we have, of our unique values.

It's hard to hold the line, to maintain our focus. There are a lot of pressures from inside and outside the organisation to make exceptions. We usually say no. We make sure people understand the strategy, especially at the most senior levels, so they will feel comfortable arguing the company's case when they are approached.

The management process

There is an annual strategy review by the main management committee for the UK company. I take to them our proposals in terms of strategy and funding. They give me direction on the proposals. It's a very healthy, educated debate.

The plan is also reviewed at European level – mainly for information and confirmation. They check that our spending is appropriate and reasonable and give some international guidance on areas to focus on.

The US headquarters has a public responsibility committee, which looks at ethical considerations and includes people from the external world. The IBM board in the UK doesn't have such a committee. Instead we have a Community Advisory Panel of four people – currently executives of National Council for Voluntary Organisations, Citizens' Advice Bureaux, the J. Rowntree Foundation and Earthwatch. It is a rolling membership (we don't want people to become too close to us) and we use it to advise my functional managers about social responsibility issues. None of the advisers receives a salary for the work, but IBM pays a contribution to their organisations instead.

The first of the four quarterly meetings sets the broad agenda for the year. Information and views from the committee members are supplemented by feedback from employees and elsewhere.

I have a central budget, but our programmes are a mixture of national

Illustration 11.3 continued

and local, so budgets are also dispersed through regional directors. They have the discretion as to whether they should pass spending authority down to the individual location managers. We've been enthusiastic to encourage location managers to develop programmes consistent with national strategy.

We tell location managers to look out for critical local issues, such as AIDS in Edinburgh, where the local office has helped provide an education programme. We also encourage them to develop their own local strategies and the systems to run them.

Bottom-up input of this kind helps drive the national and international community investment strategies. For example, a major new issue for us is ageing. The Leeds office initiated a project in that area, which has led us to review our priorities. In order to keep a strategic focus, we would normally expect to change priorities, rather than simply add another priority area.

Some locations have community investment committees, where the employees become involved in deciding what activities to get involved in.

We recognise local community investment efforts through a formal chief executive's award. Locations nominate themselves and the award is given on an assessment of good practice in strategy, project management and originality of the programmes themselves. The winning locations receive a cheque to go towards the activity their entry was based on and an additional sum is made available to hold a celebratory event with the community partner.

Local environment action teams – groups of employees who get together under their own initiative to tackle a local environmental issue, such as a derelict piece of land – can also apply for specific awards from the centre.

Another award goes to individual employee volunteers. It consists of a trophy and some money for the organisation to which they volunteer their time.

Measurement
We have two key measures:

- Is it helping the business interests?
- Is it helping the community?

We participate in a MORI survey on what people think about community investment. It's a helpful umbrella, but it doesn't tell us much else.

Last year we piloted in Bristol and Greenoch a more detailed survey of three audiences:

- employees
- opinion formers
- the general public.

We asked questions such as:

- What role should companies play in the community?
- What did they think about IBM in this context?
- What did they think about individual programmes?
- What should we be doing?

Illustration 11.3 continued

There were a lot of correlations between local and national opinions.

We also asked what people thought were the most important resources IBM had to offer. Every group put people resources first. This has helped us think through some of the strategic issues around whether to give money or time. We were also able to use some of the data on what people knew about us to refine the emphasis of some of our community activities.

At the individual project level, we aim to set clear objectives at the beginning, and gain the agreement and understanding of the partner organisations. Then we track progress closely against those objectives. For example, we regularly review the contract with the subcontractors, stipulating what's needed for our Creative Management Skills programme.

Another form of measurement is what would be called repeat business in the commercial sector. In 1991, 45 per cent of voluntary organisations using the scheme did so more than once.

We are also participating in a J. Rowntree Foundation research project to assess the impact of our community activities on the recipient organisations. Has our involvement made a real difference to them?

Individual locations provide annual reports on their activities, in which they assess their performance against broad strategic objectives.

12

Discovering and defining the process of strategy development

By Andy Bailey and Clare Avery

Editors' introduction

In Chapter 2 of *Exploring Corporate Strategy* illustrations are given of different characteristics of the strategy development process. Three broad explanations of strategy development are presented: strategy developed as managerial intent; strategy developed as the outcome of cultural and political processes in and around an organisation and strategy imposed on an organisation. However, it is also made clear that any one particular approach to, or pattern of, strategy development does not exist across organisations, rather there are likely to be a number of different configurations of strategy development processes.

The research, which is reported in *Exploring Corporate Strategy*, employed a Strategy Development Questionnaire (SDQ). This questionnaire can also be used as a tool by which managers can explore and define their view of the strategy development processes in their own organisations (see Appendix 12.1). This chapter explains the questionnaire and shows how it can be used.

12.1 Introduction

This chapter explains how processes of strategy development in organisations can be understood using a Strategy Development Questionnaire (SDQ, see Appendix 12.1). The SDQ comprises 36 statements, derived from extensive research, that relate to six dimensions of strategy development (These are outlined below and discussed in *Exploring Corporate Strategy*, Chapter 2). It is a self-administered technique, so the assessment can be carried out by each manager in approximately 15 minutes.

The output from this self-completion questionnaire is a pictorial representation which identifies the dominant processes operating within an organisation – a strategy development profile, similar to those shown in *Exploring Corporate Strategy* (see also Appendix 12.2). It is important to understand the nature of the strategy development process not least because attempts to alter strategy development need to be based on a real understanding of the existing process rather than on assumptions about that process.

The use of the SDQ has a number of benefits:

- It builds on a conceptual framework and language for explaining strategy development that clarifies the complex processes at work in organisations
- It allows such processes to be made explicit when, so often, they are taken for granted or masked by what managers think should occur rather than what does occur
- In this way it can facilitate the discussion of processes which are often not discussed
- In addition, it can be used to compare different perceptions of strategy development processes: for example, differences between parts of an organisation (e.g. SBUs or functions), differences between levels of management or differences over time, e.g. before and after a programme of strategic change.

12.2   *The dimensions of strategy development*

The process of strategy development cannot always be characterised as intentional and planned. Strategy can come about through a number of different influences or processes. The framework here uses six dimensions to describe such processes:

1   *The planning dimension.* Strategy is developed through an analytic, intentional and sequential process of planning.
2   *The incremental dimension.* Strategy is developed in an evolutionary but purposeful manner, through an iterative and adaptive process of trial and error.
3   *The cultural dimension.* Strategy is directed and guided by the cultural aspects of an organisation, its history and the shared assumptions and beliefs of its members.
4   *The political dimension.* Strategy is developed through a process of bargaining, negotiation and influence between internal interest groups.
5   *The command dimension.* Strategy is defined and determined by a particular powerful individual within an organisation.
6   *The enforced choice dimension.* Strategy is developed as a result of external pressures which limit an organisation's ability to determine its own strategic direction.

These dimensions of strategy development are discussed more fully on pages 46–63 of *Exploring Corporate Strategy* (4th edition) and key characteristics of the dimensions are summarised in Table 12.1.

Table 12.1   *Characteristics of the six dimensions*

Planning

Strategies are the outcome of rational, sequential planned and methodical procedures.
Strategic goals are set by senior organisational figures.
The organisation and environment are analysed.
Definite and precise objectives are set.
Precise plans for implementation are developed.
The strategy is made explicit in the form of detailed plans.

Incrementalism

Strategy is continually adjusted to match changes in the operating environment.
Strategy options are continually assessed for fit.
Early commitment to a strategy is tentative and subject to review.
Strategy develops through experimentation and gradual implementation.
Successful options gain additional resources.
Strategy develops through small-scale changes.

Cultural

A 'way of doing things' in the organisation impacts on strategic direction.
Strategies are evolved in accordance with a set of shared assumptions that exist in the
    organisation.
A core set of shared assumptions based on past experience and history guides strategic actions.
Organisational history directs the search for and selection of strategic options.
Strategy not in fit with the culture is resisted.

Political

Strategies are developed by negotiation and bargaining between groups.
The interest groups seek to realise their own desired objectives.
Influence in strategy formulation increases with power.
Power comes from the ability to create or control the flow of scarce resources.
Interest groups form coalitions to further their desired strategy.
The control and provision of information is also a source of power.
A strategy acceptable to the most powerful interest groups is developed.

Command

An individual is the driving force behind the organisation's strategy.
Strategy is primarily associated with the institutional power of an individual or small group.
The strategy represents the aspirations for the organisation's future of this individual.
The individual becomes the representation of the strategy for the organisation.
An individual has a high degree of control over strategy.

Enforced choice

Strategies are prescribed by the operating environment.
Strategic choice is limited by external forces which the organisation is unable to control.
Strategic change is instigated from outside the organisation.
Organisations are not able to influence their operating environments.
Barriers in the environment severely restrict strategic mobility.

12.3   *How to develop a strategy development profile*

The strategy development profile is a diagrammatic representation of the strategy development process derived from the perceptions of the managers involved in that process. The application of the tool has been particularly effective when used in management workshops with individuals from the same organisation.

12.3.1   *Context of use*

The SDQ can be used at a number of levels; however, it is especially effective when used with a coherent group of managers – for example, a top management team. It is important that the participating managers have some knowledge of strategy development within their organisation, although it is not essential that managers are actively involved in every stage of defining strategy. Another important requisite for administration of the questionnaire is that a predefined frame of reference is given to the managers prior to completion – for example, is the SDQ to be completed on the basis of the SBU, the division or the organisation as a whole? This stipulation ensures that the resulting profiles are drawn from a common origin so that comparisons made across and between individuals later are in fact valid. Further, it is important to stress that it is the general nature of the strategy development process that is of interest, not the process employed in the resolution of a specific strategy decision. This is made clear in the rubric at the front of the SDQ.

12.3.2   *Administration*

The Strategy Development Questionnaire should be given to managers for completion after the frame of reference for completion has been clearly articulated. Having followed the instructions and completed the SDQ, the self-scoring sheet should be given to managers for completion. The managers are now in a position to map their own scores onto the strategy development profile template provided (see Appendix 12.2).

12.3.3   *Interpretation of the strategy development profile*

The interpretation of the strategy development profile is based on distance from the mid-point ring (highlighted in bold). Points moving away from this ring towards the outside of the map (accompanied by a positive score) represent the degree to which the dimension is seen to be a characteristic of the strategy development process in the organisation. Points moving towards the centre (accompanied by a negative score) represent the degree to which the dimension is uncharacteristic of the process. Points at zero or low positive or negative scores indicate that the attributes associated with that dimension are not particularly characteristic or uncharacteristic of the strategy development process.

12.4   *Feedback and discussion of strategy development material*

12.4.1   *Stage one*

The first stage of the feedback is to help managers understand their own strategy development profile. The initial step to this end is for the facilitator to describe the characteristics of each dimension (as described in *Exploring Corporate Strategy*, Chapter 2 and summarised here in Table 12.1). As managers rarely see one dimension as dominant, the emphasis should be placed on the likely occurrence of combinations or configurations of dimensions.

It is important that no one dimension or configuration is presented as being representative of 'best practice'. The managers themselves should determine what would represent 'best practice' within the context of their organisation. This part of the session introduces the concepts and language with which to support deeper discussion about how strategy is developed.

12.4.2   *Questions for discussion for individual managers*

A number of questions can be put to the manager at this stage to encourage greater understanding of the process of strategy development that operates within his or her organisation (see Illustration 12.1).

1   What do you think are the potential consequences of the process you describe for strategy development in your organisation?
2   Are there aspects of the organisation that make the process the way it is? For example, in what ways do influences internal to the organisation – such as the structure, management systems, and the personality and behaviours of colleagues – promote the strategy development process in the form you describe.
3   Similarly, what impact do influences external to the organisation – such as nature of the market, maturity of and speed of change within the industry or government legislation – have upon the strategy development process?
4   What does such a profile suggest about your own role within the strategy development process? Are there certain individuals or activities that are more effective than others in gaining influence over strategic direction?

Strategy in action

Illustration 12.1
Chief Executive Officer (CEO) – public service organisation

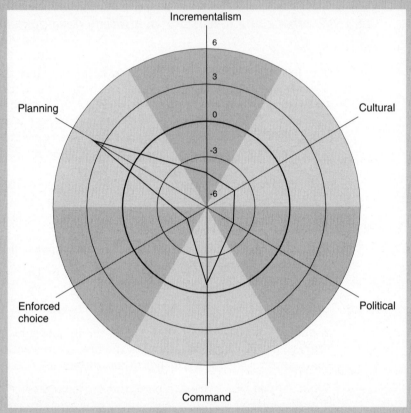

Figure 12.1 Public service CEO.

The CEO sees the process of strategy development as being distinctly characterised by planning. He indicates that the strategy followed by the organisation
is the outcome of sequential, mechanistic and deliberate procedures. This pro-

12.4.3 Stage two of feedback

The second stage of feedback is to present to the group the overview
profile for the organisation, which can be produced by summing all the
individual scores for each dimension and then dividing that by the
number of individuals. This exercise allows managers to compare their
own view against those of the aggregate or average of other mana-

Illustration 12.1 continued

file reflects the context of this public service organisation where formalised planning is a requirement imposed by the demands of powerful external stakeholders such as the government and the local authority. As a result, the organisation's Strategic Planning Unit adopts an elaborate annual planning cycle and system; internal and external environmental analyses are carried out on a regular basis using tools such as SWOT and PEST analyses, and public consultative groups are set up. The resulting strategy emerges as published documents: an annual plan and a 3–5 year strategic plan. The CEO also publishes a mission statement which provides a high-level guide for the strategy. Planning in the consultative form seen here is also believed to promote ownership of strategy, through involving internal and external stakeholders in the strategy development process. Therefore the way that strategy is developed can aid the implementation of strategic decisions. The emphasis on the command element seen in the profile reflects the hierarchical nature of the organisational structure and a recognition by the CEO that he is ultimately responsible for strategy.

In relation to this example:

1 *What do you think are the potential consequences of the process you describe for strategy development?*
The risk is that planning in such a formalised fashion can become more of a self-serving ritual rather than a means of analysis and thinking about complex strategic problems that face the organisation. The result of extensive consultation and analysis can be information overload which carries the risk of a major strategic issue being overlooked in the mass of data. The profile indicates that the CEO sees little political and cultural influence in the strategy development process. The danger here is that planning fails to take these important elements of organisational life into consideration despite the fact that strategy can only be implemented through people. It may be that the participative nature of planning in this organisation reduces the need for such processes. It is interesting that given the context of the organisation the CEO's profile does not acknowledge the influence upon the process from external bodies such as the government. Perhaps he or she believes that the planning process operates to limit or control external influences by anticipating and accommodating these within the strategy development process.

2 *Are there clear aspects of the organisation that make this process the way it is?*

gerial perceptions. In addition, the differences between individuals across dimensions could be shown to the group using a bar chart (see Figure 12.2).

Each manager is now in a position to explore his or her perception in relation to an aggregate profile and also to fellow managers. This presents a good opportunity to encourage managers to discuss the profiles and the factors which underlie them. (This could be done in a

Illustration 12.1 continued

For example, in what ways do influences internal to the organisation – such as the structure, management systems, and the personality and behaviours of colleagues – promote a strategy development process in the form you describe?
The organisation is highly complex with a regimented hierarchy, many functional specialisms and it operates from multiple sites situated across a wide geographical area. Strategic planning is set up as a specialised function in itself and the planning process as it exists provides these with clear statements of the organisational targets and purposes and values, which are then used to support control and discipline. The CEO role is that of figurehead and the CEO's authority and vision are sanctioned by all other members of the organisation.

3   *Similarly, what impact do influences external to the organisation – such as nature of the market, maturity of and speed of change within the industry or government legislation – have upon the strategy development process?*
Although the CEO's profile gives no indication of this, the organisation is heavily influenced by external stakeholders. For example, the government determines the budget for the organisation and sets national targets which impact upon the focus of the organisation. Change within the operating environment can be substantial but tends to occur gradually over time rather than suddenly. All these factors work to make planning a requirement and because change in the environment can to a large extent be anticipated, planning is a viable process for developing strategy.

4   *What does such a profile suggest about your own role within the strategy development process? Are there certain individuals or activities that are more effective than others in gaining influence over strategic direction?*
The profile describes an organisational figurehead concerned with the future direction of the organisation, spending most time in consultation and collaboration with external agencies, which promotes the strong emphasis on planning. This CEO is less concerned with the day-to-day running of the organisation, which is delegated to other members of the Top Management Team (TMT). Certain functional groups can achieve some influence over the strategy development process by demanding greater allocation of resources necessary to meet organisational targets for example, but this is not indicated by this profile. This absence is further evidence that the CEO 'is in control' of the organisation – a position influenced less by the everyday organisational realities such as political activity.

plenary session or in smaller groups.) At this stage it is necessary to reinforce the central point to the whole group that no value judgements about the profiles can be made – there is no right, wrong or best profile. Each manager's perspective is a valid picture of the process at work; what is important is to discuss the reasons for each perception.

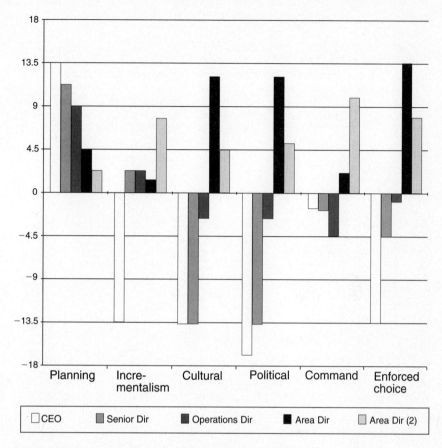

Figure 12.2 *Strategy development profiles of members of TMT.*

12.4.4 *Questions for discussion within a group* (see Illustration 12.2)

1 Compare your individual profile with that from fellow managers and the aggregate profile. To what extent is there agreement about strategy development processes. If there are differences, why do they exist?

2 How appropriate or successful is the strategy development process currently in operation?

12.5 *Further exploration of the strategy development process*

The facilitator should make certain at this point that the group understands the technique and that associated concepts are clear. Having confirmed this, the next stage builds upon the previous exer-

Strategy in action

Illustration 12.2

Profiles of members of the top management team

1   *Compare your individual profile with that from fellow managers and the aggre-*
     gate profile. To what extent is there agreement about the strategy development
     processes. If there are differences, why do they exist?

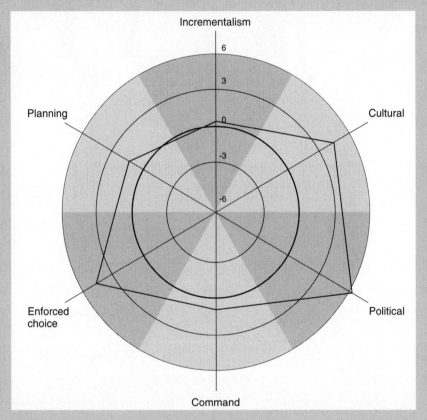

Figure 12.3   Individual profile: Area Director.

In contrast to the profile of the CEO (Figure 12.1) which emphasises the planning dimension, the Area Director perceives a number of other influences

cises and moves the managers towards using these to explore the appropriateness of the strategy development that is employed within
their organisation. Useful discussion exercises at this point could be
centred around hypothetical scenarios – e.g. What would it be like if
the CEO was the sole master of strategy? What would have to change

impinging on the strategy development process. The greatest influences are characterised by the enforced choice, cultural and political dimensions, indicating that the director does not perceive strategy development to be wholly the product of planning, but rather that the process is subject to other forces internal and external to the organisation. Such a profile reflects the fact that, unlike the CEO, the Area Director is more immediately involved with the operational levels of the organisation and, unlike the CEO, he also does not see himself 'in control'. In this position the Area Director more directly experiences political activity and cultural influences within the process of strategy development. It is also possible to account for differences in perception of the strategy development in terms of tenure. The fact that the Area Director has been with

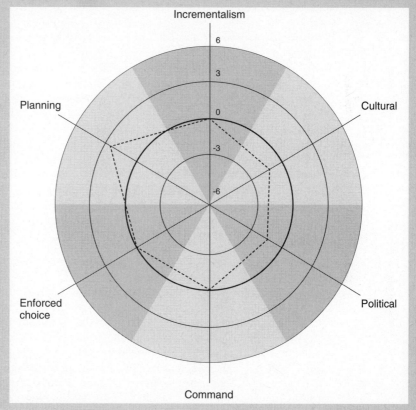

Figure 12.4   *Group profile: TMT.*

to permit that? Would that be a good way of doing things? What are the strengths and weaknesses of the current process?

An interesting exercise at this point is to ask the group to compete the questionnaire again but this time to use an 'ideal' conception of the strategy development process within the organisation as the

Illustration 12.2 continued

the organisation for longer than the CEO may allow the inference that the profile reflects greater familiarity with the organisation and the historical influences upon strategy development. The score on the command dimension reflects the role in the process of the CEO who is responsible for strategy.

When the profiles of the five TMT members are aggregated, planning emerges as the dominant characteristic of the strategy development process. It is interesting that the high scores in the previous profile on the cultural and political dimensions are not reflected to the same extent in the aggregate profile. This indicates that there is a division within the TMT between those members who perceive the strategy development process to be characterised as a deliberate and systematic process of planning and those who see the political and cultural aspects of the organisation having an affect upon the process. By looking at the bar chart (Figure 12.2), which represents individual member's scores, it is possible to see where these differences lie. As discussed earlier, the impact of organisational culture and of political activity upon the strategy development process is perceive most by those members of the TMT who are more immediately involved at an operational level, and this is seen in the profiles of the two Area Directors and to a lesser extent by the Operations Director. In contrast the CEO and the Senior Director see the process as much more uni-dimensional with the focus on planning. This can be accounted for in part by the fact that they are relatively new members of the team and are detached from the organisational history; their high-level role is more about considering the nature of the organisation in the future and the CEO is charged with shifting the existing traditional culture to a new culture founded upon openness between members and greater individual responsibility. The scores for the incremental dimension reveal that all members of the TMT with the exception of the CEO perceive an incremental element to the strategy development process.

2   *How appropriate or successful is the strategy development process currently in operation?*

The current process runs the risk of being less about strategy development and more concerned with smoothing the path for the implementation of strategy. The process is construed by some members of the organisation as a cynical attempt to achieve a widespread ownership of an intended, predetermined strategy rather than an information-gathering exercise on which to base strategy development. It is possible that the process fosters negative political behaviour. Organisation members have argued that the process becomes ineffective because too many people are consulted during the planning process, making it cumbersome and inefficient.

common frame of reference. The most likely outcome will be profiles that will strongly emphasise the planning dimension. It is common for managers to believe that the 'best' way to develop strategy is through planning, and they aspire to this without considering many of the potential consequences associated with planning. This provides the opportunity to debate not only the pros and cons of planning but also the assumptions held by the managers that promote this view (see Section 2.3.1 in *Exploring Corporate Strategy* (4th edition)). As in the example earlier (see Stage 1) it is easy to present planning as *the* means by which strategy is developed; however, the reality can be that planning is an unrealistic desire which disguises or ignores the inevitability of other processes.

It is important to consider that other dominant dimensions make very good sense in particular circumstances. For example, the increased projection of command when the organisation is under threat. Incrementalism might be the dominant characteristic of the strategy development process when the organisation's operating environment is relatively stable or when small-scale changes can be used to experiment with new approaches and strategies. The dominance of the cultural dimension is appropriate where there is a legacy of proven success; consider Marks & Spencer for example.

Managers might also be encouraged to recognise the inevitability and importance of *configurations* of strategy development processes. They might wish to debate which dimensions usefully complement each other. For example:

- Strong planning combined with a strong command dimension can act as a mechanism for checking and challenging the strategy and its development
- High enforced choice and strong command are complementary if a CEO acts as lobbyist to the external stakeholders
- High planning or command is likely to be found in combination with low political and cultural influence if change within the organisation is to occur. This, in turn, requires the managers to consider how these influences can be managed.

12.6 *Monitoring change using the SDQ*

Since the framework is easily administered and minimally intrusive, it may also permit ready access to organisations over time. A longitudinal approach employing the questionnaire at intervals of time to access the strategy development process may indicate the stability of the process and the dimensions as perceived by managers; and may be especially useful in illuminating procedural issues at times of strategic change in organisations (see Illustration 12.3).

12.7 *Summary*

Executives often complain that they spend too little time discussing strategic issues, and when such discussions do take place, they are

Strategy in action

Illustration 12.3
An example of a change in pattern of strategy development over time

A professional service firm had, within a period of three years, undergone a major strategy review to address an increasingly competitive market, had changed its managing partner, and restructured its organisation. Figures 12.5

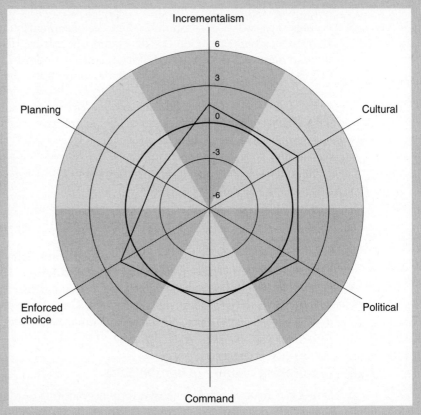

Figure 12.5   Professional service firm (1).

typically about what the strategy should be. This is indeed important. However, it is also important to discuss how strategies come about. The Strategy Development Questionnaire is an easy-to-use tool with which managers can become aware of, and understand, the strategy

Illustration 12.3 continued

and 12.6 depict the strategy development process at the commencement and after these changes as seen by partners taking part in a strategy development programme.

Unlike many corporations where an individual's involvement in decision making at an operational level may be strongly influenced by role and function, partnerships operate less rigidly. This is reflected in Figure 12.5. Processes of negotiation, debate and compromise around particular issues characterise the way in which strategic problems are defined and strategies developed. The

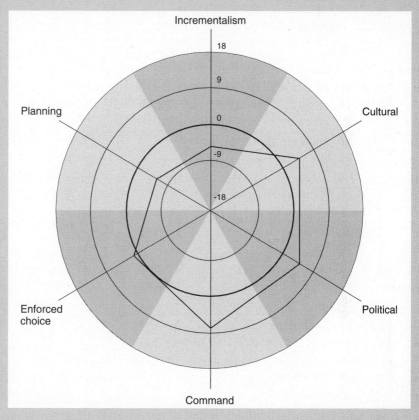

Figure 12.6   *Professional service firm (2).*

development processes that operate in their organisations. It is not intended as a means to prescribe a 'best' way of developing strategy but rather as a means to understand the reality of strategy development, consider the pros and cons of such processes and encourage debate about improvements to such processes.

Illustration 12.3 continued

same individuals or groups may not be involved in each decision. The strategy developed, then, reflects the interests of groups within the organisation.

The firm's long professional history and associated culture also influenced the identification of issues and options, and mediated the choices of strategy. Further, commonly held beliefs and assumptions allowed the various power groups to relate to each other within routines which were taken for granted. Within this culture, the strategies pursued emerged in an adaptive manner through a series of continual small-scale changes and steps which those in the organisation believed enabled the firm to keep in line with a business environment which it could merely respond to rather than influence. Indeed, strategies were not seen to develop in any systematic planned manner; little in the way of set procedures for the development of strategy existed.

However, the appointment of a new managing partner associated with changes in strategy and structure appear to have changed this situation, as illustrated in Figure 12.6. The process of strategy development is no longer characterised by an adaptive approach; rather strategy is seen to relate primarily to the power of the 'big man'. It is the aspirations for the future of the organisation which this individual holds that are seen to provide the focus for strategic direction.

Although influence over strategy development is still seen to be closely related to processes associated with the possession and utilisation of power, the importance of this dimension has diminished. Similarly, the influence of the organisation's culture on strategy development also appears to be less strong and might be associated with a programme of 'culture change' initiated by the managing partner. However the relationship which exists between political and cultural dimensions and command is, in itself, of significance. The professional ethos which permeates the organisation and its members provides a common understanding and an established power structure through which political activity can be exercised: indeed the command figure has emerged from this structure. Thus, even though the managing partner is seen to have ultimate control, his power is moderated. In addition, as this individual has developed and progressed through the same professional and organisational structure as his colleagues, he is likely to hold a similar view of the world and the strategic issues faced.

Appendix 12.1   *Strategy Development Questionnaire*

This questionnaire considers the process by which strategy is developed within organisations. It is designed to discover **your perceptions** of how strategic decisions are made in your organisation. Strategic decisions are those which are characterised by a large commitment of resources and deal with issues of substantial importance to the organisation usually with longer rather than just short-term impact or significance; they usually involve more than one function and involve significant change.

The following pages comprise a number of statements. When considering these statements please:

- assume each applies to _____, and respond to the statements as such
- think of your organisation as it **exists at present**, not as it has existed in the past or how you would like it to exist in the future
- evaluate each statement in terms of the extent to which you **agree** or **disagree** with it in relation to your organisation.

Thank you for your cooperation.

How to complete the questionnaire

- *Please answer all the statements (it will take approximately 5–10 minutes to complete)*
- *Give the answer that first occurs to you. Do not give an answer because you feel it is the right thing to say or you feel it is how things should be*
- *Respond to each of the statements by circling the appropriate number on a scale of 1 (you **strongly disagree** with the statement in relation to your organisation) to 7 (you **strongly agree** with the statement in relation to your organisation).*

Your name:_____

Name of your organisation: _____

What industry does your organisation mainly operate within?

_____

	Strongly disagree						Strongly agree
1. We have definite and precise strategic objectives	1	2	3	4	5	6	7
2. To keep in line with our business environment we make continual small-scale changes to strategy	1	2	3	4	5	6	7
3. Our strategy is based on past experience	1	2	3	4	5	6	7
4. The influence a group or individual can exert over the strategy we follow is enhanced by their control of resources critical to the organisation's activities	1	2	3	4	5	6	7
5. The strategy we follow is directed by a vision of the future associated with the chief executive (or another senior figure)	1	2	3	4	5	6	7
6. Our strategy is based on past experience	1	2	3	4	5	6	7
7. We evaluate potential strategic options against explicit strategic objectives	1	2	3	4	5	6	7
8. We keep early commitment to a strategy tentative and subject to review	1	2	3	4	5	6	7
9. Our organisation's history directs our search for solutions to strategic issues	1	2	3	4	5	6	7
10. The information on which our strategy is developed often reflects the interests of certain groups	1	2	3	4	5	6	7
11. Our strategy is closely associated with a particular individual	1	2	3	4	5	6	7
12. Our freedom of strategic choice is severely restricted by our business environment	1	2	3	4	5	6	7
13. We have precise procedures for achieving strategic objectives	1	2	3	4	5	6	7
14. Our strategies emerge gradually as we respond to the need to change	1	2	3	4	5	6	7
15. There are beliefs and assumptions about the way to do things which are specific to this organisation	1	2	3	4	5	6	7
16. Our strategy develops through a process of bargaining and negotiation between groups or individuals	1	2	3	4	5	6	7
17. The chief executive determines our strategic direction	1	2	3	4	5	6	7
18. We are not able to influence our business environment; we can only buffer ourselves from it	1	2	3	4	5	6	7
19. We have well-defined procedures to search for solutions to strategic problems	1	2	3	4	5	6	7

	Strongly disagree						Strongly agree
20. We tend to develop strategy by experimenting and trying new approaches in the marketplace	1	2	3	4	5	6	7
21. The strategy we follow is dictated by our culture	1	2	3	4	5	6	7
22. Our strategy is a compromise which accommodates the conflicting interests of powerful groups and individuals	1	2	3	4	5	6	7
23. Our strategic direction is determined by powerful individuals or groups	1	2	3	4	5	6	7
24. Barriers exist in our business environment which significantly restrict the strategies we can follow	1	2	3	4	5	6	7
25. Our strategy is made explicit in the form of precise plans	1	2	3	4	5	6	7
26. Our strategy develops through a process of ongoing adjustment	1	2	3	4	5	6	7
27. The strategies we follow develop from 'the way we do things around here'	1	2	3	4	5	6	7
28. The decision to adopt a strategy is influenced by the power of the group sponsoring it	1	2	3	4	5	6	7
29. Our chief executive tends to impose strategic decisions (rather than consulting the top management team)	1	2	3	4	5	6	7
30. Many of the strategic changes which have taken place have been forced on us by those outside this organisation	1	2	3	4	5	6	7
31. We make strategic decisions based on a systematic analysis of our business environment	1	2	3	4	5	6	7
32. Our strategy is continually adjusted as changes occur in the marketplace	1	2	3	4	5	6	7
33. There is resistance to any strategic change which does not sit well with our culture	1	2	3	4	5	6	7
34. Our strategies often have to be changed because certain groups block their implementation	1	2	3	4	5	6	7
35. A senior figure's vision is our strategy	1	2	3	4	5	6	7
36. Forces outside this organisation determine our strategic direction	1	2	3	4	5	6	7

Strategy Development Questionnaire scoring sheet

Instructions

Please transfer the number circled for each statement of the Strategy Development Questionnaire to the corresponding box on the grid below. The number at the left of each box indicates the questionnaire statement to which it refers.

Having transferred the number for all statement to the grid, sum each column. Subtract **24** from each of the column totals to produce a score for each of the perspectives. This score can then be plotted on the strategic development profile by marking a cross on the appropriate one of the six axes. Finally, join all the crosses together by moving clockwise around the profile.

Planning	Incrementalism	Cultural	Political	Command	Enforced choice
1	2	3	4	5	6
7	8	9	10	11	12
13	14	15	16	17	18
19	20	21	22	23	24
25	26	27	28	29	30
31	32	33	34	35	36
Column Total	Column Total	Column Total	Column Total	Column Total	Column Total
−24	−24	−24	−24	−24	−24

Score = Column total −24

Appendix 12.2   *Strategy development profile*

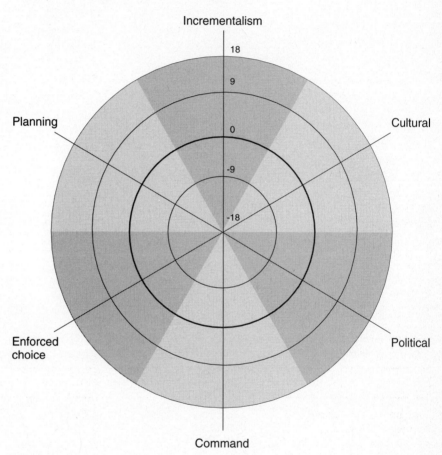

Notes

Part IV
Evaluating and choosing strategic options

13

Portfolio matrices

By David Faulkner

Editor's introduction

Portfolio analyses can facilitate an organisation's assessment of the balance of its mix of services, products or businesses. Section 4.5 of *Exploring Corporate Strategy* illustrates the ideal of portfolio analysis by using the examples of the 'BCG' and other matrices. David Faulkner's chapter usefully extends the traditional use of matrices by taking the attractiveness matrix (*Exploring Corporate Strategy*, Figure 4.11(b)) and asking a further 'question' concerning the relatedness of the competences needed to sustain the various SBUs. In this respect he is engaging with important issues about the overall basis of the organisation's strategy – as addressed in Chapter 6 of *Exploring Corporate Strategy*, particularly Section 6.2.3. This chapter proposes the use of a 'portfolio cube' using the three dimensions of *market attractiveness, organisation's strength* and *relatedness of comptences*. He illustrates this analysis in the case of the Xerox Corporation.

13.1 Introduction

What businesses to be in is a fundamental issue for the corporate board. Traditionally, or at least since the early 1970s, the issue has been addressed by employing one or more of the strategic consultancy company portfolio matrices, the 'box' of the Boston Consulting Group, the directional policy matrix of McKinsey or the life-cycle matrix of Arthur D. Little. However, none of these matrices explicitly takes into account the resource-based theory of the firm (see Chapter 4 of *Exploring Corporate Strategy*) or makes any rigorous attempt to determine the firm's key or core competences (1) in order to discover the area in which the company is most likely to succeed. This chapter briefly describes the three most common portfolio matrices and identifies their respective limitations. It then suggests how the addition of a third axis for 'mesh' can take account of the weakness referred to above.

13.2 The Boston box

The Boston box (2) was the earliest of the matrices to hit the market, and being perhaps the easiest to understand is probably still the most popular in the business world. As shown in Figure 13.1, it has four quadrants and two axes: market growth and relative market share.

The Boston box has the attraction of its simplicity, but it suffers from a number of problems and weaknesses and should be used with caution. The two axes attempt to relate the attractiveness of a market to the inherent strength of the business unit. However, market growth rate is only a very approximate surrogate for market attractiveness. The five forces competitive intensity model (3) illustrates the complexity of the attractiveness concept in which market growth has only one part to play in one of the five identified key forces determining attractiveness. Whether growth is important also depends on whether the business unit concerned has strategic advantage in the key competences that enable the growth to lead to improved results for the company.

Relative market share is also an uncertain surrogate for company strength. Market share can be bought easily by pricing below cost without the possession of any real internal strength. It also refers to the past, not the future and could be said to be more the result than

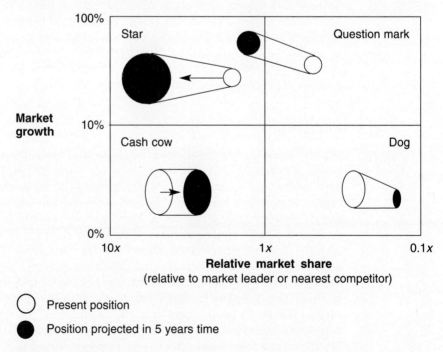

Figure 13.1 The Boston box.

the cause of business unit strength. Economic research almost unfailingly correlates high market share with high profitability (hence strength) but correlations do not of course indicate the direction of causality. Does business strength lead to high market share, does high market share lead to high business strength, or does some third factor cause them both?

The Boston box does not allow for declining markets, applies mostly to fast-moving consumer goods companies and certainly does not apply easily to industrial goods companies, to fragmented industries or to industries in which the experience curve and scale economies give small unit cost advantages. It is also not evident why companies in slow-growth industries who are not market leaders should be divested. Many may still make good profits without requiring large investment funds. Indeed, in many industries it would not be difficult to find examples for the concept of the 'cash dog'. Furthermore, even slow-growth industries exhibit investment opportunities in particular segments or niches, and many well-focused companies in this box may well be acceptably profitable, e.g. Imperial Tobacco. This company is not the market leader, and its industry is in decline. Since it joined the Hanson Group, however, it has shown ever-increasing profitability year on year.

13.3   *The McKinsey directional policy matrix*

The McKinsey matrix (2) attempts to overcome some of the weaknesses of the Boston box by selecting more realistic multidimensional axes to represent industry attractiveness and business strength, as shown in Figure 13.2.

McKinsey are careful not to be over-prescriptive regarding the dimensions of industry attractiveness or of internal business strength. Indeed, they emphasise that the relevant factors will vary from industry to industry. However, if the matrix had been developed after the publication of Porter's *Competitive Strategy* (3) and *Competitive Advantage* (4), it may well be that the five forces industry attractiveness model would be recommended as a means of assessing one axis, and the value chain the other.

This matrix has its axes in reverse to those of the Boston box. They are, however, conceptually similar in that the box where high industry attractiveness meets high business strength leads to a recommendation of investment with the objective of growth, similar to that of the 'star'. Correspondingly, low attractiveness/low strength as with Boston's 'dog' leads to the recommendation 'harvest/divest'. The other boxes follow a similar logic. Although the McKinsey matrix purports to be an investment matrix in contrast to Boston's cash matrix, the distinction is more a formal than a real difference.

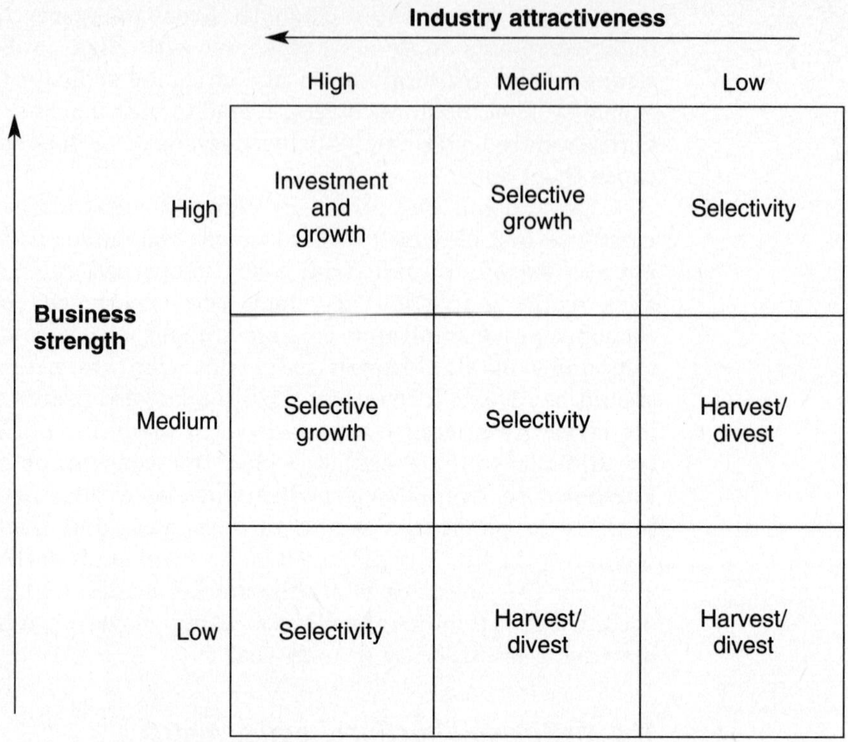

Industry attractiveness

	High	Medium	Low
High	Investment and growth	Selective growth	Selectivity
Medium	Selective growth	Selectivity	Harvest/ divest
Low	Selectivity	Harvest/ divest	Harvest/ divest

Business strength

Figure 13.2   The directional policy matrix.

The major weakness of the McKinsey matrix is that there is no easily applied means of establishing the appropriate weightings for the many dimensions of attractiveness and business strength, and this enables practitioners to bias weightings to meet their already established ideas if they are so inclined. Therefore, in the wrong hands, it can be more of a demonstration tool than an analytical model capable of giving surprising insights. This same criticism can, however, also be levied against the Porter five forces model.

13.4   *The Arthur D. Little life-cycle matrix*

A third variant of the portfolio matrix is the Arthur D. Little life-cycle matrix (ADL) (2). Following the customary internal axis, it chooses competitive position as its measure of the firm's strength, not a far cry from McKinsey's business strength axis although measured somewhat differently. Its other axis is quite different, however. It selects market maturity as its external measure (see Figure 13.3).

This requires it to aver that there are appropriate strategies for any maturity, and therefore that no particular maturity is 'good' or

Stages of industry maturity

	Embryonic	Growth	Mature	Ageing
Dominant	Fast grow Start-up	Fast grow Attain cost leadership Renew Defend position	Defend position Attain cost leadership Renew Fast grow	Defend position Focus Renew Grow with industry
Strong	Start-up Differentiate Fast grow	Fast grow Catch-up Attain cost leadership Differentiate	Attain cost leadership Renew, focus Differentiate Grow in industry	Find niche Hold niche Hang-in Grow with industry Harvest
Favourable	Start-up Differentiate Focus Fast grow	Differentiate, focus Catch-up Grow with industry	Harvest, catch-up Find niche, hold niche Renew, turnaround Differentiate, focus Grow with industry	Retrench Turnaround
Tenable	Start-up Grow with industry Focus	Harvest, catch-up Hold niche, hang-in Find niche Turnaround Focus Grow with industry	Harvest Turnaround Find niche Retrench	Divert Retrench
Weak	Find niche Catch-up Grow with industry	Turnaround Retrench	Withdraw Divest	Withdraw

Competitive position

Figure 13.3   The life-cycle portfolio matrix.

'bad'; indeed, diversified groups such as Hanson or Tompkins seem to prefer that their acquisitions be in mature rather than growth markets, since this often means greater stability and lower demand for investment funds.

Very deterministic rules are applied to this matrix for the calculation of competitive position and market maturity, leading to a positioning on the matrix which, in turn, leads to the recommendation of a very limited range of 'natural' strategic thrusts. A problem here exists in that if every business unit in a particular matrix position adopts the same strategic thrust in a given market, it is difficult to see how competitive advantage will be gained. In business, as in life generally, the winner is often the competitor who does something unusual, rather than the one who applies rigorously a formula known and available to all.

There are other problems attached to this matrix. It is possible through the use of the ADL methodology to determine the maturity of the market concerned. It is not possible, however to determine how quickly the maturing process will take place, or indeed whether it will take place at all. Some products/markets mature very rapidly, e.g. personal computers; others don't seem to mature at all, e.g. houses, staple foods or non-fashion clothing; while others, due to fashion, technology breakthroughs or strong marketing activity, reverse maturity, e.g. watches or sports shoes. As a predictor of the ageing of markets, the matrix is of little use. Its value for strategy guidance must be similarly limited for the same reasons.

13.5   *Other problems*

All three matrices have basic flaws that attach to each of them individually. They also have some limitations that apply to them all collectively. All assume that each business unit has no achieved synergetic relationship with any other. Indeed, if this were not the case it would not be possible to regard the positioning of a strategic business unit (SBU) on a matrix as implying any particular strategic implications, without considering carefully any relationship one SBU might have with any other, be it supplier, distributor, joint economy of scope achiever, or whatever. Strictly speaking, therefore, the portfolio matrix approach to corporate resource allocation can only be used effectively where no synergies are sought between the units. Yet one of the major justifications for the existence of a corporation over and above that of SBUs is the belief that such synergies can be realised and thereby give competitive advantage.

Such matrices are also, by their nature, an example of comparative statics and do not enable accurate insights necessarily to be gained into enduring future trends, but perhaps this is to expect too much. Other criticisms of the portfolio matrices are that they assume that corporations have to be self-sufficient in capital, and must find a use for all internally generated cash, and are incapable of raising more finance for attractive projects. The matrices are also silent on the question of the competitive advantage a business received from being owned by a corporation compared with the costs of owning it.

However, a more fundamental criticism is that, in purporting to provide an aid to the corporate chief executive in his difficult resource allocation decisions involving the product/markets on which to concentrate, they play little if any attention to the growth of risk with increasing unfamiliarity, and of the wisdom of getting involved only in new businesses whose key factors for success relate closely to the corporation's already demonstrated competences. Indeed all three matrices can be used to justify totally unrelated acquisitions based on no clearly existing competences within the corporation whatsoever. As Collis and Montgomery (5) point out:

> 'The problem with the portfolio matrix was that it did not address how value was being created across the divisions. . . . The only relation between them was cash. As we have come to learn, the relatedness of businesses is at the heart of value creation in diversified companies.'

13.6   A new approach to resource allocation

The portfolio matrices described above ignore the question of how the various SBUs in the corporate portfolio might be expected to help each other create value. It is proposed, therefore, to add an additional axis to the normal two axes representing market attractiveness and business strength (1). The third axis will illustrate the closeness of the corporation's core competences to each other, and thus indicate how value may be created in the corporation through the relatedness of the corporation's competences in one market to those in another. The matrix will therefore answer the questions: Which markets are we or should we be in? How attractive are they? How strong are we in the key competences required for success in these markets compared with our competitors? How close are these competences to the core competences of the corporation?

13.6.1   The portfolio cube

Figure 13.4 illustrates the portfolio cube. The position of each SBU in the corporation can be assessed on the market attractiveness axis in the following way. First, a Porter five forces analysis should be carried out to determine the level of competitive intensity in the market and the key structural forces. The future might then be considered by applying a PEST factor checklist, and reviewing the five forces analysis in the light of this. It is important to define the market appropriate to this analysis. In order to do this the degree of substitutability of the products concerned with their nearest needs neighbours should be the guiding factor. Thus a Mini is only substitutable for a Rolls Royce if the would-be traveller is in desperate straits, and should therefore not be considered to be members of the same market for analysis purposes.

Two other key factors need to be considered when assessing the attractiveness of particular markets. Firstly, market size is important. A market may be structurally attractive but very limited in its size and therefore not attractive to a broadly based corporation for that

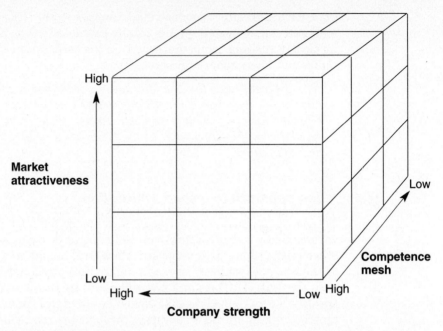

Figure 13.4   *The portfolio cube.*

reason. Indeed, when considering new markets, their potential size is often the first thing a businessperson will consider, as only markets of a substantial size will justify investment of time and resources. The second factor is the price elasticity of demand for the product. Thus if demand is totally price elastic, firms are limited to the role of price takers and no differentiation of product is possible, thus eliminating the opportunity for establishing added value and thus competitive advantage by branding or other similar differentiating methods. As the demand elasticity reduces, however, the opportunity for product differentiation increases, and to that extent the attractiveness of the market to a firm with appropriate key competences.

The second axis of the cube is, as is consistently the case in portfolio matrices, a measure of the strength of the firm in relation to its competitors. The Boston Consulting Group attempt this by measuring relative market share, McKinsey by a range of measures many of which approximate to value chain analysis (4), and ADL estimates the firm's competitive position by means of their own rubric, which includes market share and an evaluation of many internal factors. It is proposed here that the appropriate measure of a firm's competitive strength lies in the level of its possession of the key competences required for success in each particular market. Key competences are those capabilities in a firm measurable in terms of effectiveness (value adding) and efficiency (unit cost reducing) required to succeed in a particular market. They may be contrasted or related to a firm's core competences which are capabilities similarly measured but defined purely as the functions in which the firm is most proficient. Thus, for example, Burroughs might have had excellent core competences in mechanical engineering, which might also have been some of the key competences to succeed in the mechanical adding machine market. They ceased to be key competences, however, with the onset of the electronic age, and core competences that were closely aligned with the required key competences suddenly ceased to be so, and the firm found itself needing to develop new and sometimes alien competences if it was to survive.

The position on the company strength axis of the cube can be determined by constructing a producer matrix, as described in Chapter 2 of *Exploring Corporate Strategy* (1997) (or in Bowman and Faulkner (1)). This will position the firm in terms of its key competences relative to its competitors in each market in which it operates.

The third axis is necessary in order to develop a view on the degree to which the portfolio of SBUs in the corporation's ownership are able to add value to each other by the relatedness of their competences, and thus justify their existence within the same corporation, according to the dictates of the resource-based view (RBV) of the firm. This view suggests that firms are unique bundles of physical and intangible assets, capabilities, and organisational cultures. The configuration of the factors determines how well a company performs its activities, and it is best positioned to succeed where these internal factors are the most appropriate ones for particular markets. The RBV therefore combines both the external and the internal aspects of competitive strategy (see Chapter 4 in *Exploring Corporate Strategy*).

It also suggests that investing in resources that are valuable because they are in high demand in particular markets, are scarce and are difficult to imitate is a good route to corporate success. Some competences may be specific to markets and hence to competitive strategy. Many corporation competences are, however, likely to apply across the board and thus be linchpins of corporate strategy. Thus Disney's brand name, and its skills in characterisation and in animation, apply across more than one potential product/market SBU. The corporation's core competences therefore represent the basic high-level capabilities that should guide it in determining the businesses in which it is most likely to succeed. Some core competences are extremely wide in their application, e.g. Hanson's ability to identify undervalued mature businesses and increase their profitability through tight financial control and strong motivation of SBU managers. Others are much narrower, e.g. when Xerox tried to use its strong brand name to diversify into a complete range of 'office of the future' products, it discovered that the market saw it principally as a photocopier company. By building outwards from limited core competences the corporation can, however, deliberately extend its range of capabilities in an incremental fashion. It is this aspect of the portfolio matrix that the third axis aims to capture.

Xerox and the portfolio cube

The Xerox Group portfolio as at 1982 provides a good example of how the portfolio cube works. During the period prior to that date Xerox had been conscious that its pre-eminence in the plain paper photocopier market was coming to an end. Its patents were running out and the Japanese, with Canon in the lead, were eating away at its market share. In order to combat this assault, Xerox decided to diversify its product range and attempt to become the leading office automation company. As the 'office of the future' took longer to become translated from concepts into actual sales volume, Xerox then decided that they were credible as a major diversified corporation with a wide and varied industry portfolio, and bought into the financial services industry through the acquisition of Crum & Forster, the insurance company. Later in the 1980s, having discovered that such diversification did not lead to high corporate performance, Xerox divested themselves of most of their acquisitions unrelated to xerography, and concentrated on fighting the competition in the areas of their competitive strength, i.e. reprographics. In this they were successful, but only after billions of dollars of shareholders' funds had been lost on unrelated diversification.

In three-dimensional form the Xerox portfolio looked something like Figure 13.5. Xerox's core competences lay in the skills associated with designing, manufacturing, selling and servicing photocopiers. In more detail they could be said to be understanding and operating with electrostatic processes, particularly the process of xerography, providing all the necessary services in relation to photocopiers from design through manufacture to after-sales support services, research and development skills concentrating in this and related areas, and the marketing and distribution of photocopiers and related paper and chemicals. More general competences, or at least strengths, were to be found in the financial strength of the company and its strong brand name, although this latter factor proved problematic, since the company believed its name to be instantly transferable to other products, whereas the market identified it only with photocopiers.

The Xerox portfolio cube attempts to measure on the vertical axis the attractiveness of the market for each of Xerox's products. Along the

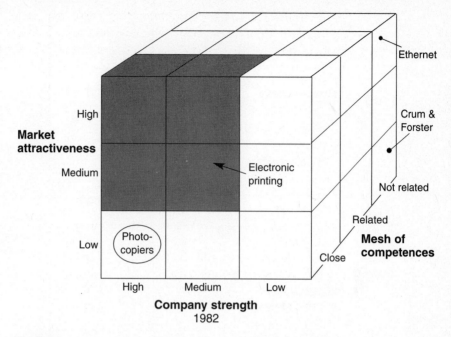

Figure 13.5 *The Xerox portfolio cube.*

Portfolio
- Photocopiers – reprographics
- Paper
- Electric typewriters
- Word processors
- Small computers – Shugart (floppy disk drives) Diablo Systems (daisy wheel printers)

- Fax machines
- Toner and other supplies
- Publicity educational material
- Electronic printing, combining computer technology and xerography
- Ethernet

horizontal axis it measures company strength as in the product matrix by measuring each SBU's competitive strength in the key competences required for success in each segment, and adds to this its market share in order to determine the degree to which the SBU's competences have been successfully translated into success in the marketplace. The third axis assesses the mesh between an individual SBU's core competences and the core competences of the corporation, in this case the competences associated with the xerography business. Using the resource-based view of an appropriate portfolio for a corporation, the shaded area of the cube represents the sub-cube within which it would be recommended that the majority of the portfolio should fall. It can be seen from the figure that only electronic printers (that use electrostatic technology) join the core reprographics business within that sub-cube. Ethernet, while in an attractive market, is not closely related to reprographic technologies, and Xerox are not strong in it. Crum &

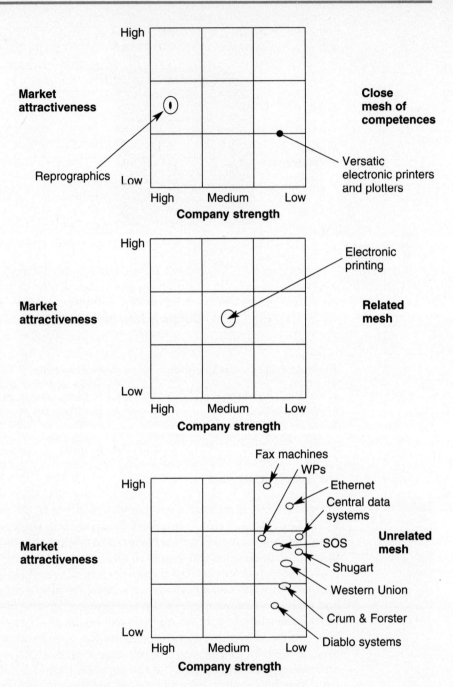

Figure 13.6　Xerox's portfolio.

Case study 13.1

Forster are neither in an attractive market nor particularly strong, and they are quite unrelated to Xerox's known competences. It is, perhaps, not surprising that the stock market marked Xerox shares drastically down when news of the intended purchase reached it.

Figure 13.6 breaks the cube out into its three planes to project a better view of the individual SBUs of the portfolio. It can be seen that only the Versatic product range of electrostatic printers and plotters are closely meshed to Xerox technology, and the company is not strong in this market, nor is the market particularly attractive. Electronic printing comes within the related mesh plane, but the vast majority of the acquisitions and developments fall within the unrelated plane and suggest, therefore, on the basis of the RBV a poorly constructed portfolio, with few synergies between the SBUs and an excess of products in areas in which Xerox cannot demonstrate high degrees of core competence.

Despite the disapproval of Wall Street of its acquisition of the insurance company Crum & Forster against all RBV logic, Xerox went further and acquired Furman Selz, an investment bank, and Van Kampen Merritt, a mutual fund business. The remainder of the 1980s saw Xerox working hard to improve the performance of its traditional core business, with some success, and devoting an increasing level of resources to its new love, financial services. Indeed, by 1991 financial services operations contributed one-third of Xerox's revenues, but only 3 per cent of its profits. In 1991, under a new chairman, Xerox decided to divest itself entirely of its financial services arm. Xerox shareholders have thus had to pay a heavy price for Xerox's directors' decision to ignore the dictates of RBV theory and develop a corporate portfolio without reference to the corporation's core competences.

13.7 Summary

The three traditional portfolio matrices show, in their different ways, how business strength and market attractiveness can be combined in relation to a portfolio of SBUs to give a picture of the balance and potential of a corporation's businesses. They do not, however, give any indication of how the SBUs relate, in terms of their contributions, to each other and to the corporation as a whole. The addition of a third axis labelled 'mesh' attempts to address this question and makes portfolio matrices usable for advocates of the development of strategy through the resource-based view of the firm.

References

(1)   Bowman, C.C. and Faulkner, D.O. (1996). *Competitive and Corporate Strategy*, London: Irwin.
(2)   Hax, A.C. and Majluf, N.S. (1991). *The Strategy Concept and Process: A Pragmatic Approach*, New Jersey: Prentice Hall.
(3)   Porter, M.E. (1980). *Competitive Strategy*, New York: The Free Press.
(4)   Porter, M.E. (1985). *Competitive Advantage*, New York: The Free Press.
(5)   Collis, D.K. and Montgomery, C.A. (1995). 'Competing on resources', *Harvard Business Review*, July/August, 118–128.

14

Gap analysis

By Jon Billsberry

Editor's introduction

In assessing strategies for the future, managers are usually concerned with understanding the *incentive to change* – in other words, the extent to which current strategies (if unchanged) would fall short of meeting the organisation's aspirations and/or obligations. Gap analysis is one approach to assessing the need for change, as explained in Section 8.2.2 of *Exploring Corporate Strategy*. Jon Billsberry's chapter takes the general idea of 'bridging the gap' and looks in detail at the various different 'elements' of future strategies which might contribute to filling the gap. He does this through a systematic identification of what he calls 'market structure profile growth opportunities'.

14.1   *Introduction*

Gap analysis can help the manager better understand the dynamics of the competitive environment. Importantly, it can be used to reveal where an organisation has weaknesses, and where it has strengths, in relation to its competitors. Such an analysis helps the manager develop strategies to catch market leaders, or strategies to stay ahead of the chasing pack.

Following this introduction, the chapter is divided into four sections. In the first section, gap analysis is defined, and it is noted that gap analysis is interpreted in many different ways. For example, there are descriptive and analytical variations and each has its use. The second section looks at performance gap analysis and shows how the manager can use the idea to gain an overview of the organisation's strategy. The third section looks at a more detailed model of gap analysis which concentrates on product and market analysis. The final section discusses some of the practical considerations that the manager should be aware of when using gap analysis. These practical considerations include the need to use both quantitative and qualitative performance indicators and the fact that 'gaps' are dynamic and ever-changing.

14.2   *What is gap analysis?*

Gap analysis is a technique that can be understood in many different ways. The common theme running through all of the definitions of gap analysis is, not surprisingly, the word 'gap'. The dictionary defines the word 'gap' in a number of ways:

- as a physical space between things
- as a period of time when not involved in a particular activity
- when something is missing that prevents the successful completion of an activity
- as a great difference between two things, people or ideas.

The analysis of all four of these forms of 'gap' can be considered as gap analysis. However, there are some usages that are more common, and generally of more use to the manager, than some of the others. The simplest useful form of gap analysis merely involves a search for 'gaps' in the market. In many respects, when gap analysis is used in this way, the term is being used as a surrogate for market research and segmentation. An alternative simple usage is as a tool to look at the differences between competitors. Again, when used in this context, gap analysis is being used as a surrogate. In this case, it is being used as a surrogate for competitor analysis (see Chapter 7).

More usefully, gap analysis is less concerned with the fact that there is a gap between things, than with how to close the gap. Recognition of the fact that a gap exists is only one stage in the process. Having recognised that there is a gap, the manager needs to develop strategies that will close the gap, manage the process of change, and finally, monitor the process to ensure that the same gap does not reappear and, if possible, to open a favourable gap with the competition. The process of gap analysis can thus be portrayed pictorially (Figure 14.1).

14.3   *Performance gap analysis*

A simple, but very powerful, approach to gap analysis centres around three questions:

1   Where are we now?
2   Where do we want to get to?
3   How can we get there?

These three questions can be portrayed graphically, as shown in

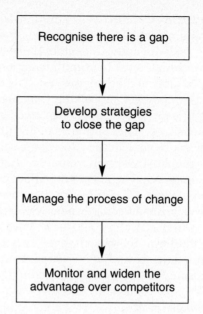

Figure 14.1   *A model of gap analysis.*

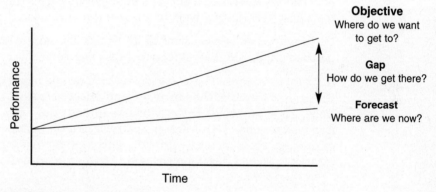

Figure 14.2   *Performance gap analysis.*

Figure 14.2, which illustrates how simple performance gap analysis can be. Used in such a manner, the three questions have relevance in almost every planning and forecasting scenario. Their usage tends to frame the nature of the planning and forecasting problem being faced and allows the application of other strategic planning techniques, such as STEP, SWOT (Chapter 8), culture web (Chapter 9), portfolio matrices (Chapter 13), with a purpose and direction.

When gaps are found, the manager has three alternative courses of action:

1 *Redefine the objectives.* The first thing to do when a discrepancy between objectives and forecast is found is to check that the objectives
   are realistic and achievable. If objectives have deliberately been set at
   a very high level to stimulate action, it is usually advisable to set less
   high, intermediate objectives. This course of action avoids the problem
   of the manager perceiving that his or her actions will not make any
   significant impact upon objectives which can lessen motivation.
2 *Do nothing.* This option is under-utilised by the manager, but should
   always be considered. Reorganisation and redirection is commonplace
   in the business environment, but it is clear that people become
   'change-weary' and that continual change can lead to defensive behaviour, increased staff turnover, decreased levels of satisfaction and
   lower levels of commitment. Sometimes giving people time to 'bed in'
   to a new structure and new ways of doing things pays greater divi-
   dends than another change. This is particularly the case, when previous initiatives have centred around the development of talent, the
   training of staff, or the introduction of new staff, as all of these will
   take time to have an effect.
3 *Change the strategy.* When a gap is found between objectives and forecast and the first two options have been considered and rejected, the
   only alternative is to change the current strategy and develop a new
   one. Having identified a gap, the manager now uses the other strategic
   tools described in this book to analyse the various options available.

Performance gaps consist of three segments: improvement gaps, expansion gaps, and diversification gaps (Figure 14.3).

* *Improvement gaps.* These are gaps which can be narrowed by internal
  changes to improve the efficiency and effectiveness of existing operations: 'How can we do better what we already do?'
* *Expansion gaps.* These are gaps which can be narrowed by internal
  strategies that increase growth, such as increasing market penetration, product development and targeting new markets

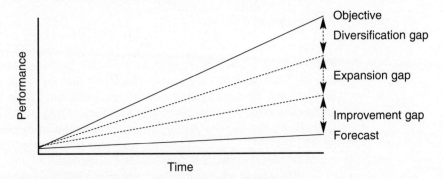

Figure 14.3 Diversification, expansion and improvement gaps.

- *Diversification gaps.* When improvement and expansion strategies have been considered and found not to close the gap fully, the manager has to conclude that the objective cannot be met from existing businesses and therefore must consider strategies of organisational-level growth. These strategies include growth strategies of both diversification and integration, the stability strategy of harvesting, and the defence strategies of divestment and liquidation.

14.4 Product and market gap analysis

Weber (1) proposes an alternative model of gap analysis that examines the gap between an organisation's sales potential and its actual performance. Although Weber's approach to gap analysis is from a marketing perspective, it is clearly relevant as it provides a framework for addressing the type of gaps commonly experienced by strategic managers.

Rather than analyse the gap between objectives and forecasts, Weber is interested in the gap between the potential in the market and the firm's current sales. To begin to use his model you therefore need to measure these two variables. Hopefully, the manager should know the current level of sales. The second variable, industry market potential (IMP), is calculated in the following way:

IMP = (No. of relevant consumers) × (No. of *use* occasions per relevant consumer which arise per relevant consumer per operating period)

When conducting product and market gap analysis, it is important to distinguish every market that the organisation's products and services supply, because analysing multiple markets as an amalgam hides influences. To avoid this, the manager should only combine products or services in a market gap analysis when they perform the same function, i.e. they are functional substitutes. If a product or service addresses more than one market, the manager should conduct an analysis of the market structure profile for every market.

The potential of every market is not static. Weber contends that markets can be enlarged in four ways:

- natural changes, such as for demographic reasons
- new uses of the product, or new user segments
- innovative product differentiation
- adding new product lines.

By forming an understanding of the current position and the potential of the market, the manager is in a position to analyse the gap between the two. There are four components to this gap, and each of these gaps can be addressed by the internal strategies, detailed below and outlined in Figure 14.4.

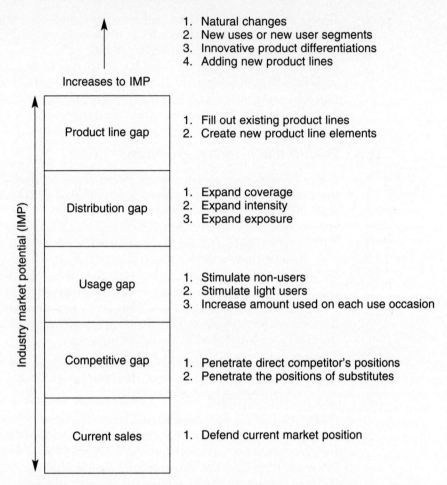

Figure 14.4   *A summary of market structure profile growth opportunities (adapted from Weber (1)).*

14.4.1   Product line gaps

To analyse product line, or indeed service line, gaps, the manager begins by specifying all the possible alternative elements that can be recognised within the product. These elements might include price, size, quality, colour, flavour, value or anything else that differentiates one product from another. Once this has been done and compared to the competition, the manager has two options:

- Develop products or services where the organisation is under-represented.
- Create new products or services through innovation or significant product differentiation.

14.4.2 Distribution gaps

A distribution gap exists when customers are unable to purchase an existing product or service when they would like to. There are three reasons why this can occur:

- *Coverage gap*. This is when a geographical region is not served by the organisation
- *Intensity gap*. This occurs when a product or service is not offered for sale in a region where the organisation has a physical presence
- *Exposure gap*. This occurs when products or services are available for customers but cannot be seen for such reasons as inadequate shelf space, poor location or inappropriate promotion.

14.4.3 Usage gaps

A usage gap occurs when customers are not using the product or service to the full when they have a need to do so. Customers can be segmented into three categories: those that could use the product or service but do not; those who use the product or service occasionally, but not on every occasion when they need to use it; and those using the product or service to its full extent. There are three growth strategies, each of which addresses a separate segment:

- Encourage non-users to use the product or service
- Encourage light users to use the product or service more often: i.e. encourage loyalty and repeat buying
- Encourage greater use of the product or service: this might involve augmenting the product or service, or simply an encouragement to use more (e.g. 'Can you eat *three* shredded wheat?').

14.4.4 Competitive gaps

The competitive gap is the gap left when the product line, distribution and usage gaps (the amalgamation of these three gaps is broadly similar to Ansoff's (2) portfolio gap') have been closed. There are three strategies that can be adopted to narrow competitive gaps:

- Penetrate the market share of direct competitors
- Penetrate the market share of those who sell substitutes
- Defend the existing market position.

The strategies outlined are summarised in Figure 14.4, and Illustration 14.1 presents a case study for J. Sainsbury plc.

Strategy in action

Illustration 14.1

J. Sainsbury plc

In Spring 1996, J. Sainsbury plc announced financial results that saw them slip from the position of number one UK food retailer for the first time. Commenting on the results, David Sainsbury, chairman of J. Sainsbury plc, said: 'In the 1970s and 1980s, Tesco was larger in terms of market share but we were still seen as the market leader. . . . We would always like to be market leader leading in innovation, quality and customer service rather than market share. That is not to say we wouldn't want to be leader on market share as well.' In assessing the results, BZW's food retail analyst, David McCarthy, suggested that 'The company needs to reposition and to match competitor initiatives.'

In the early 1990s, it is clear that Sainsbury's failed to respond to the market, product and service innovations of competitors. This 'taking the eye off the ball' was uncharacteristic for an organisation that had introduced many exciting food-retailing concepts that had disadvantaged their competitors. An example of such innovation included the introduction of quality own-label products. When the poor results were announced in spring 1996, Sainsbury's unveiled plans about how they would close the gap with the market leader, Tesco. The main weapon in their armoury would be the launch of a nation-wide loyalty card. Tesco had been operating such a scheme for the past year and had attracted more than five million members. Clearly, Sainsbury's viewed this as a major reason why Tesco had overtaken them. In an effort to improve on Tesco's scheme, Sainsbury's said that they planned, in addition to a loyalty card, a credit card and other financial services such as deposit accounts, pensions and personal equity plans. Interestingly, within a month of this announcement, Tesco had launched its own form of credit card (actually a form of budget account) on the back of its Clubcard, ahead of the launch of the Sainsbury's card.

Food retail analyst at NatWest Securities, Tony MacNeary, said the following about the proposals of Sainsbury's: 'One has to wonder how much bang for their buck they are going to get.'

The thinking of Sainsbury's seems quite transparent. If they measured

14.5 Practical considerations

There are three practical considerations which are important to remember when analysing gaps:

1 *How do you assess performance?* First thoughts tend to go to quantitative methods such as measures of profit, return on capital employed, sales volume, market share, and so on. Of course these are important, and you will find help on these topics elsewhere in this book, but it is worth briefly stressing the importance of qualitative performance indicators. These can be most illuminating and will explain much cus-

Illustration 14.2 continued

the gap with the market leaders using the model of gap analysis presented above, the decision to launch a customer loyalty card appears a sensible and natural choice. Distribution gaps were largely negligible, given the penetration of all major stores across the country. However, Tesco's purchase of the William Low supermarkets in Scotland, plans to enter European markets, and the introduction of Metro stores – a city centre mini-supermarket concept – reminded Sainsbury's that this might be the next gap to increase. Product line gaps with Tesco's were being addressed with the development of an own-label Economy range in response to Tesco's. However, this highlighted another issue for Sainsbury's: half of the 20,000 product lines sold in each supermarket were own-label, resulting in relatively little choice of branded goods. In regard to the competitive gap, Tesco's marketing campaign 'Every little helps' had successfully changed customer perceptions of the supermarket from one of 'pile it high, sell it cheap' to one of 'quality and value' at a time when these factors had become a priority for customers. Sainsbury's marketing campaign 'Everyone's favourite ingredient', where mannered celebrities related their favourite recipe using Sainsbury's ingredients, reinforced its middle-class, high-quality image, but distanced itself from a 'value for money' supermarket. Ironically, while sales of the mentioned ingredients increased in Sainsbury's, they also increased in the stores of competitors. But it was the Tesco Clubcard that had had most impact on the usage gap. It stimulated light users by encouraging them to do all their shopping in Tesco through the offer of generous money-off vouchers related to the amount spent (effectively money-back vouchers). In addition, Clubcard members received not inconsiderable money-off vouchers against 'mainstream' products. The Clubcard might also have had a small impact on ticket values as well. But Clubcard was effective because once tried and used, the vouchers had the effect of 'converting' customers from other retailers, which is the ultimate prize in supermarket retailing. It is not surprising, therefore, that Sainsbury's decided that it had to bite the bullet and launch its own loyalty card. It was not, after all, as David Sainsbury had described Tesco's Clubcard on its launch, 'electronic Green Shield stamps'.

tomer reaction. For example, in the J. Sainsbury illustration, Tesco will almost certainly have used focus groups to assess customer attitudes and impressions of quality. The decision to launch a budget card is difficult to justify in quantitative terms, but in-depth interviews with customers and focus groups could gauge reaction to the Clubcard and suggest enhancements (e.g. to allow petrol purchases to count towards Clubcard points) and developments (e.g. the Clubcard plus budget card scheme).

2   *Gap analysis is used by market leaders as well as followers. How can the performance gap with followers be increased?* The J. Sainsbury example illustrated how a follower, J. Sainsbury, could use gap analy-

sis to find ways (i.e. launching a loyalty card) to close the gap with the market leader. However, within the illustration there are examples of the market leader using gap analysis to develop initiatives to pull away from the followers. The extension into Europe, the budget card, and the Metro stores all have the goal of increasing the gap with followers.

3   *Gaps are dynamic.* This point follows on from the previous one. It is important to remember that while one organisation is trying to close or increase a gap, other parties are trying to improve it for themselves. When reading the J. Sainsbury example you may have thought 'too little, too late'. This seems most apt and the point was made most sharply when Tesco's launched a budget card before Sainsbury's, even though Sainsbury's had announced it first. Followers should not just analyse where market leaders are now, but where the market leaders will be by the time their own new initiatives have had time to have an effect. As a result, new initiatives should address the gap between where the market leader is and will be by the time the initiatives have come to fruition. You have to work twice as hard as the leaders to catch them.

14.6   Summary

At first glance, gap analysis might appear a little superficial. But such an impression mistakes the purpose of the tool. Unlike many of the other techniques discussed in this book, it is not the honed analytical tool from finance, management science or marketing. Instead, gap analysis is a 'first stage' technique that gives the manager a 'feel' for the size and nature of the strategic problem. Gap analysis frames the problem and informs the manager about the directions in which to look for solutions. Once this direction has been established, other techniques can then come into play. As such, gap analysis is a vital weapon in the strategic manager's armoury.

References

(1)   Weber, J.A. (1977) 'Market structure profile analysis and strategic growth opportunities', *California Management Review*, **XX** (1), 34–46. Fall.

(2)   Ansoff, H.I. (1987) *Corporate Strategy* (revised edition), London: Penguin.

15

Understanding and using shareholder value analysis

By Roger W. Mills

Editor's introduction

Shareholder value analysis (SVA) is concerned with assessing whether strategic developments are likely to result in an increased value for the shareholders. This involves an analysis of how value is created and managed in the organisation – starting with the identification of the key value drivers. This is explained in Section 8.3.1 of *Exploring Corporate Strategy*. Roger Mills's chapter shows in detail how such an analysis can be done. His worked example shows both the 'mainstream' analysis and the associated questions, issues and assumptions which link the financial analysis to the decisions and judgements about future strategies. He also gives some useful advice as to when SVA analysis is likely to be most useful.

15.1 *Introduction*

The terms shareholder value and shareholder value analysis (SVA) have been attracting considerable interest in the UK in recent times (1–3). All too often shareholder value is associated with traditional earnings-based measures of performance, such as earnings per share, while SVA is a generic term given to a number of approaches which, for a publicly traded corporation, are used to relate its share price to managerial perceptions of future cash flow performance. This is achieved by focusing attention upon the present value of estimated future short- and long-term cash flows.

In fact, the principles which underpin SVA are not new. It is well established in project finance and investment appraisal procedures for major projects, such as acquisitions (4). However, what is different about SVA is its application in valuing the corporation and the use of such a valuation approach in managing the business. Often this involves developing a new – or, at the very least, modified – set of performance measures to replace the previous dominance of accounting performance indicators for managing the business. More broadly, and what is often not well appreciated, is the usefulness and adaptiveness of the approach for such issues as evaluating joint ventures and not-for-profit organisations (5).

SVA has all the appearances of being just a financial tool, but it is really multidisciplinary. It draws not only on corporate finance, but also on strategy, marketing and scenario analysis. It also comes in different forms, although most share one common feature – an emphasis upon discounted cash flow analysis. The different forms often relate more to the particular focus of attention of the originator than to substance. In this chapter, the main alternative forms will be reviewed, followed by an overview of an SVA calculation and its application. Merger and acquisition analysis will be used to illustrate the potential value and power of the approach as a tool for assessing its underlying benefit in evaluating strategic options of all types.

15.2   SVA frameworks

Alternative SVA frameworks for assessing potential value creation include:

- shareholder value analysis
- strategic value analysis
- economic value added (EVA)
- 'spread' methods.

The framework known as shareholder value analysis is reliant upon the net present value approach commonly used for purposes of investment appraisal (6). Using this method, projected cash flows for a planning period and beyond for each business unit in a corporation can be estimated by management, converted into a present value and aggregated. When divided by the number of common shares, the result provides an estimate of the shareholder value per share. Strategic value analysis has much in common with this approach and focuses substantially upon issues relating to the time period over which value may be created, the implications associated with the selection of an appropriate planning horizon and the strategic implementation of the approach within business units (7). It has a very strong link with scenario analysis and the analysis of business- and market-specific risks (8).

Economic value added (EVA) also draws upon the principles of discounted cash flow. EVA for any time period is the product of total capital and the difference between net operating profit after taxes (expressed in cash flow terms) as a percentage of capital and the weighted average cost of capital (WACC). While EVA focuses upon a given time period, its proponents use market value added (MVA) to show long-term total value creation or destruction, where MVA is defined as capital plus the present value of projected EVA. In fact, the results of applying shareholder value analysis, strategic value analysis and economic value added can be shown to be the same (9).

In addition to frameworks which draw upon the net present value principle, there are those which view value creation or destruction by comparing the 'spread' between the return generated and some measure of the cost of capital. Approaches to calculating the return generated may differ. They can be measured using an internal rate of return calculation or by adjusting accounting returns into cash flow terms.

15.3 Value drivers

Irrespective of the framework adopted, potential future benefits are typically translated into financial forecasts using the key business factors that drive value creation. These are often known as 'value drivers'. In generic terms, using the shareholder value frameworks, these can be expressed as:

1 Sales growth.
2 Operating profit margin.
3 Cash tax rate.
4 Working capital investment to support future growth, known as incremental working capital investment (IWCI).
5 Fixed asset investment to support (a) current levels of activity, known as replacement fixed capital investment (RFCI), and (b) future growth, known as incremental fixed capital investment (IFCI).
6 Cost of capital.
7 Growth duration (planning) period.

Cash flows are determined with reference to the first five value drivers. These cash flows are estimated over the growth duration (planning) period, and then discounted to a present value using the cost of capital.

A good illustration of the use of these seven value drivers has been provided by Price Waterhouse (3). It developed ValueBuilder with the primary objectives being to validate and evaluate current business strategies, and it draws extensively upon these seven value drivers. Using its software, Price Waterhouse benchmarks a company's performance in terms of these seven value drivers against key competitors. This is then used to indicate where strategies can be modified to enhance value and to formulate and implement courses of action necessary to achieve the business goals.

In fact, one of the key distinguishing features of most shareholder value approaches is the focus of attention upon using managerial judgements, as expressed in the form of value drivers to generate value estimates. By understanding what it is that drives performance in terms of shareholder value, it is considered that management will be able to focus upon what really matters. However, not all value drivers will be equally important, and by building a value model it is generally possible to identify those which have the greatest impact upon value.

15.4   *Calculating shareholder value*

Using these seven value drivers a relatively crude, but effective, initial valuation can be undertaken. In Table 15.1 the seven value drivers are shown for a business with a growth duration period of five years, and in Table 15.2 they are used to produce the future cash flow and value forecasts illustrated for year 1.

The free cash flow line in Table 15.2 is calculated as follows. Current sales receipts are £100m and are expected to grow by 5 per cent at the end of year 1. Of the £105m, 90 per cent has been assumed to be consumed by cash outflows in the form of costs, resulting in the 10 per cent operating profit margin of £10.5m. Cash tax, the sum expected to be paid out as distinct from that to be provided in the accounts, must be deducted from the operating profit and then depreciation added back to determine operating cash flow. Such a cash flow requires expenditure on assets which wear out or become obsolescent if it is to be sustainable in the future. If the intention is to increase the business, as implied in this case by a sales growth rate, then an allowance for incremental fixed and working capital must be included. This is calculated in the example below using the percent of sales method. For year 1, IFCI is 4 per cent and IWCI is 3 per cent. Given the 5 per cent sales growth rate, sales increase by £5m with IFCI being 4 per cent of this increase (£0.2m) and IWCI 3 per cent (£0.15m). Of course, many different methods can be used for

Table 15.1   *Five-year growth period*

	Year					
	1	2	3	4	5	Beyond
Value drivers	(%)	(%)	(%)	(%)	(%)	(%)
1. Sales growth rate (SGR)	5	10	10	15	15	0
2. Operating profit margin (OPM)	10	10	12	12	14	14
3. Cash tax rate (CTR)	30	30	30	30	30	30
4. IFCI	4	6	3	2	2	0
5. IWCI	3	3	4	3	2	0
6. Cost of capital (COC)	12	12	12	12	12	12

Table 15.2   *Future cash flow and value forecast*

	Year 1 (£m)
Sales receipts (currently £100m)	105
Operating profit	10.5
Less: Cash tax	3.15
Profit after tax	7.35
Add: Depreciation	5.00
Operating cash flow	12.35
Less: RFCI	5.00
Less: IFCI	0.20
Less: IWCI	0.15
Free cash flow	7.00
Discount factor (12% cost of capital)	0.89
Present value (Free cash flow)	**6.25**

these calculations and their size will be contingent upon many factors. For example, in a start-up situation one would expect these to be very large and often much greater than the cash inflows. Once determined, they are deducted to arrive at the free cash flow. This is then discounted at the cost of capital to express it in present value terms.

By using the same method for calculating cash flows and value over a five-year planning period and beyond (assuming zero sales growth after year 5), the result is a present value of £112.86m, made up of £35m from the planning period and £75.86m from the period beyond. As indicated, the £35m from the planning period is the result of discounting the free cash flows for the five-year planning period, these free cash flows having been calculated from the value drivers shown in Table 15.1. The value beyond the five-year planning period is known as the residual value and, as the illustration reveals, this value may account for the largest proportion of total value. For our example company, using the data provided in Table 15.1, it accounts for 69 per cent of the total present value (cumulative present value from the planning period plus the residual value) at the end of year 5. Using the SVA framework this value is calculated by assuming that sales growth ceases at the end of the five-year planning period and that the resulting cash flows from the period immediately beyond can be valued as a perpetuity.

The seven value drivers are rarely adequate for specific valuation applications. Questions about the composition of each of the seven value drivers for specific businesses need to be asked and the value for the whole organisation typically needs to be analysed as a number of valuations, say by principal lines of business (PLBs).

Some value drivers can be broken down by activity and process. For example, the operating profit margin – which, for any given year, is the difference between revenues and costs – may be heavily influenced by competitive factors which may or may not be controllable. However, we cannot ignore the influence capable of being exerted by management in terms of activities and processes. This being so, the costs could be looked at in terms of activities that influence them.

All value drivers should be capable of being disaggregated in similar fashion, the purpose being to make them meaningful in managerial terms. This is because the key objective is to link value creation with managerial action. Only by looking at the value drivers in such terms can a meaningful SVA system be seriously contemplated.

The application of the seven value drivers in the manner described does not produce the measure known as shareholder value. The result of adding the present values from the planning period, and thereafter, is known as 'business value'. Thus, in the earlier example, we could imagine the value of £112.86m as being that relating to just one business unit. By aggregating the values for all other business units the result is an aggregate business value. If we imagine two other business units with a combined value of £200m, the total business value is £312.86m.

In order to calculate shareholder value two adjustments to this business value are necessary. First, if the business holds any investments from which income is derived, but which are not included in the free cash flows, then the value of these investments must be added to the business value to determine what is known as corporate value. That part of corporate value actually receivable by shareholders will be calculated *after* any outside debts or obligations have been repaid. Therefore, by deducting the market value of external debt and obligations shareholder value can be found. If we assume that the value of investments is £87.14m, corporate value is £400m. If we also assume that the value of debt is £100m, the shareholder value is £300m. By dividing this shareholder value by the number of issued ordinary shares, an estimate of shareholder value per share can be calculated. For a quoted company this means that a comparison can be made with the published share price, and any potential value gap can be identified. So, in our example, if the number of ordinary shares is 100m, the shareholder value per share is £3. Assuming the share price to be £2.20 there is a value gap of £0.80, implying some potential value capable of being 'unlocked'. Such situations are the fabric of acquisition activity. If value from a potential target looks substantially greater than the existing share price, there is a potential opportunity not currently being realised. In different hands, this position might be changed with the new acquirer standing to benefit substantially, provided of course that the price paid is right. More will be covered on this shortly when the framework for acquisition analysis is reviewed and its potential explored more broadly for the analysis of all manner of strategic options.

15.5 *Growth duration period and residual value*

One very important influence upon value is the time period to be taken into consideration. Its importance can be understood if we consider two very simple statistics – the price earnings (PE) multiple and the planning periods frequently used by UK companies. The average PE multiple for UK publicly quoted company shares has been reckoned to be 16 times. Crudely, this can be interpreted as implying that the market puts a value of 16 years on the current after-tax earnings attributable to shareholders. Given that many businesses plan for somewhere in the region of five years, there is the potential for what can be thought of as a 'value gap'. To prevent such a gap, a longer term business planning horizon is required by managers. This raises a problem because planning for five years can often be difficult enough. To avoid this, shareholder value approaches include the estimated value beyond the planning period, which has been introduced as the residual value.

You will remember, in the earlier example, that by using the same method for calculating cash flows and value over a five-year planning period and beyond (assuming zero sales growth after year 5), the result was a present value of £112.86m made up of £35m from the planning period and £75.86m from the period beyond. As indicated, the £35m from the planning period was the result of discounting the free cash flows for the five-year planning period, these free cash flows having been calculated from the value drivers shown in Table 15.1. The value beyond the five-year planning period, known as the residual value, calculated using a perpetuity calculation, accounted for the largest proportion of total value: 69 per cent of the total present value (cumulative present value from the planning period plus the residual value) at the end of year 5.

Business strategy frameworks can be used in principle to help to understand the issues associated with identifying an appropriate valuation period in the form of two related time periods – a planning period, the limit of which is the point in time where competitive advantage will disappear, and the continuing period beyond it. By estimating the planning period, the total value-creating potential of a business can be estimated relatively straightforwardly (in principle). These are discounted at the required rate of return (cost of capital) and aggregated. To the resulting net present value of the planning period, the residual value is added (Figure 15.1).

Of particular importance is the value beyond the planning period, which may be estimated by calculating the perpetuity value of the

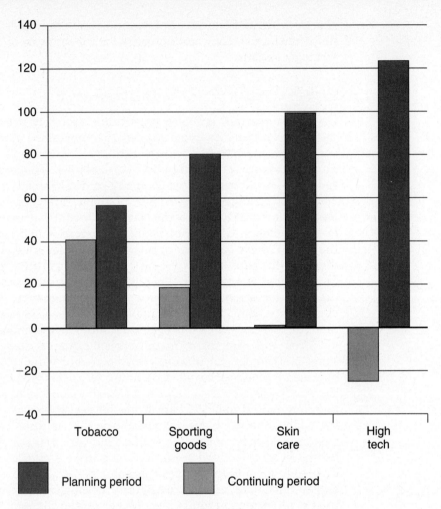

Figure 15.1   Value creation beyond a planning period.

cash flow in the period immediately following the planning period. This is then discounted to express it in present-day terms.

In fact, a noteworthy feature of the shareholder value approach is the emphasis it places upon value creation beyond the planning period. As McKinsey and Company have shown, the contribution of such value to the total may be very significant (10). They illustrate (Figure 15.1) that, in four industries, continuing (often called residual) value accounts for anywhere between 56 and 125 per cent of total value.

Typically, the perpetuity calculation used in a shareholder value calculation assumes that the cash flow in the last year of the planning period allowing for capital expenditure to finance replacement needs is representative of the future into infinity. While many at first sight take exception to the valuation of an infinite cash flow, it is important to recognise that very little value is generated in the very long term. This can be appreciated if we consider the present value of £1 at a rate of 15 per cent. At the end of year 1 the present value is £0.87, at the end of year 5, it is £0.497, and at the end of 20 years it is only £0.061. The higher the rate selected, the greater is the fall-off in value. For example, at 30 per cent the values for these time periods are £0.769, £0.269 and £0.005, respectively.

There may be occasions where the view is held that even beyond the planning period there will be continued growth. In such a case, the perpetuity can be calculated by assuming that growth in free cash flows will occur. This involves the estimation of a growth factor which is deducted from the cost of capital to allow for growth in the free cash flows. Assuming a free cash flow of £10m, a cost of capital of 12.5 per cent and a growth factor of 2.5 per cent, the perpetuity with growth would be £100m (£10m/(12.5−2.5 per cent)) as opposed to £80m (£10m/12.5 per cent) without.

Approaches other than the perpetuity are also used. Where the time horizon is seen as being finite, an annuity calculation may be used. Alternatively, any of the following might be adopted:

- price earnings multiple
- market book multiple
- estimated market value of assets.

15.6 The cost of capital

The cost of capital used typically has a significant impact upon shareholder value. This is particularly so where a perpetuity calculation is used to determine the residual value component. Use of the perpetuity is based on the assumption that a company that is able to generate returns above the cost of capital (i.e. achieve excess returns) will attract competitors, whose entry into the business will drive down returns to the minimum acceptable cost of capital rate. Thus, the assumption is made that after the forecast period, the company will earn, on average, its cost of capital on new investments. The perpetuity does not necessarily assume that all future cash flows will be identical. It assumes that the rate of return on future cash flows is equal to the long-term cost of capital.

While the perpetuity approach is one of the most conservative methods, its use in a shareholder value calculation will make the valuation particularly sensitive to the cost of capital. For example, in the analysis of the Glaxo–Wellcome acquisitions by James Capel, each one percentage point increase in the group's cost of capital decreased the shareholder value to the base case value they estimated by 75p (11).

In studies of practice, companies have been found to use a company-wide cost of capital. For example, a survey conducted in the USA showed that roughly one-third of Fortune 1,000 US companies used a single cost of capital (12). Similar results were found in a UK study of practice referred to earlier (4). The problem of using a company-wide rate is that it may overstate the risk associated with low-risk projects leaving managers with what has been termed a 'lie or die' choice – that is, either lie about the real situation or have no chance of obtaining future investment and growth.

Estimating the cost of capital is difficult in practice, particularly if the risk–return relationship is to be incorporated on a business unit basis. At the least, the steps that need to be followed in estimating the cost of capital are:

1 Estimate the cost of equity.
2 Estimate the cost of debt.
3 Determine the cost of capital by weighting the cost of equity and the cost of debt by the projected proportion of debt and equity in the capital structure.

Of these three steps the most difficult and controversial concerns the estimation of the cost of equity. Modern financial theory suggests that the cost of equity can be estimated from analysing the return investors require when buying a share. Their requirement can be estimated using the capital asset pricing model, known as CAPM. The underlying premise of the approach is the more risk an investor is required to take on, the higher the rate of return that will be expected. In fact, CAPM is in a class of market models called risk-premium models which rely on the assumption that every individual holding a risky security will demand a return in excess of the return they would receive from a risk-free security. This excess return is the premium to compensate the investor for the risk. Put in everyday terms, a UK investor could invest in UK government securities which are reckoned to be risk free. Logically this can be thought of as a benchmark against which to compare other investment opportunities – more risk will have to be compensated by more return.

The risk premium in CAPM is measured by the beta. Betas for quoted companies can be extracted typically from published sources, such as the London Business School Risk Measurement Service. This risk is called systematic, market, or non-diversifiable risk. This risk is caused by macroeconomic factors such as inflation, which affect the returns of all companies. If a company is affected by these macroeconomic factors in the same way as the market, then it will have a beta of 1, and will be expected to have returns equal to the market. Similarly, if a company's systematic risk is greater than the market, then the company will be priced such that it is expected to have returns greater than the market.

Perhaps it is easier to think of the beta as being a relative measure of volatility, the relative volatility being determined by comparing a share's returns to the market's returns. The greater the volatility, the more risky the share is said to be, which relates directly into a higher beta. For example, if a share has a beta of 2.0, then, on average, for every 10 per cent that the market index has returned above the risk-free rate, the share will have returned 20 per cent. Conversely, for every 10 per cent the market index has returned below the risk-free rate, the share will have returned 20 per cent below.

To obtain a CAPM estimate of the cost of equity, two other pieces of data are required, these being the risk-free rate and the equity risk premium. The risk-free rate represents the most secure return that can be achieved. From a UK perspective, anyone wishing to sleep soundly at night might invest all available funds in government bonds which are largely insensitive to what happens in the share market and, therefore, have a beta of nearly zero. The risk-free rate within CAPM is theoretically defined as an investment that has no variance and no covariance with the market. This means that a perfect proxy for the risk-free rate is a security with a beta equal to zero, and no volatility. To find a perfect proxy is empirically impossible. So a proxy is used that meets these requirements as closely as possible. In developed economies government securities tend to be the best candidates, since the government in many countries guarantees payment.

The equity risk premium represents the excess return above the risk-free rate that investors demand for holding risky securities. The risk premium in the CAPM is the premium above the risk-free rate on a portfolio assumed to have a beta equal to 1.0. If an individual security is more (or less) risky, then it will have a higher (or lower) risk premium.

Research has revealed the market risk premium for the UK to be between 3.36 per cent and 15.52 per cent historically, depending upon the time period chosen (see Table 15.3). Clearly the premium selected will have a very significant effect upon the cost of capital.

Once the beta has been determined, together with the risk-free rate and the equity risk premium, the cost of equity can be found from the CAPM formula:

Cost of equity = Risk-free rate + (Beta × Equity risk premium)

For example, a company with a risk-free rate of 8.5 per cent, a beta of 1.1, and an assumed equity risk premium of 4 per cent, would have the following cost of equity :

Cost of equity = 9% + (1.1 × 4%) = 13.4%

This cost of equity estimate should be undertaken on a business-by-

Table 15.3   *Historical estimates of excess returns*

Time period	Average equity premium
1931–1940	6.58
1941–1950	13.84
1951–1960	15.52
1961–1970	4.68
1971–1980	3.36
Annual average excess returns	8.28

business basis and the results combined with cost of debt and gearing estimates to produce appropriate cost of capital estimates.

15.7   How SVA can be used and who is using it

SVA can be applied to an organisation as a whole to gain a corporate perspective of value-creating potential. However, it offers greater potential benefit when applied at business unit level to evaluate the value-creating potential of the parts of the overall organisation which together make up the whole. As indicated, this involves viewing the overall organisation as a portfolio of business units, each of which has responsibility for the generation of business value. When seen this way, shareholder value is the aggregation of the value generated by each business unit. To calculate this it is necessary to estimate the cash flow for each business unit and, ideally, for the principal lines of business. These cash flows are converted to a value which ideally involves the estimation of the return required by the providers of funds for individual business units together with appropriate planning periods.

There are well-publicised examples of quoted UK companies, (e.g. Lloyds Bank) which are pursuing the development of the shareholder value approach in this way. In addition, some unquoted companies are using the approach, one good example being ICL which has been implementing business value since the beginning of 1994. Smaller organisations both within and outside the UK are also embarking on the 'value journey'. For, example, Cultura Inglesa in Rio de Janeiro, Brazil, is in the preliminary stages of introducing the approach as a managerial planning tool.

SVA can be used very effectively in acquisition and divestment analysis for estimating the value to be created (13). Taking the example of an acquisition, this corresponds with undertaking a valuation of the newly combined organisation and a comparison with its value beforehand, referred to as the 'stand-alone value':

Value created by acquisition
= (Value(s) with synergies) − (Stand-alone value(s))

Using SVA, the relationship between the assumptions and the value outcomes can be clearly explored in terms of the key 'value drivers'. This approach to acquisition analysis was used by James Capel (11). Analysts using the approach in evaluating the Glaxo–Wellcome bid estimated a value for Glaxo with Wellcome of approximately 575p, compared to Glaxo's existing share price of 732p.

The benefits of applying the approach for acquisition analysis can be seen if we consider issues associated with the control premium, the value of synergies and the question of perspective together. The control premium is the amount over and above the traded share price that has to be paid to gain control of an acquisition target. In terms of assessing how much this premium should be, there are many views which may often relate more to an assessment of historical benchmarks than to any assessment related to the potential value to the acquirer. The norm for the UK appears to be around 30 per cent, but there may often be exceptions. For example, *Acquisitions Monthly* produced a table relating to the last few years, which is summarised in Table 15.4 (14). This illustrates the bid premiums paid by UK firms in the years 1991–1995.

A good example of a higher bid premium was the Glaxo–Wellcome deal referred to earlier. Glaxo made a £9 billion cash and share offer for Wellcome. When announced in January 1995 it constituted the UK's largest ever completed public takeover and it resulted in shareholders accepting 53 per cent one-day and 51 per cent one-month premiums (13).

What might be an appropriate control premium can be estimated by looking at the valuation of potential synergies from the perspective of the acquirer using the SVA approach. For example, in the acquisition of one quoted UK chemical company, the target company's share price had been fluctuating around the 50p mark. As a result of apply-

Table 15.4   *Bid premiums in UK acquisitions*

Period	Premium one day before offer (%)	Premium one month before offer (%)
1991	33	44
1992	39	46
1993	31	34
1994	36	36
1st quarter, 1995	32	27

ing SVA to the target company on a stand-alone value basis the resulting share price was 63p. During the process of the acquisition a number of offers were made, the last one being 120p which, by any standards, is a substantial control premium. However, the SVA value with synergies resulted in 165p when looked at solely in terms of immediate benefits that could potentially be achieved via the target, such as margin improvements.

Value created by M&A
     = (Value with synergies) − (Stand-alone value)
   102p   = 165p − 63p

The implications of this example are that the control premium of 140 per cent may not seem unreasonable if the synergies are actually achievable. (In fact, by all accounts, the margins achieved have exceeded expectations.)

As illustrated, the framework can be used simplistically by focusing solely upon the target to be acquired, but if it is to be used to its full effect, then this will typically involve valuations of the acquirer, i.e.:

Value created by merger or acquisition
     = (Value of combined companies) − [(Stand-alone value of
        acquirer) + (Stand-alone value of target)]

In relation to the earlier example, when benefits to the acquirer in terms of restructuring potential were also taken into consideration, the resulting SVA value was 240p!

Greater potential accuracy can be achieved by looking in more detail. This is achieved by calculating the cash flows corresponding with each business unit for both the acquirer and the target, discounting the business unit cash flows by the relevant cost of capital, and summing the results. The value to be created by a merger or acquisition can then be estimated at the same time as the price to pay.

Last, but by no means least, a significant benefit of SVA is that it does not suffer from many of the shortcomings associated with using accounting measures for valuation purposes. These include:

- Being short-termist in perspective, typically focusing upon profitability in the near term
- Ignoring risk
- Ignoring fixed and working capital requirements to maintain the existing level of activity and to support future intentions
- Ignoring the cost of equity. The servicing costs of equity are treated conventionally as after tax distributions and not a cost to the business.

The reality is that unless the cost of equity is taken into consideration, the true performance of a company cannot be understood.

15.8 Summary

Shareholder value analysis draws upon cash flow analysis and assumes, in broad terms, that the value of a business can be determined by discounting its future cash flows using an appropriate cost of capital. These cash flows are captured within a number of value drivers and relate to the dynamics of business. SVA does not have the shortcomings of more traditional accounting-based approaches for measuring value which:

- may be influenced by creative accounting practices
- tend to be very short-term
- do not effectively capture risk and uncertainty
- fail to recognise that money has a time value
- are poorly associated with firm performance.

Notes and references

(1) Thomson, R. (1995) 'Who needs earnings?', *Management Today*.
(2) Houlder, V. (1995). 'A value system for shareholders', *Financial Times*, 20 March, p. 11.
(3) Price Waterhouse (1995). *ValueBuilder – Increasing Shareholder Value*, Press release, 2 February.
(4) Mills, R.W. and Parker, D.R. (1995). *The Use of Shareholder Value Analysis in Acquisition and Divestment Decisions by Large UK Companies*, Chartered Institute of Management Accountants, November.
(5) Mills, R.W and Chen, G. (1996). 'Evaluating Chinese joint venture opportunities using strategic value analysis', *Journal of General Management*, January.
(6) Rappaport, A. (1986). *Creating Shareholder Value: The New Standard for Business Performance*, New York: The Free Press.
(7) Mills, R.W. (1994). *Finance, Strategy and Strategic Value Analysis: Linking Two Key Business Issues*, Mars Business Associates Ltd, p. 49.
(8) Mills, R.W. and Weinstein, W.L. (1996). 'Valuable scenarios: estimating value in a turbulent environment, *Long Range Planning*, January.
(9) Mills. R.W. and Print, C. (1995). 'Strategic value analysis, shareholder value and economic value added – what's the difference?', *Management Accounting*, February, pp. 35–37.

(10) Copeland, T., Mueller, I. and Murrin, I. (1992). *Valuation*, McKinsey & Co.

(11) James Capel Equity Research (1995). *Pharmaceuticals: In Search of Shareholder Value*, May, p. 16.

(12) Gitman, L.J. and Mercurio, V.A. (1982). 'Cost of capital techniques used by major US firms: a survey and analysis of Fortune's 1000', *Financial Management*, Winter.

(13) Rappaport, A. and Friskey, E.A. (1990). 'The Quaker Stokely deal: boosting shareholder value through M&A', *Mergers and Acquisitions Europe*, March/April.

(14) Atkins, E. (1995). 'A step in the right direction', *Acquisitions Monthly*, May, p. 38.

16 Corporate-level strategy

By Andrew Campbell and Michael Goold

Editors' introduction

Effective corporate parenting is a challenge which faces any organisation with multiple businesses. It is a complex matter, concerned as it is with the bridge between business- and corporate-level strategies. The discussion in Chapter 6 of *Exploring Corporate Strategy* is a summary adaptation based on the work of parenting carried out at the Ashridge Strategic Management Centre and explained in their book *Corporate-Level Strategy*. In this chapter Andrew Campbell and Michael Goold, who have undertaken so much work in the field of corporate strategy, provide an extended discussion, with examples of the challenge of corporate parenting based on their research. The chapter deals with the principles of corporate parenting and gives examples of how these principles can be applied in practice.

16.1 Introduction

Current thinking on corporate-level strategy (1–3) focuses on the importance of achieving alignment between three elements: the value creation logic of the corporation, the portfolio of businesses owned by the corporation, and the skills and processes used by the centre to manage the portfolio. The rationale for this way of thinking is straightforward.

Corporate portfolios differ from investment portfolios (a collection of shares in a number of different companies) because the corporation owns a controlling stake in its businesses (normally 100 per cent) and has managerial control over the businesses. Managerial control only makes sense if it can be translated into additional value creation. Hence, every corporate portfolio needs to be built around a value creation logic that requires managerial control to implement. The value creation logic then drives choices about what skills and processes are needed at the centre and about what businesses should be included in the portfolio.

This way of thinking contrasts with the portfolio management ideas of the 1970s and early 1980s. Portfolio management concepts –

balance, risk spreading, sound investments, growth, portfolio renewal – are similar to the concepts used for an investment portfolio and do not require managerial control to implement (4–5). The 'value creation logic' way of thinking encompasses the concept of synergy developed by Ansoff in the 1960s and is fully compatible with the resource-based view of strategy: superior returns are derived from the possession of valuable corporate resources (6–8).

One version of the value creation logic way of thinking is called 'Parenting Theory'. Described in detail in *Corporate-Level Strategy* (1), this theory argues that the value creation logics of successful multi-business companies are based on the insights, skills, management processes and other resources of the corporate parent. (The corporate parent is defined as the management hierarchy above the level of the businesses.) Corporate-level strategy, this theory argues, is about developing a corporate parent which has insights, skills and other resources that are superior to those of other corporate parents for adding value to the particular collection of businesses in the corporate portfolio. While these insights and skills are superior when applied to certain types of businesses, they are likely to be inferior when applied to other businesses.

This chapter shows how to analyse the businesses and the management hierarchy of a corporation so as to understand its current value creation logic, if it has one, and think about what its future corporate-level strategy should be. The chapter is based on the 'framework for developing corporate-level strategy', shown in Figure 16.1. We will start by describing the framework and an analytical matrix called the 'Ashridge portfolio display'. We will then list the analytical techniques that are appropriate for developing corporate-level strategy. Finally, we will describe a format for documenting corporate-level strategies and discuss the implications a particular strategy has for decisions about the portfolio of businesses and the organisation, processes and staffing of the parent organisation.

16.2   Framework for developing corporate-level strategy

The objective of corporate-level strategy analysis is to develop a value creation logic that gives the corporate parent an advantage over rival corporate parents. The advantage – called 'parenting advantage' – is measured by the amount of value the company can create from owning a business. While the ideal is to have parenting advantage with respect to all businesses in the portfolio, in practice even the best companies usually have disadvantage with respect to some of their businesses.

The framework places the search for parenting advantage in the middle circle. Four inputs help with this search:

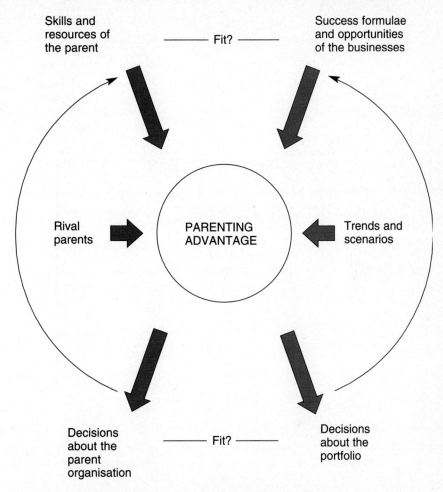

Skills and resources of the parent ——— Fit? ——— Success formulae and opportunities of the businesses

Rival parents → PARENTING ADVANTAGE ← Trends and scenarios

Decisions about the parent organisation ——— Fit? ——— Decisions about the portfolio

Figure 16.1   Framework for developing corporate-level strategy.

- Understanding the skills and resources of the parent organisation
- Understanding the success formulae and opportunities of the businesses
- Understanding the skills and resources of rival parents
- Understanding the scenarios and trends that might affect any of the above factors.

These four inputs provide the understanding needed to think creatively about parenting advantage. One way of capturing the essence of these four inputs is the Ashridge portfolio display (Figure 16.2). The display captures the degree of fit between each business in the portfolio and the current skills and resources of the parent organisation. There are two dimensions of fit: 'critical success factor fit' and 'parenting opportunity fit', both of which will be explained later in the chapter. The matrix is divided into five sections:

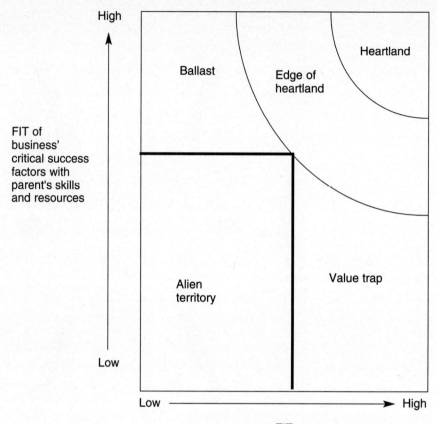

Figure 16.2   Ashridge portfolio display.

- *Heartland*. These are businesses for which parenting advantage probably already exists and, hence, which are likely to be at the core of any future strategy
- *Edge of heartland*. These are businesses where the parent may be able to develop an advantage. They are also likely to be part of any future strategy
- *Ballast*. These are businesses where the value creation logic is weak. They can be sold if a better parent exists, or they can be moved into the heartland if a new value creation logic can be developed for them
- *Alien territory*. These are businesses which do not fit and need to be sold as soon as it is convenient
- *Value trap*. These are businesses in which there is a value creation logic but the parent's strengths and weaknesses do not fit well with the

business's critical success factors. These businesses need to be sold unless the parent is able to change its skills and other resources in a way that reduces the misfit.

The development of the Ashridge portfolio display can be based upon an analysis of the current portfolio and the parent's current skills and resources. It can also be developed with a forward-looking view, planning for changes in the portfolio and in the parent's skills and resources. The display is an aid to synthesis. It summarises much of the detailed work and gives the analyst a pictorial display to help with the task of communicating and choosing a future strategy.

Once a strategy has been chosen, decisions need to be made to implement it. This involves specific changes to the parent organisation and the portfolio of businesses.

16.3 *Success formulae and opportunities of the businesses*

The best place to start with an analysis of corporate-level strategy is with the businesses. There are two questions that need to be answered. First: In what ways might a parent organisation be able to create additional value from or add value to each business? Each business has a market value as an independent company. The issue is about ways in which the parent organisation can create additional value, over and above the independent market value, from owning the business.

- If the business needs to expand into Asian markets to become an effective global competitor or to fully exploit its product technology, then a parent organisation with experience in Asia, a cadre of Asian-tested managers, and contacts with Asian governments and partners will be likely to be able to add value to the business.
- If the business has underexploited technologies developed as part of some previous product development project, then a parent with other businesses able to exploit these technologies will be able to create additional value.
- If the business is in branded, consumer products, but has weak brands and poor advertising, then a parent with strong brands and strong competence in consumer marketing is likely to be able to add value.

In parenting theory, these opportunities to create additional value are called 'parenting opportunities' – opportunities for the parent company to influence or help a business create more value than the business team would be likely to create if left undisturbed.

The second question that needs to be answered is about the critical success factors (success formulae) of each business. It is important to understand the critical success factors because a judgement needs to be made about how well these factors fit with the skills and resources of the parent. If they fit badly, the influence of the parent is likely to make the business perform less well and result in value destruction rather than value creation.

Strategy in action

Illustration 16.1

Sony and Columbia Pictures

When Sony acquired Columbia Pictures, it gained ownership of a Hollywood studio that had critical success factors very different from the consumer electronics business. Not surprisingly, Sony managers made a number of mistakes in their decisions over Columbia Pictures. They did not have a good feel for the type of managers needed to lead a Hollywood studio and were forced to change the chief executive three times. They had no way of judging what was an appropriate level of investment in major films or which scripts had most potential. As a result, Columbia had a run of expensive flops. The Sony culture and ways of doing business were alien to those of Hollywood, making communication between the two sets of managers difficult.

Strategy in action

Illustration 16.2

Oil companies

When the oil companies acquired minerals businesses, they gained ownership of another 'extractive' industry, but one which had surprising differences in critical success factors. Success in oil is mainly about exploration. In minerals, it is about buying into a share of the best mines. Vertical integration is a good strategy in oil, but a poor one in minerals. Central functions and services make sense in oil, but decentralisation is better in minerals. As a result of these differences, the oil companies made a number of operating and strategic mistakes in minerals.

As Illustrations 16.1 and 16.2 show, listing the critical success factors of each business can help point to areas of likely misfit with the parent, leading to potential value destruction.

Both these analyses – critical success factors and parenting opportunities – can be undertaken together. Figure 16.3 is an example summary sheet that needs to be produced for each business. Most of the information is readily available from each business's strategic plan or by talking with the business's management team.

- 'Critical success factors' are the main features which distinguish the best competitors in the business from the less good
- 'Special features' are any other aspects of the business that it might be

Business name: BASE CHEMICALS	
Critical success factors • Low cost feedstocks • Low cost side stream management • Low cost conversion/ infrastructure/logistics • Low use of capital • Product technology • Global business structure • Managing derivatives portfolio	**Special features** • Handful of competitors

Major tasks
• Build on feedstock strength
  – drive down costs
  – optimise assets
  – add low cost capacity
• Maintain good co-producer
  relationships, etc
• Develop Pacific strategy
	Common mistakes
	• Failure to focus on cost
	  fundamentals
	• Geographic influence too strong
	• Overbuild capacity
	• Forecasting errors

**Parenting opportunities
from major tasks**
• Support for cost reductions
• Help with capacity decisions
  – analysis checks
  – integration checks
  – culture of integrity
• Senior relationships with industry
  players
• Central technical support
• Help with Pacific strategy
	Other
	• Vertical integration
	• Horizontal integration
	• Global structure
	• Cycle management
	• Derivatives management

Figure 16.3   Business summary sheet.

useful to record to help the analyst distinguish the strategic priorities of this business from those of other similar businesses
• 'Major tasks' are the major action plans that the management team of the business needs to execute well if it is going to be successful over the next three to five years
• 'Common mistakes' are the typical errors that managers in this industry (i.e. this business and its competitors) have made. They may be strategic errors or operating errors.

Parenting opportunities are identified by thinking about the major tasks, common mistakes and critical success factors. For each major task, the analyst asks: 'Will the managers of the business do a good job of executing this task; and could they benefit from help?' 'If the parent company had the appropriate skills and resources, could it add value to the efforts of the business managers?' If value can be added, a parenting opportunity exists. In our experience, there are few major tasks where business managers could not benefit from help, *provided* that the parent company has deep experience and relevant skills for the task.

Once parenting opportunities have been defined by looking at the major tasks, additional opportunities can be derived from common mistakes and critical success factors. The analyst asks: 'Could a parent company help business managers avoid the typical mistakes?' 'Could it help build the appropriate critical success factors?'

Finally, the analyst needs to think more broadly about parenting opportunities. 'Are there any skills or resources currently possessed by the parent (or by any corporate parent) that could help this business?' 'Are there any resources owned by the business that would be better exploited by linking with other businesses or by changing strategy or investment policy?' In other words, are there any other ways in which additional value could be created?

Typically the analysis will generate 5 to 20 parenting opportunities for each business. Some of these will be large: the parent's influence could enhance the value of the business by 50 per cent or more (e.g. help with distribution of products in Asia). Some will be small: value enhancement is likely to be less than 5 per cent (e.g. centralised pension support and salary payments).

Each parenting opportunity and each critical success factor can, therefore, be graded by its importance. One grading system is to allocate a 0 for minimal importance, 1 for impact of up to 20 per cent on value and 2 for impact of more than 20 per cent on value. Tables 16.1 and 16.2 illustrate how a grading system like this might be used in a forest products company.

Table 16.1 *Summary of critical success factor analysis*

Critical success factors	Business units		
	Pulp	Bulk paper grades	Speciality paper grades
Low cost forests	2	2	1
Low cost side stream management	1	n/a	n/a
Low cost conversion	1	2	0
Low use of capital	2	1	0
Process technology	1	1	2
International business structure	0	1	1
Professional marketing	0	1	2
Downstream integration	2	1	0
Application technology	0	0	1
Application sales	0	1	2

Scores deliberately do not reflect a real situation

2 = impact on profit more than 20%; 1 = impact on profit less than 20%; 0 = minimal impact

Table 16.2 *Summary of parenting opportunity analysis*

	Business units		
Parenting opportunities	**Pulp**	**Bulk paper grades**	**Speciality paper grades**
Support cost reductions	2	12	0
Help with capacity decisions	1	2	0
Senior relationships	1	1	0
Central technical support	1	2	0
Help with overseas strategy	0	1	2
Support international structure	0	1	1
Encourage integration	2	1	0
Superior cycle management	1	1	0
Help with integration interfaces	1	0	0
JV management skills	0	1	1
Professional marketing skills	0	1	2
Innovative financing	0	0	0
Long-term planning support	0	1	0

Scores deliberately do not reflect a real situation

2 = impact on profit more than 20%; 1= impact on profit less than 20%; 0 = minimal impact

16.4 Skills and resources of the parent

The parent's skills and resources can only be judged effectively in relation to particular businesses, because a given skill can be a strength if applied to business A but a handicap if applied to business B (Illustration 16.3).

Strategy in action

Illustration 16.3
Research attitude

Shell is renowned for its long-standing policy of investing in research as a way of gaining competitive advantage. In some businesses, this is a highly effective strategy and Shell's corporate research skill is a major strength. In other businesses – for example, bottled gas where marketing and distribution are key to success – Shell's attitude to research is likely to be a weakness, encouraging the business unit to over-invest in a dimension that is unlikely to produce advantage.

Rather than attempt to create a careful analysis of skills and resources, we have found it more useful to document some broad characteristics and then consider the degree of fit between the parent organisation and particular businesses. Figure 16.4 is a useful framework for capturing some of the broad characteristics of the parent.

1   What are the main *mental maps* that dominate the parent's thinking?
    • insights about value creation?
    • biases and predetermined views about industries or ways of competing?
    • values and beliefs?
2   What is the company's *structure* and what are the main *systems and processes* used by the parent to manage the portfolio?
3   Which *central functions or services* are influential and what influence do they have?
4   Who are the most powerful *people* in the parent and what are their *skills*?
5   What degree of autonomy do business units have? Which decisions are made by the parent and which by the businesses? These questions define the *decentralisation contracts* between the businesses and the corporate parent.

The following list gives a summary of the main parenting characteristics of an example company. A list such as this can only be a sum-

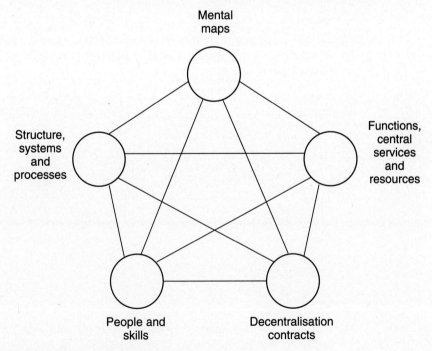

Figure 16.4   Characteristics of the parent.

mary as it will not include all aspects of parenting that may be relevant to the 'fit' analysis.

- Global business structures
- Brand and reputation
- Size and muscle
- Long-term orientation
- Belief in integration
- Belief in technology
- Tight operation cost management
- Value-based planning
- Functional barons
- Weak marketing skills.

With these characteristics in mind, it is then possible to make the two fit judgements that form the axis of the Ashridge portfolio display:

- How well do the critical success factors in each business fit with the parenting characteristics?
- How well do the parenting opportunities in each business fit with the parenting characteristics?

Tables 16.3 and 16.4 show how these judgements can be made in a semi-quantified way. But it is important to realise that these are still judgements; managers can disagree about the exact position of an individual business within the matrix. The portfolio display is not a scientific tool, it is an aid to synthesis. Figure 16.5 is an example portfolio display.

16.4.1 Skills and resources of rival parents

Rival parent analysis involves identifying, for each business, other parent companies that might add more value. The list of rival parents should include both direct competitors and other multi-business

Table 16.3   *Misfit analysis*

Critical success factors	Degree of misfit
Low cost forests	0
Low cost side streams	0
Low cost conversion	−2
Low use of capital	−1
Process technology	0
International business structure	0
Swap skills	0
etc.	

−2 = major misfit between parenting characteristics and critical success factor
−1 = minor misfit
  0 = no misfit

Table 16.4   *Fit analysis*

Parenting opportunities	Degree of fit
Support cost reduction	0
Help with capacity decisions	1
Senior relationships	2
Central technical support	2
Help with overseas strategy	1
Support international structure	2
etc.	

2 = The parent is likely to be good at addressing the parenting advantage.

1 = The parent will make some contribution to the parenting opportunity.

0 = The parent will make no contribution.

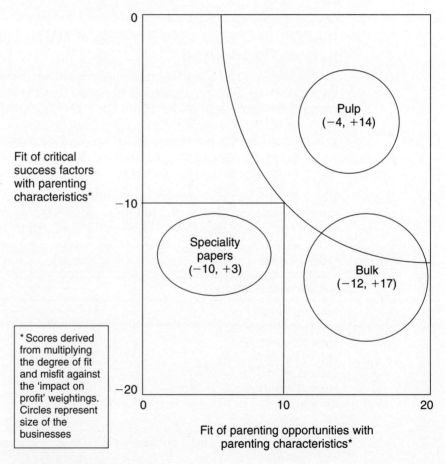

Figure 16.5   *Summary portfolio display.*

companies whose parenting approach might be appropriate for the relevant business. For the companies identified as rival parents, a review of parenting skills and resources, similar in concept to that just described, should be carried out.

We suggest four ways of developing names for the list of rival parents:

1 List all the obvious rivals: companies of similar size with similar port-folios of businesses.
2 For each business in the portfolio, list all the parents that own direct competitors to the business.
3 For each business in the portfolio, list all the companies that could have beneficial linkages with the business and note the parents that own these companies. Take particular care to note parents that own similar businesses in different countries. These similar businesses often provide opportunities for skill and technology sharing.
4 For each business in the portfolio, consider the different types of value that could be added to the business (e.g. tight financial controls to improve cash flow, or linkages with sister companies in Europe), and describe the type of parents that could add this kind of value. Then identify companies that match this type.

A list of rivals should be compiled, such as that shown below for a diversified construction company:

1 *Similar businesses*
   • Construction industry generalists (e.g. Tarmac)
   • Construction industry focused (e.g. Blue Circle)
   • Construction industry specialists (e.g. Barratt)
   • Global construction companies (e.g. Bechtel)
   • European diversified construction companies (e.g. Bouyges)

2 *Companies with some competing businesses*
   • Engineering consultancies (e.g. water companies)
   • Waste management (e.g. water companies)

3 *Companies with possible linkages*
   • International linkages (e.g. Bouyges)
   • Raw material linkages (e.g. British Industrial Sand)

4 *Companies with relevant value adding skills*
   • Cross-Europe coordination (e.g. Unilever)
   • Tight financial control (e.g. Hanson Industries)

Once the list of rival parents has been developed, the next step is to select the companies that will be analysed in more detail. It will be impossible to do a full analysis of all the rival parents on the list. We suggest focusing on the most 'obvious' rivals and then creating categories of less obvious rival parents, selecting one company to analyse from each category.

As with competitive analysis at the business level, rival parent analysis is a process of getting to know the rivals better and better, so that it is possible to use them as a benchmark of value creation. The benefits of this benchmarking are not limited to major strategy reviews. Like all benchmarking exercises, benefits can accrue in many small ways as new ideas are gained from studying rivals (Illustration 16.4).

Strategy in action

Illustration 16.4
Rival parent analysis

One company in the electrical equipment industry noted that one of its rivals had less than a quarter of the number of managers in country head offices and yet appeared to be able to achieve as much country presence and coordination. By reverse engineering the country organisation of this parent and understanding how the coordination was achieved, the first company was able to cut tens of millions of dollars from its country organisations. By decentralising some of the functional tasks to businesses within the country and centralising other activities to the corporate centre, the country organisation was able to focus on a few essential coordination activities, such as liaising with the government, coordinating marketing to major customers, and coordinating graduate recruitment. Even these tasks were mainly led by the larger businesses, with the country organisation providing some administrative support and impetus for action.

Most managers view rival parent analysis as a daunting task. Yet we can vouch for its value and practicality. Companies are not as secretive about their management philosophy as they are about their product technology. Normally accessible sources – company literature, ex-employees, recently sold businesses, direct contacts, studies by investment analysts, and other public sources – can provide considerable information. Moreover, it is often not necessary to devote more than a few days' work to each company to produce useful results.

Table 16.5 displays the rival parent analysis carried out by one manufacturing company of its two most obvious rivals. The work took two days and the results can be summarised on one page. Yet the implications are clear. Company A, a US-based company, is likely to be a better parent for certain kinds of businesses – for mature, US-based businesses with good cash flow potential. Company A is also likely to be better at rationalisation opportunities. Company B, on the other hand, is likely to be a better parent for businesses with long investment lead times, such as technology-driven businesses, particularly those requiring complex global management structures and bold strategies.

Table 16.5   *Rival parenting analysis: manufacturing*

Company A	Company B
Financially driven	Strategically driven
Quick to pull out of low profit investments	Long-term outlook
Few 'international' managers	Large 'expatriate' group
Few non-nationals	International senior management group
Authoritarian management style	Consensus management approach
Strong systems	Discussion culture
Risk averse	Willingness to joint venture
Prefer equity control	Need for operational control

16.4.2   Trends and scenarios

All the analyses so far involve current or historic data. Yet good corporate strategy options need to contain some vision: some view about how trends are evolving, about opportunities that will exist in ten years' time, about how the world is going to be. The danger with all analytically based approaches to strategy is that they are over-influenced by historic data.

One of the methods for analysing the future is the scenarios technique. The technique involves developing scenarios of two or more different and yet possible future worlds. These worlds represent different ways in which current trends and influences could move. They can be used to help the process of creating ideas about future sources of parenting advantage in three ways.

First, the scenario worlds can be used to judge the rival parents that are likely to do well or badly in each scenario. This can help focus attention for further analysis of rival parents and contribute to the creation of strategic options. For example, a scenario that predicts a smooth transition to a common currency in Europe and the lowering of trade barriers world-wide may favour parent companies seeking to create value through internationalising businesses. An opposite scenario may favour parent companies seeking to create value by linking businesses within national boundaries.

The second way to use scenarios is to compare the company's list of parenting skills and resources against each scenario. Each parenting characteristic can be scored as positive, negative or neutral against each scenario, giving a deeper understanding of the match between the company's parenting characteristics and the scenarios. This analysis also provides useful insights for developing options.

The third use of scenarios is to generate different ways of adding value under the different scenarios. For example, a scenario that predicts an increase in retailer brands would also predict that a number of branded manufacturers will run into trouble by attempting to resist the trend. This suggests a parenting opportunity: buy companies with good product technology that are resisting the trend and change their strategy to be more supportive of the retailers. The insight would be the prediction that some companies will underperform because they will be locked into an outdated way of marketing. Assuming that other parents have not spotted the opportunity, the company ought to be able to buy companies with poor strategies and create value by re-directing their strategies.

Building a complete scenario is expensive and time-consuming because of the need to think through the impact of many different forces of influence. However, the alternative to scenario analysis – studying individual trends – has dangers. It can cause the analyst to overlook the impact an individual trend may have on the broader system. Frequently, a seemingly obvious trend fails to emerge in the way predicted due to other factors in the system. The scenario approach attempts to look at the whole system and the total impact of all the trends. Individual trends analysis is most useful when it takes account of the likely influences of the broader system.

16.4.3   *Generating options and selecting a corporate strategy*

Ideas for corporate strategies are developed by thinking about the value creation logic that will underpin the strategy. If the company already has some strong value creation logic and has many businesses in the heartland or edge of heartland, then the current value creation logic is likely to form the basis of future strategy.

If, however, the world is changing so that the current logic is no longer sustainable (as was the case for Hanson plc prior to its four way demerger), or if there is no substantial value creation logic at present, new logics need to be generated and evaluated.

The analyst must examine all the parenting opportunities, looking for some that might provide the basis for a new logic. The analyst must also reconsider the skills and resources of the parent, paying particular attention to any insights in the minds of senior managers, to see if any of these might provide the basis for a logic. Finally, the analyst must do some independent creative thinking, drawing on knowledge of current trends, the strengths and weaknesses of rival parents, and the summaries of parenting opportunities and critical success factors.

Table 16.6 describes the logics that underpin the strategies of some successful multi-business companies. These logics have mostly grown up with the company over a number of years as a result of experience, leadership and luck. Some have been brought to companies with the arrival of a new chief executive from another company. But few have come from a process of careful analysis and reflection. This is

Table 16.6   *Example logics*

Company	Strategies
3M	Build new businesses in high tech niches related to the company's core coatings technology.
ABB	Improve the profit focus and commercial skills of engineering-intensive, electro-technical businesses. Rationalise production across borders. Help with expansion in Asia and Eastern Europe.
Canon	Build new businesses by combining technical and market skills in precision mechanics, fine optics and micro electronics.
RTZ	Help businesses invest in the best mines with financing, deal doing and risk management skills. Provide support in key specialist areas.
Unilever	Improve the marketing of mass market consumer goods companies and increase their commitment to new product development. Link similar product areas into an international network that shares product and market information and creates international brands.
Virgin	Create businesses to compete in 'institutionalised' markets, using the Virgin brand and PR skills.

not to say that the analyses we are suggesting are a waste of time; rather we are implying that most corporate strategies will be built around some existing source of value creation.

In our experience, typical options include the following:

- demerge or starburst
- focus on division A, become more global and develop parenting skills to build more synergies
- focus on country A and develop some country-based skills
- focus on parenting skill A and test how wide an array of businesses it can add value to.

The final choice of which strategy to follow should be based on the option that is most likely to lead to the greatest degree of parenting advantage. Superior returns come from having an advantage, and the best performance will come from the option that gives the biggest advantage over rival parents.

Two other criteria also need to be considered when choosing between options: implementation risk and stakeholder objectives. Implementation risk is about how easy it will be to make the portfolio or parenting changes that will be needed to implement the strategy. A choice often needs to be made between a strategy that has the potential to deliver more parenting advantage, but with high implementation risk, and a strategy that will yield low parenting advantage, but will be easier to implement. As in any strategy development process, the managers concerned must then weigh up the degree of implementation risk they are willing to run, relative to the potential benefits each strategy could yield. Stakeholder objectives are about the desires primarily of shareholders, the board and senior executives. Unless the strategy is likely to meet most of these desires it will not be approved or supported, even if it does promise the best returns. Frequently the ambitions of senior executives – 'to be a Fortune 100 company' or 'to be a leader in the construction industry' – are not considered appropriate inputs to the decision process. However, since these same executives will need to implement the strategy, it is better to get their personal desires on the table early in the selection process.

16.4.4   Documenting and implementing the strategy

Once a strategy, in the form of a value creation logic, has been chosen, it needs to be documented in a way that is helpful both for communication and implementation purposes.

A 'parenting advantage statement' is a useful way to do this. The strategy is broken down into three elements. First, the statement lists the key insights that underpin the value creation logic. These insights concern the opportunities or problems that the businesses are not fully addressing, making it possible for a skilled parent to add value. The second part of the statement describes the parenting skills and resources that will enable the company to make a distinctive contribution to these opportunities or problems. The third part of the statement describes the type of business on which the company should focus. These heartland criteria are in effect the company's acquisition criteria. They describe the type of business the company is most interested in owning: the type of business the company can add most value to. Table 16.7 gives parenting advantage statements for three very different companies.

The value of a parenting advantage statement is that it forces the strategist to be crisp and clear. There is no opportunity for loose thinking or padding. Weak logic is quickly exposed. This helps with communication, and also helps with implementation.

The current portfolio of businesses can now be scored against the heartland criteria and businesses that do not fit well can be examined more closely or put up for disposal. A few businesses may not fit in their current form and may need to be restructured before they can be given a lasting place in the portfolio. Acquisition candidates can also be scored against the heartland criteria and a list of targets developed.

The existing staffing, structure, processes, skills and culture of the parent organisation can also be reviewed against the desired skills and resources. Where weaknesses exist, changes need to be made. Where strengths exist, they need to be identified and bolstered. An agenda for changing the parent organisation can be developed from comparing current skills and resources with required skills and resources.

Table 16.7   *Parenting advantage statements*

Parent	Advantage statements
ABB	
Value creation insights	Most companies make direct trade-offs between centralisation and decentralisation, or scale and focus. There are opportunities for a parent that can combine the various benefits in new ways.
	Many European engineering businesses have been relatively fragmented in global terms. Consolidation can reduce costs while increasing coverage and global muscle.
	Many engineering businesses do not have a strong commercial focus, and are prone to increase sales volume and product range at the expense of margin. A parent can help redress the balance.
	Many engineering companies need help developing an effective presence in Asia.
Distinctive parenting characteristics	Ability to combine decentralised small business units into a global network through the ABB matrix structure.
	Systems and corporate initiatives that focus on profitability, customer needs, and simplification of operations.
	Ability to integrate acquisitions and improve their performance rapidly.
	Ruthless approach to cutting of overhead costs.
	Growing presence in Asia.
Heartland businesses	Engineering-intensive, electro-technical businesses, usually involving complex integration into systems. Customers are large industrial or governmental institutions.
CANON	
Value creation insights	Individual businesses have resourcing difficulties in pursuing a range of technologies in depth and can benefit from shared resource within the parent.
	Businesses find it difficult to create linkages and cross-fertilisation between different areas of technology, between technologies and market needs, and between different markets; and there is a role for a parent in facilitating these linkages.
	An inspiring corporate vision can help businesses to stretch for growth beyond the confines of each business.
Distinctive parenting characteristics	Ability to manage cross-fertilisation • across different technologies • between technical and market specialists • across different markets. A high level of corporate commitment to technology and learning. Company vision that energises staff towards growth and stretch without prompting inappropriate risks.
Heartland businesses	Businesses in which overall performance depends heavily on product performance and new product development, which in turn are driven by superior understanding and linking of three core technology areas: precision mechanics, fine optics, and micro-electronics; where technology advantage is embodied in certain key components; where international presence and ability to manage multiple channels to market provide a major advantage; selling business machines, cameras, and specialist optical products.
UNILEVER	
Value creation insights	By creating a network of operating companies in FMCG businesses in different countries, a parent can generate value through the exchange of product, marketing and technological information, ideas and skills.
	By promoting investment in new products and research, a parent can improve performance, since most independent FMCG businesses tend to under-invest in these areas.
Distinctive parenting characteristics	Decentralised structures: • developed countries • LDCs. Mechanisms to encourage networking across businesses and countries: • expatriate cadre and HR development • category management and information flows • corporate culture Balance of centralised and decentralised research: • fat technology skills • close relationship between research and marketing.
Heartland businesses	Fast-moving consumer packaged goods for the mass market, where opportunities exist to gain advantage by centralised research and product development and international linkages between country-focused business units.

The value creation insights provide additional guidance for implementation decisions. Businesses in the portfolio should be those where the insights point to major opportunities to create value. Changes to the parent organisation should be those that make the company better at exploiting the insights, moving always towards the objective of parenting advantage – being the best possible parent for each business in the portfolio.

16.5   Summary

Developing a corporate-level strategy is, in summary, little different from developing any strategy. Some analysis needs to be done on strengths, weaknesses, opportunities and threats. Some creative thinking needs to be done to develop a concept that exploits the best opportunities and the most valuable strengths. This concept needs to be documented in a way that aids communication and implementation. Finally, an agenda for action is required to make the strategy work.

There are clear similarities between the development of corporate-level strategy, and business-unit strategy. Both are about searching for competitive advantage. Both involve analysis of opportunities and strengths. Both involve considering problems and weaknesses. Both involve peering into the future. The main difference is the focus of the analysis. The focus for business-unit strategy is the product ranges and market segments in which the business unit is capable of competing profitably. The focus of corporate-level strategy is the type of business unit to which the parent organisation is capable of adding value. The different focus makes it necessary to use different analyses and frameworks. Underneath these, the strategic problems are surprisingly similar.

References

(1)   Goold, M., Campbell, A. and Alexander, M. (1994). *Corporate-Level Strategy: Creating Value in the Multi-Business Company*. New York: John Wiley & Sons.
(2)   Collis, D.J. and Montgomery, C.A. (1997). *Corporate Strategy: Resources and Scope of the Firm*, Burr Ridge, IL: Irwin/McGraw-Hill.
(3)   Prahalad, C.K. and Doz, Y. (1997). *CEO: A Visible Hand in Wealth Creation*, Working Paper.
(4)   Hedley, B. (1977). 'Strategy and the "business portfolio"', *Long Range Planning*, February.
(5)   Hofer, C.W. and Schendel, D. (1978). *Strategy Formulation: Analytical Concepts*, St Paul: West Publishing.
(6)   Ansoff, I. (1965). *Corporate Strategy*, New York: McGraw-Hill.

(7)   Grant, R.M. (1991). 'The resource-based theory of competition advantage', *California Management Review*, Spring.

(8)   Collis, D.J. and Montgomery, C.A. (1995). 'Competing on resources: strategy in the 1990s', *Harvard Business Review*, July–August, 118–128.

17

Strategy and creative thinking in business

By Stephen Reid

Editor's introduction

Innovation and change are at the very heart of successful strategic management. *Exploring Corporate Strategy* (Chapter 2) warned that the 'taken-for-granted' assumptions in organisations – although a strength in supporting current strategies – are also likely to 'blind' an organisation to the need for change and how new strategies could be developed. Stephen Reid's chapter is concerned with helping managers overcome this problem through improving processes of creative thinking while analysing and developing strategies.

17.1 Introduction

'Know yourself and conquer' is an old Chinese proverb. In this context, personal strategy precedes grand strategy.

Creative thinking is vital if a business strategy is to achieve surprise, gain a significant advantage or dominate a market. In an age where information flows more freely, the old maxim of 'Information is power' begins to look like a recipe for drowning in data. All the research in the world will not produce a successful strategy if it lacks the power to surprise. In today's information-rich society, when most competitors have access to key data, it requires ingenuity and creativity to deliver a 'break out' conferring strategic advantage.

In essence, a winning strategy will evolve if it is based not on information but on the creative ways it can be interpreted and used to gain advantage. This principle applies just as much to products as it does to services, and to the private as well as the public sector.

This chapter is about how individuals and teams can acquire a more creative perspective and develop more imaginative strategies. Learning how to think more creatively about strategy (or anything else for that matter) is not difficult. Anyone can do it. Creative thinking skills can be acquired by individuals; however teams need to understand and adopt creative thinking behaviours if a company is to harness its latent strategic advantages.

17.2   *Applying creativity to strategy*

Chapter 2 of *Exploring Corporate Strategy* (4th edition) looked at the importance of having enough awareness in the organisation to actually 'hear' weak signals, while Chapter 8 asserted the need for a wider appreciation and for a higher quality of thinking behind strategy. A higher quality of thinking can be achieved in addition to raising the general level of creativity in strategic management by teaching staff how to apply divergent thinking skills. Developing additional thinking tools opens up the possibility of forming new frames of reference through which we can, as individuals or as teams, *choose* to view the future. A frame of reference may be thought of in three dimensions as either a lens through which we view the world or as a box of familiar reference points within which we choose to be confined intellectually.

We will first look at a basic model of thinking process in Section 17.2.1 and in Section 17.2.2 we will move on to a practical example.

17.2.1   *How we think*

Knowing ourselves in order to conquer. We have briefly considered the lenses or frames of reference through which we automate a large portion of our thinking. In what follows we will look at the preferences we develop and our habitual thinking pathways. Once we grasp how we think, we can knowingly reshape the patterns to elicit creative strategies.

'HOW' to think is rarely taught in school. 'What' to learn is clearly given; but 'HOW' to think is left up to each one of us to acquire as we go along. Usually, people eventually adopt a preferred thinking pattern or style and stick to it for most of their lives.

Our preferred thinking pattern will develop in one of two predominant directions, as shown in Figure 17.1:

1   *Convergent thinking* is to do with focus and logically arriving at a result. Avoiding uncertainty and ambiguity are important. The payback for using focused thinking is a higher degree of certainty and comfortable habits. Socially skilled people who can filter out essential data and arrive at conclusions quickly are often selected in business and government as managers and leaders. They have focus as a constantly rewarded and reinforced thinking style. Rightly so, because these people 'get the job done'. They are, at their most focused, seen as hard edged and sometimes ruthlessly successful.

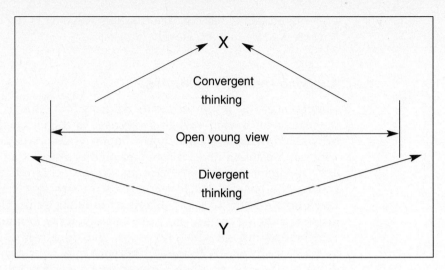

Figure 17.1   *Consolidated map of thinking options.*

2   *Divergent thinking*, on the other hand, is more concerned with inter-
    esting departures and the intellectual journey. Arriving is not import-
    ant. In this mindset uncertainty and ambiguity are enjoyable.
    Divergent thinkers do not focus, and constantly expand the scope of
    enquiry. Divergent thinkers are curious, inventive people who enjoy
    experimentation, exploration and creativity over precision. The ben-
    efits of using the good divergent thinkers is that they excel at gener-
    ating ideas and alternatives.

We all retain the skill to think in the opposite direction. It is just that
we prefer one major direction over the other. To use an analogy, most
people are either left or right handed. A few are ambidextrous. It is the
same with thinking. Most of us develop the convergent focus pattern,
some are creative using divergent thinking while a few employ holistic thinking patterns. Entrepreneurs such as Walt Disney are said to
be holistic thinkers.

Creativity has a lot to do with divergent thinking. To develop a
complete or holistic pattern, however, it has been proposed that an in-
terim thinking pattern exists somewhere between convergent and divergent thinking. Dilts *et al.* (1) refer to this as a 'realist' phase in Walt
Disney whilst de Bono (2), in his six hats model, gives it the colour
yellow. Walt Disney was believed to possess three preferred thinking
patterns, namely dreamer, realist and critic. Walt Disney would not
embark upon a project until he had satisfied himself in all three thinking realms.

17.2.2 *Thinking creatively: thinking outside the box*

Imagination skills simply lie dormant in most people; however, individuals do vary in how creative they are. I believe it is a matter of how individuals tolerate ambiguity and uncertainty. For some, generating and playing with ambiguity is great fun. In most people creative thinking skills can be enhanced if a tolerance of ambiguity is developed. Tension is normal during a creative development and is usually expressed as relief in joy or laughter when the frame of reference is expanded to include new insights (Figure 17.2).

Most good creative thinking processes involve an acceptance that we have a boundary to our thinking. Creative thinking involves testing and moving beyond these boundaries or frames of reference. This can evoke a variety of responses. Once a creative thinking workshop takes off the group begins to laugh and the pace of laughter speeds up as ideas become more abstract. In order to think more creatively we promote thinking outside of the traditional frames of reference. Ideally, the further away from the frame we get the higher the level of freedom to generate new ideas.

Making the familiar strange

Between the 1950s and 1960, William J.J. Gordon presented or published papers in the *Harvard Business Review* and elsewhere based on research experience gathered from 1944 onwards. Much of his work on creative thinking pointed towards a key intellectual process of 'making the familiar strange' (3).

Many methods invoking creative thinking involve a strong divergent thinking component and tap into different ways of 'making the familiar strange'.

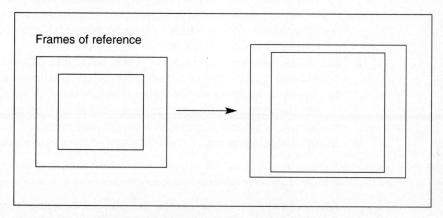

Frames of reference

Figure 17.2 *The frame of personal reference has been expanded to include new knowledge or insight, releasing tension.*

One of the easiest ways to access this creative pathway is to dismantle a frame of reference into its component parts. The next step is to make the various parts as strange as possible and then imagine the consequences. Reversing the assumptions is suggested by some (4, 5) while Edward de Bono's method (6), 'PO' or 'provocative operation', suggests that each assumption is turned into something ridiculously provocative. Turning each assumption into the biggest lie possible also works well in my experience.

17.2.3   Setting up a creative thinking process

Creative strategies only survive in the hearts and minds of committed champions. It is therefore important to identify a champion and then ensure that he or she has the power and the will to act. If working in a group ask those present to:

- identify from those present who precisely will own the implementation
- establish that the individual has the will to implement the resulting strategy
- establish that he or she has the power to act.

Then, either as a group or alone, process your thinking using the following four phases. These phases are outlined briefly below and then given in more detail.

1   State clearly the strategic need that must be met. Examine the statement to check any other issues that are connected. Consider context and any assumptions. Ask the champion if any of these make a better starting point.
2   Allow a divergent thinking process to address a specific element of this need (see 'Assumption busting' below). During this phase, judgement must be suspended. Anything is possible. Money and technology are freely available. No one asks questions of others. Obstacles when encountered are restated as 'how to . . .'
3   Collect rough ideas and improve them. Return to phase 2 if more work needs to be done. Make sure the ideas are considered in the widest contexts and for their internal/external implications. A group may need to do additional research to gather more information on new concepts and revisit phases 2 and 3 again. When satisfied move to phase 4.
4   Apply critical judgement and test the concepts and strategies.

Phase 1: Contexts and assumptions

Often our frames of reference are shaped in some way by some assumed limit of what is possible **for us**. The assumption may be correct for us, but not from someone else's perspective.

Figure 17.3   *Context map and limits of perception.*

For example, the market for doughnuts may be perceived as having expanded from markets 1 and 2 to 3 in Figure 17.3. Feint signal exist from 4 but current preoccupation is with maximising market 3. There is minimal awareness of 4, but 5, which will eventually challenge 1, 2 and 3, does not exist in the mind of this trader.

As another example: the prospect of high-quality shirts emerging from Hong Kong to threaten the northern European market was not even on the scale of thinking in 1965. The cost of air freight was not seen as a strategic threat to the clothing industry when most freight was sent by sea container. As a key strategic issue the cost of air freight was outside most European manufacturers' scale of thinking in context '5'.

The entry of unusual new players from another market has recently brought to the fore the need to test assumptions concerning what is needed to be in a particular business. For example, the prospect of food retailers becoming financial traders or banks is difficult to foresee unless one looks at them as highly cash generative with more person-to-person contact than banks achieve with their customers. Furthermore, smart retailing through loyalty cards allows a high potential for data mining to profile customers and to facilitate micro marketing. Precise data also allows an advantage in cherry picking of profitable customers for premium financial services products.

All of these are difficult to predict unless fundamental assumptions are exposed and tested. To identify the context in which the assumptions sit, and to unearth as many assumptions as possible, try drawing concentric circles around the strategic issue and place fundamental related issues in each circle. The outermost circles should include extreme issues such as invasion by aliens! This exercise may stimulate some abstract thinking simply by mapping out the issues. For instance, if our doughnut maker had played with the idea of an alien invasion of his business, he might have expanded his view of possible threats and their 'secret weapons'. For more on assumption busting, see below and Illustration 17.1.

Phase 2: Assumption busting, working guidelines

The objective of this phase is only to arrive at broad-brush options; usually five or six very rough concepts may emerge within 1 to 2 hours. First work alone, then as a team.

1   List as many obvious assumptions as you can down the left-hand side of a piece of paper, leaving plenty of space between each entry. Then try for a few more. Try to get at the really **obvious** assumptions that underpin the subject. These assumptions are so obvious that they are difficult to think about.
2   Distort all of the assumptions in some way. For example, flip/reverse/ exaggerate or make a huge lie out of them. Only a few will be stimulating, the rest will be nonsense. Once you have done this pick the most bizarre, or those you like best to work on.
3   Treat two or three of these bizarre 'busts' that you like as if they were serious living proposals. Make them real. No matter how absurd these new starting points sound, treat them as 'possible or achievable'. For a while suspend judgement about legality, technological limitation or other constraints.
4   Try to imagine the effects of each of these and write down what each one develops into via several steps.
5   Now choose the best/most bizarre example that you liked and share it with the team.
6   Discuss with the team the favoured ideas. The team should then expand and develop their favoured concepts probably via several more steps.

The group should treat each suggestion as absolutely real and should attempt to imagine what it would mean practically to implement any given wild strategy. Extend the consequences as widely as possible, in society, in general, and see what associated concepts emerge.

The ideas should bounce through several steps before any attempt to legitimise the results as a strategy. When you have explored your new options sufficiently, bring them back to reality, retaining as much originality as possible. Take care not to lose the value of the new strategy on the way back. Remember, the objective of this phase is only to arrive at a modest number of broad-brush options

A *few tips*

- Dig out and look for the most basic assumptions
- Several changes can be made to any one assumption
- Go for volume first (there is lots of wastage, don't worry about that)
- When picking a 'lie' to play with, use your intuition to select one or two. Don't work slavishly down a list, testing each one. The more ridiculous the lie the better!

One trap I often see people falling into is that, in a hurried attempt to legitimise a creative strategy, novelty gets thrown over in favour of convention. This results in nothing new. Therefore, when new concepts are being made realistic, try to retain the power of novelty and originality at every step.

Phase 3: Improve ideas

In phase 2 of the development it is usual to find huge amounts of material produced. Rooms are quickly re-papered with flip charts, notes and purposeful drawings. Creative thinking can produce lots of output but it can be alarming to step back and wonder what this all means! When the task changes from creative thinking to a more rational level some people will say they are lost, but others will want to carry on because being creative is great fun. Phase 3 is about making a selection of ideas more robust.

In moving to the next stage it is also easy to slip back and start to axe ideas because they have a flaw. This must be resisted because ALL the ideas at this stage are new-born and will look vulnerable. They will be vulnerable because most will have flaws and often the ideas will demand further research into a new subject area. It is important to do the research and to try to buttress the ideas before they are subjected to harsh criticism.

Phase 3 is not about free flow or harsh critical judgement. In effect this phase is about striking a balance between an open mind and a search for meaning from among the mess. Phase 3 is about extracting the best from the creative mess and reinforcing each idea or concept until it looks stronger.

Essentially I encourage people to pick up 'threads' (Illustration 17.2) or components of ideas and to combine different parts of ideas with other ideas. Intellectually this involves asking about the

Strategy in action

Illustration 17.1

Assumption busting: education strategy

To illustrate how this technique can work, consider a theoretical strategic problem I often give a group, i.e. 'How would you develop a policy for education in a small nation state given a steady rising population and slowly falling revenues?'

Assumptions exposed initially typically include these three amongst many others:

- Buildings
- Teachers
- 9–5, etc.

The technique relies heavily on the ability to suspend judgement long enough to arrive at new possibilities. To do this the group is asked to treat the 'lies' as if they were real. From this comes the lies or 'busts' of: No buildings / 1 building / 1,000 × more buildings, out of which flow ideas about putting education into the workplace / into the environment / pupils building their own schools / nomadic learning principles which sometimes leads to the idea of exporting pupils / and so on.

What proves more difficult to uncover are the more deeply rooted assumptions that people call ' obvious', e.g. that pupils (of whatever age) *learn* or that school is a *safe* place to be. From the latter comes schools which teach violence. This eventually can lead to thinking about military schooling or a model in which harsh peer group pressures are encouraged as usual social/cultural norms to drive learning forward (as in Japan). One imaginative soul flipped this idea again and suggested a school for love in which human interaction skills were placed foremost, the notion being that pupils were taught how to love and interact succesfully with others above all else. The earlier 'learn' assumption evolved into a lie about 'Denial of learning' which, in turn, led to thinking about self-tuition and self-reliance which eventually complemented the school for love concept.

The group is then reminded to expand their thinking to include impact on society as a whole, i.e. examine against a wider context. For example, the advantage of encouraging pupils to go abroad is that they build contacts for future commerce and bring back valuable technologies as well as developing skills in other languages. A downside is cost, but this could be met in a variety of ways. A more serious downside is the risk of the country's finest leaving for good. Generous incentives might be needed to encourage scholars to return or to remit their income or knowledge (e.g. Egypt relies on several billion dollars in remittances from its massive expatriate graduate workforce).

At any stage the thread of thinking could easily have been broken because someone thought the germ of an idea was too much of a threat to their personal frames of reference. The trick is to suspend judgement long enough to give the idea a chance to lead to something better.

Strategy in action

Illustration 17.2

Phase 3 – Schools budget

Using the small nation state's education budget problem, we developed a range of individual ideas. It is essential NOT to dismiss anything at this stage, no matter how repugnant or extreme the idea may seem. First we look for threads. Then we see how they might combine in clusters. Then we see how to extend the concept or idea into something better. Several 'threads' emerged and these include:

- some things to do with military/regimentation
- some things to do with going overseas
- some things to do with other governments
- some things to do with violence or its opposite love/relationships
- some things to do with someone else paying/sponsoring.

Considering a combination of the above it is easy to get to the concept of alliances with other governments to permit students to enrol for service abroad. So another concept emerges as 'some things to do with alliances' which, when added to the concept of teaching students about relationships, suggests a complementary policy on integrating education with global military/global commerce and scientific opportunities.

Looking inwards, perhaps an alliance between the ministry of commerce and the military (and religious) arms of government could benefit the education authority in the long term. So the question of solving a longer term budget problem is how to make our students be highly desirable commodities to other nation states or to their global enterprises.

Education policy could outwardly be directed to striking alliances with global companies, foreign universities, foreign charity foundations. Inward policy might be directed at producing vigorous minds and super-fit bodies.

This idea can be further bolstered by extending the thinking further. Extensions to this line of thinking might be to limit TV to six hours per week and to establish social norms for ideal behaviour and posture as being either physically fit or mentally fit or ideally both, for all ages. Education might reflect a higher physical content with intellectual dexterity placed higher than rote learning skills. For example, orienteering, chess and interpersonal/relationship skills could be repositioned as being as important as maths and language.

Education could then be directed to produce soldiers for another country's use or perhaps, in a more enlightened world, to produce worldly wise diligent, multilingual traders and arbitrators whose education has largely been paid for by companies and institutions outside. There is no reason why both policies might not be followed during a 25-year strategy alongside a complementary 50-year strategy to reduce dependency on foreign resources while maintaining good commercial links.

essential features of the better ideas. What makes this particular idea powerful? How does this idea suggest a big opportunity? What gives it strength? Can I use this feature somewhere else? By mixing and matching individual features it is possible to steadily improve the ideas to a point at which they become more defensible.

The thinking outlined in Illustration 17.2 is not without precedent. For example, one of the British army's most feared regiments was composed of Ghurkas. Also, Egypt produces thousand of multilingual graduate engineers, medics and scientists for export, many of them working hard for several years with foreign companies with the aim of returning home richer (and more skilled). While they are overseas they remit billions of dollars and create an example for others to follow. Singapore and the island of Penang have both worked economic miracles using increasing standards as the driver to encourage inward investment.

When making ideas more robust it also helps to think through the consequences and wider implications. No idea works in isolation. Once ideas have been re-enforced they should be subjected to critical review.

Phase 4: Critical judgement

In many respects this phase is often easier to grasp because the more common daily mindset of 'focus' requires reductive or selective thinking. Critically judging one's own ideas is a useful way of identifying weaknesses before someone in authority does so. Well-considered ideas have a better chance of surviving the ultimate review of criticisms by people in positions of power. Whom you involve during the development process may influence the quality of thinking and the final approval. For example, it may be prudent to ask other senior managers for advice (not judgement) during development. That sometimes can gain 'buy in' and help to circumvent later problems that appear more obvious to your new collaborator.

The bias in phases 1 to 3 is in favour of the possibilities. In phase 4 we are more interested in what can go wrong, despite the opportunities presented. Critical judgement will require you to weigh the positives alongside weaknesses.

Listing pros and cons and interesting issues can expose where strengths and weaknesses lie (see Illustration 17.3). In some cases the weaknesses will be so bad that the cluster of ideas is simply dumped. In other cases more research or creativity may help resolve the difficulty.

Another way of resolving the problem is by looking at 'the art of the possible', or the political dimension. Actions can be defined as absolute or variable, so one could look at individual proposals or ideas as if they operated on a sliding scale. Sometimes moving the slider creates a better or more acceptable option. By operating in this way the desired end point is arrived at later and by a series of imperceptibly small but acceptable steps.

Strategy in action

Illustration 17.3

Phase 4 – The schools budget problem

Issue	Good points	Weak points
Health and fitness, i.e. more exercise	Less cost to health service Longer life spans Raised IQ?	Some people will resist Higher pension cost Will take time to implement
Travel abroad	Increases intellectual capital	Mothers will miss them
Students sent/ encouraged to leave and return	Reduces local unemployment Creates alliance opportunities Remittance brings in currency	Cost to set up/start Slow to build up Risk of losing our best people
TV 6 hours/week	More time for fitness/study Demands for other activity	Social unrest No other activity defined

Moving the proposals from absolutes to variables helps make some of them more practical. For example, it would be politically acceptable to propose initiatives designed to increase health and fitness. Immediate legislation (an absolute decision) would probably be contentious, however slower implementation through a variety of health and fitness initiatives led by respected icons allows the idea to survive.

Selling better opportunities abroad again will appeal to some but not all, so again a slow oblique approach may be required initially so that people 'learn' that this is a good idea.

The proposal to restrict TV viewing to six hours would also be a major weakness in a society where the TV is central to many people's habits. This needs, therefore, to be changed or ditched to save the core proposal. Legislation is not an option here and the idea on its own does not lend itself to slow introduction. A little more creativity and a few new ideas are needed to exploit the principle behind this idea. For instance, a concerted campaign to show improved IQ and better attention span in those children exposed to less TV and more healthy pursuits is one slow political option which, together with additional initiatives, can be used to progressively attack sedentary habits. The aim becomes one of helping to show people that the decision to reduce TV watching is the preferred individual choice (smoking in public has been cut using this sort of slow consensus-building approach).

The four-phase approach defined above has been sanitised so that it appears logical, neat and tidy. In reality there will be lots of movement between the different phases. The real process is not linear, it is often a question of revisiting the various stages of development until all conditions are satisfied.

The real trick is to know when to draw in the ambiguous bits of information and to distil meaning from apparent nonsense. Fortunately our species has a brain that will subconsciously try to make a pattern of sense out of the chaos presented to it by daily life. All we have to do is exercise this side of our thinking – i.e. our intuition – more often. Practice does help and the process of developing creative concepts in strategic management is iterative.

17.3 *Practical barriers to creative thinking, and summary*

Even when viable strategic concepts emerge, other staff will want to have their say, so sustaining an original idea in the face of diluting pressures can be problematic. Chapter 8 in *Exploring Corporate Strategy* summarises by saying that evaluation of strategic choices is about suitability, acceptability and feasibility. The problem with creative strategic concepts is one of interpretation. Creative strategic concepts are easier to kill off than to pursue because, by virtue of their originality, they lack history, precedent or some detail that fits someone else's wrong paradigm. In the context of suitability, acceptability and feasibility an original strategy can be even more easily dismissed as 'unsuitable' if the strategy lacks a motivated owner.

A good creative strategy can only survive in the heart and mind of an enthusiastic champion. The survival possibilities for a creative strategy escalate dramatically if the same clear, powerful vision of what may be possible is held in the minds of **a team** of enthusiastic champions. As a strategist, once you know yourself, seek first to find and motivate that team. *Know yourself and conquer. In this context, a personal strategy precedes a corporate one.* Having mastered the self, then find powerful sponsors.

In the end, the use of creativity tools will throw up several strategic possibilities and sharp decisions will still have to be made.

The benefit of using a creative route, however, is that the choice will not be so obvious to others and the options exposed should at least have widened the appreciation of what might be possible. Creative thinking can therefore generate more strategic options and open up the possibility to surprise. Any decision can then be considered as informed and not imposed by circumstance. Then you may conquer.

References

(1) Dilts, R.B., Epstein, T. and Dilts, R.W. (1991). *Tools For Dreamers,* Cupertino CA: Meta Publications.

(2) De Bono, E. (1985). *6 Thinking Hats*. First published in USA, later published by Penguin.

(3) Gordon, W.J.J., (1961). *Synectics*, New York: Harper & Row.

(4) Grossman, S.R. (1984). 'Releasing creative energies', *Training & Development Journal*, **38**, 94–98.

(5) Michalko, M. (1991). *Thinkertoys,* Berkeley CA: Ten Speed Press, 46–47.

(6) De Bono, E. (1994). *Serious Creativity*, London: Harper Collins.

Index